Essential
Catholic
Social Thought

Essential
Catholic
Social Thought

Bernard V. Brady

ORBIS BOOKS
Maryknoll, New York 10545

Founded in 1970, Orbis Books endeavors to publish works that enlighten the mind, nourish the spirit, and challenge the conscience. The publishing arm of the Maryknoll Fathers and Brothers, Orbis seeks to explore the global dimensions of the Christian faith and mission, to invite dialogue with diverse cultures and religious traditions, and to serve the cause of reconciliation and peace. The books published reflect the views of their authors and do not represent the official position of the Maryknoll Society. To learn more about Maryknoll and Orbis Books, please visit our website at www.maryknoll.org.

Published by Orbis Books, Maryknoll, New York 10545-0308.
Manufactured in the United States of America.
Manuscript editing and typesetting by Joan Weber Laflamme.

Library of Congress Cataloging-in-Publication Data

Brady, Bernard V. (Bernard Vincent), 1957–
    Essential Catholic social thought / Bernard V. Brady.
        p. cm.
    Includes bibliographical references and index.
    ISBN 978–1–57075–756–3 (alk. paper)
  1. Christian sociology—Catholic Church. 2. Church and social problems—Catholic Church. I. Title.
    BX1753.B665 2008
    261.8088'282—dc22

                                                                    2007032026

Contents

Texts of Official Documents

Acknowledgments

After twenty-five years of teaching, I still remember *my* teachers. I thank particularly my teachers at St. Patrick and Our Lady of the Angels grade schools and St. Ignatius High School in Cleveland, Ohio. I also owe a great deal of gratitude to my students. They helped me learn how to teach this tradition. Laura Stierman, Katie Boran, and Dr. Anthony Langenfeld were particularly helpful in offering student-friendly reviews of the book. And I thank my faculty colleagues at St. Thomas who participated in a semester-long discussion group on Catholic social thought that used some material from this book.

I thank D. Claudio Rossini, SDB, Director of Libreria Editrice Vaticana, and Dr. Francesca Angeletti, Secretariat of Libreria Editrice Vaticana, for their assistance in securing permission to use these texts.

Finally, I thank the many talented people at Orbis Books for their tireless work.

Introduction

Essential Catholic Social Thought

This book title includes *Catholic Social Thought* because it addresses the fundamental moral questions of persons and their social nature as understood within the Catholic tradition. The subject matter of Catholic social thought is the relationship between Christian morality (virtues, rules, and ideals) and the concrete social patterns, practices, and institutions within which persons live. It is about work and politics, culture and economics, and the general social structures of communities. To quote the Pontifical Council for Justice and Peace, it is about the "crossroads where Christian life and conscience come into contact with the real world" (*Compendium of the Social Doctrine of the Church*, #73). Catholic social thought is a dramatic and challenging tradition that includes both official church teaching and the complementary lived practices of many Catholics. This tradition has responded throughout history to human relations too often characterized by poverty, war, oppression, injustice, and violence.

This book title includes *Essential* because its fundamental objective is to provide the reader with a broad view of the basic features of this rich tradition of Catholic reflection and action on social issues. The book presents an appropriate depth and breadth of the tradition in order to give the reader a solid understanding from which to think and to act.

OFFICIAL CATHOLIC SOCIAL THOUGHT IN THIS BOOK

There are four usual ways official Catholic thought is studied. The first is to read the documents in their entirety. This is certainly a worthwhile project. It does, however, take a good deal of time. The texts are many and long (and frankly, often not the most engaging read). A second way is to study excerpts from the documents. Through this method one can concentrate on particular issues while working through the whole tradition. A third way is to read summaries of and commentaries on the texts. While there are many helpful sources (indeed, I have profited greatly from reading them), summaries and commentaries are best read as complements to the texts and not as substitutions for reading the texts. The final way is through reading the principles. Studying the principles helps us organize and understand the tradition. They are good teaching tools but ought not be seen as a way to understand the tradition in a deep or full way.

The method presented in this book to study official Catholic social thought is different from the four usual ways. First, this book is a study of official Catholic social teaching as well as the broader Catholic social tradition. It presents the teaching of the church in relation to other sources in the Catholic tradition. The book includes the work of significant influences on the teaching and significant interpretations and applications of the teaching.

Second, the book contains most of the official Catholic social documents presented in an unusual way. Instead of the complete text or excerpts from the texts, each document is presented here in an abridged and clarified form. The abridgement was done in a way that captures the substance of each work in a shorter and more readable manner. For example, Pope John Paul II's *Centesimus annus* was abridged from about 27,500 words to approximately 7,400 words. Abridging papal documents is a sensitive task. Several criteria were followed. First, given that many of the sentences and paragraphs in the original texts are complex and very long, the texts were abridged for clarity. Second, in the original texts the authors frequently spend several paragraphs explaining an idea. These sections were abridged for brevity. Third, the documents often reviewed or summarized earlier texts. These sections were abridged. Fourth, if there were instances where the topics were historically dated, these texts were abridged. Two methods of clarification were used in reproducing the texts. First, when the term *man* was used to refer to all people, the word *person* or *human* was used in its place (this, of course, was the intention of the original). Second, many section headings and subheadings were added to direct the reader through the texts.

There are several advantages to the method in this book. Reading abridged texts gives the reader a view of the whole in a way that reading excerpts does not. The reader sees the sustained interests and arguments of the authors. Reading these chapters also gives one a sense of the characteristic way of thinking in Catholic social thought. That is, the careful reader learns how the tradition approaches issues, interprets situations, and justifies its positions. This is impossible to understand if one studies only principles.

The other advantage to the way this book is structured is that alongside the official texts are complementary readings from nonofficial sources in the Catholic social tradition. This brings to life the ideas from the official texts and makes them more concrete. It also serves as an encouragement to Catholics to pursue these teachings in their own lives.

All the official texts are taken from the Vatican website (© Libreria Editrice Vaticana, 2007). Readers who want to explore a full text are encouraged to consult that site or one of the many books in which the texts are available.[1]

The biblical quotations used in this book are from the New Revised Standard Version published by Oxford University Press.

AN OVERVIEW OF THE BOOK

Chapter 1 provides a brief overview of social Catholicism. It distinguishes official Catholic social teaching from "nonofficial" Catholic social thought. That is to say, it notes the differences between contributions from the Magisterium (popes, bishops, councils) and the work of Catholic activists, theologians, pastors, and philosophers. This chapter includes several lists. The first contains the principles of Catholic social thought in two forms, one presented by the U.S. bishops and the other prepared by the Pontifical Council for Justice and Peace. The chapter concludes with a "Who's Who" of contributors to social Catholicism through the ages. Students could research and report on their works and their relevance for today. The other lists are meant to help students think about the texts presented in this book. The objective here is to provide a vocabulary to help students analyze the methodology, types of moral argument, and forms of moral discourse in the readings. A footnote in this chapter includes definitions of basic terms in social ethics.

Chapter 2 is about three words: *personalism, conscience,* and *vocation.* After reading this chapter students should have an understanding of the nexus of Catholic social thought, namely, a particular understanding of human nature and being a person. The chapter invites readers to consider moral decision-making and conscience. The "see-judge-act" model of social Catholicism presented here could be used on a personal level and as a way to study the various texts in this book. Finally, the chapter invites readers to consider the nature and expressions of vocation from the perspective of social Catholicism. The chapter concludes with a list of Catholic organizations doing social justice and peace work. Students could explore these and other groups in greater detail.

The focal point of Chapter 3 is Pope Leo XIII's encyclical *Rerum novarum.* The chapter begins with a consideration of the roots of contemporary Catholic thought, the writing of Thomas Aquinas on law and justice. A basic understanding of Thomas helps set the theoretical context for studying the social tradition. *Rerum novarum* continues to be a compelling text. Themes emerging from it include the rights to and responsibilities of private property, just wages, the just work place, and the just economic order. The chapter ends with selections from John Ryan, an American priest who, following Leo's ideas, pushed for economic reform and the right to a living wage. There is much in the writings of Thomas, Leo, and Ryan that ties them to their historical periods; much of what they write about, however, has striking relevance today.

The writings in Chapter 4 include some of the most significant names in American Catholic life and practice: Jacques Maritain, John F. Kennedy, John Courtney Murray, and Dorothy Day. Each offered a distinctive contribution to social Catholicism in the middle decades of the twentieth century: Maritain on the Catholic understanding of the person and the common good, Kennedy on the role of Catholics in American political life, Murray on the Catholic understanding of the "American Proposition" and religious freedom, and Day on a "radical" Catholic challenge to American views of war, economics, and poverty. The centerpiece of this chapter is Pope John XXIII's encyclical *Pacem in terris,* which offers a strong defense of human rights as the basis for a just social order and just international relations. With *Pacem in terris,* social Catholicism's concern, while never losing track of the individual person, becomes global.

Chapter 5 presents the social teaching of the Second Vatican Council. It includes the first part of *Gaudium et spes* and excerpts from *Nostra aetate, Lumen gentium,* and *Dignitatis humanae.* The chapter concludes with Pope Paul VI's 1967 encyclical *Populorum progressio.* These texts are the church's contribution to the global dialogue on significant questions of the day. We read, for example, the church's view on human and social development. The texts also include reflection on the meaning of freedom and the place of freedom in a just social, political, and economic order. Finally, the chapter considers that critical question plaguing Catholics in a pluralistic and secular society: how should we view and relate to followers of non-Christian religions?

Chapter 6 includes Paul VI's *Octogesima adveniens* and the World Synod of Bishops' *Justice in the World.* It contains a review of the contributions to the Catholic social tradition from Latin America in the 1960s through the 1990s. In this section are excerpts from the 1968 Medellín Conference of Latin American Bishops as well as writings from individual bishops, namely, Hélder Câmara of Brazil and Oscar Romero of El Salvador. The chapter also has selections from Gustavo Gutiérrez's *A Theology of Liberation* and a discussion of liberation theology.

The seventh chapter is the first of three that center on the writing of Pope John Paul II. The central text in this chapter is John Paul's 1981 encyclical *Laborem exercens,* a thoughtful and thought-provoking reflection on the nature of work. The chapter then considers the contribution of official Catholic social thought to environmental ethics. It concludes with a short section on migration and immigration in the tradition.

The eighth chapter focuses on John Paul's 1987 encyclical *Sollicitudo rei socialis.* As that document considers the nature of social sin and the virtue of solidarity, the chapter moves to address the issue of Catholic thought on racism. Also in this chapter are short sections on the tradition's view of capital punishment and the "consistent ethic of life" as championed by Cardinal Bernardin of Chicago.

Chapter 9 addresses what are perhaps the two most pressing and fundamental questions in social ethics, namely, the moral ramifications of economic systems and the use of lethal violence to pursue justice. The primary
text is Pope John Paul's 1991 encyclical *Centesimus annus*. The chapter
also includes a review of contemporary Catholic thought on war and peace
that highlights the work of the U.S. bishops.

SOME THOUGHTS BEFORE YOU BEGIN

Catholic social thought has often rejected a simplistic either/or approach
to complex issues. In stark contrast to a view that seems so dominant in
public discourse today (namely, that there is an answer for every social
issue that can be stated on a bumper sticker), the Catholic tradition offers
thoughtful and reasoned positions on social issues. The tradition is decidedly addressed to the whole person and indeed to all people. As such it is
multidimensional. The Catholic social tradition is about action (on a variety of levels) *and* contemplation (prayer, worship). It calls on people to take
responsibility for themselves *and* for their neighbors. It aims to reach hearts
and minds. It has strong moral expectations for Catholics *and* non-Catholics. It addresses individuals *and* communities. It seeks personal conversion
and social transformation. It takes seriously Jesus' commandment to "love
the Lord your God with all your heart and with all your soul, and all your
mind . . . and your neighbor as yourself" (Matt. 22:37–39).

As a representation of this tradition, this book then invites you to think
and to feel. It invites you to look inside yourself and to examine the values
that structure your views on poverty, violence, and relationships with people
who do not share your national, ethnic, or religious identity. The book also
invites you to look outside yourself at the various communities in which
you live, love, and work, namely, your family, your circle of friends, your
school or work place, and your city, state, and nation to examine the values
that hold these groups together.

Chapter One

The Catholic Social Tradition

Papal Prayer for Peace and Justice
Immaculate Heart of Mary, help us to conquer the menace of evil,
which so easily takes root in the hearts of the people of today, and whose
immeasurable effects already weigh down upon our modern world and
seem to block the paths toward the future. From famine and war, deliver
us. From nuclear war, from incalculable self-destruction, from every kind
of war, deliver us. From sins against human life from its very beginning,
deliver us. From hatred and from the demeaning of the dignity of the
children of God, deliver us. From every kind of injustice in the life of
society, both national and international, deliver us. From readiness to
trample on the commandments of God, deliver us. From attempts to
stifle in human hearts the very truth of God, deliver us. From the loss of
awareness of good and evil, deliver us. From sins against the Holy Spirit,
deliver us. Accept, O Mother of Christ, this cry laden with the sufferings
of all individual human beings, laden with the sufferings of whole societ-
ies. Help us with the power of the Holy Spirit to conquer all sin: indi-
vidual sin and the "sin of the world," sin in all its manifestations. Let
there be revealed once more in the history of the world the infinite saving
power of the redemption: the power of merciful love. May it put a stop
to evil. May it transform consciences. May your Immaculate Heart re-
veal for all the light of hope. Amen.

—POPE JOHN PAUL II

In his 2006 encyclical *Deus caritas est (God Is Love)* Pope Benedict XVI
wrote:

The Church's deepest nature is expressed in her three-fold responsibility:
proclaiming the word of God, celebrating the sacraments, and exercising
the ministry of charity. These duties presuppose each other and are in-
separable. For the Church, charity is not a kind of welfare activity that

7

could equally well be left to others, but is a part of her nature, an indispensable expression of her very being. (#25)

The "ministry of charity" is an "indispensable expression" of Catholicism. This ministry includes two types of activities. The first is what most people think of when they hear the word *charity,* namely, an active concern for the poor and marginalized in society. Since the earliest days of the church, Christians have, as an expression of their faith, cared for and provided direct services for the poor. Christians have also, from the very beginning of the church, reflected on their place, role, and responsibility within society. Many "social" questions have troubled Christians through the ages; for example, What is the authority of government? Should Christians be involved in war? Can Christians own property?

This chapter serves as a basic introduction to social Catholicism and the study of this tradition.

OFFICIAL CATHOLIC SOCIAL TEACHING

This book is concerned with the church's "ministry of charity" broadly understood. At the heart of this ministry is a set of documents written by the Magisterium (those, usually the pope and the bishops, who by their position can officially speak for the church). Over the last 120 years the Magisterium has issued many official documents on the role and responsibilities of Christians in the world. These documents form the official Catholic social thought or Catholic social doctrine. In the words of Pope John Paul II, this body of teaching concerns "the crossroads where Christian life and conscience come into contact with the real world."[1]

As official Catholic social thought is at the heart of the Catholic social tradition, it is the central focus of this book. Below is the list of those documents normally included in this tradition. All originated with the Vatican. The list includes the Latin and English titles, the authors, and the dates of publication. The Latin title is the first few words from the original text. The English title is usually associated with the content of the letter. (A page number following the reference indicates a text that is addressed in this book.)

- *Rerum novarum (On the Condition of Labor),* 1891, by Pope Leo XIII (68)
- *Quadragesimo anno (After Forty Years),* 1931, by Pope Pius XI
- *Mater et magistra (Christianity and Social Progress),* 1961, by Pope John XXIII
- *Pacem in terris (Peace on Earth),* 1963, by Pope John XXIII (94)
- *Gaudium et spes (Pastoral Constitution on the Church in the Modern World),* 1965, by the Second Vatican Council (115)

- *Dignitatis humanae (Declaration on Religious Freedom)*, 1965, by the Second Vatican Council (132)
- *Populorum progressio (On the Development of Peoples)*, 1967, by Pope Paul VI (135)
- *Octogesima adveniens (A Call to Action)*, 1971, by Pope Paul VI (148)
- *Justicia in mundo (Justice in the World)*, 1971, by the Synod of Bishops (172)
- *Laborem exercens (On Human Work)*, 1981, by Pope John Paul II (186)
- *Sollicitudo rei socialis (On Social Concern)*, 1987, by Pope John Paul II (213)
- *Centesimus annus (The Hundredth Anniversary of* Rerum Novarum), 1991, by Pope John Paul II (241)
- *Compendium of the Social Doctrine of the Church*, 2004, by the Pontifical Council for Justice and Peace

Most of the documents listed above are letters from popes on topics of social justice. Such letters are called encyclicals. While the term *encyclical* now refers to an official teaching document of a pope, the literal meaning of *encyclical* is "circular." The term refers to the ancient tradition in the church of popes sending letters that were to be circulated among bishops.

Also included in this list are documents from the Second Vatican Council (a general meeting of the bishops of the world directed by the pope) and the Roman Synod of Bishops. These documents make up the core of this book.

The official Catholic social tradition also includes documents issued by local bishops and groups (or conferences) of bishops. The significant texts by American bishops are

- *Program of Social Reconstruction*, 1919
- *Discrimination and Christian Conscience*, 1958
- *Brothers and Sisters to Us*, 1979
- *The Challenge of Peace: God's Promise and Our Response*, 1983
- *Economic Justice for All*, 1986
- *The Harvest of Justice Is Sown in Peace*, 1993
- *Global Climate Change*, 2001
- *Faithful Citizenship*, 2003.

WHY ARE THERE SO MANY DOCUMENTS?

Why are there so many documents? This question is best answered by looking at the process by which Catholic social thought has developed. The paradigm can be seen in the publication in 1891 of the first modern social encyclical (addressed in the next chapter), Pope Leo XIII's *Rerum novarum*.[2]

In this encyclical Leo responded to the great challenges that the Industrial Revolution brought to social life in the late nineteenth century. His encyclical did not initiate Catholic concern for justice in general or for workers and their families in particular.[3] Years before the publication of *Rerum novarum* prominent Catholic leaders in America, England, and Germany worked to address the injustice caused by industrialism. Leo was responding in an official way to problems long identified by many Catholics involved in social issues. The publication of the encyclical did serve to validate the work of these earlier Catholics, and it also spurred many others into action.

The development of the tradition, then, is the creative mix between the already established Catholic tradition (Pope Leo relied heavily on the writings of Thomas Aquinas to assist in his interpretation and proposed resolution of the problem), the work of contemporary thinkers and activists, and a reading of what has come to be called the "signs of the times." This phrase has biblical reference (Matt. 16:1–3) indicating a theological interpretation of the present days. The encyclicals that followed *Rerum novarum* built on ideas articulated by Pope Leo.

This method of referring always to tradition while meeting the particular issues of the day gives a rare richness to the writings. The simple reason that there are so many documents is that new situations and issues arise. In its *Compendium of the Social Doctrine of the Church,* the Pontifical Council for Justice and Peace calls Catholic social doctrine a "work site." It is a tradition "always in progress, where perennial truth penetrates and permeates new circumstances, indicating paths of justice and peace" (#86). Even though these documents appear within particular historical contexts, in many ways (but not all) they are classic texts. A classic text, in the words of David Tracy, has "a permanence and an excess of meaning." The possibilities of meaning and truth expressed in classic texts have a certain timelessness that invites continual reflection and appropriation.[4] You will see in reading *Rerum novarum*, for example, that many of the themes Pope Leo articulates are relevant in today's world.

CATHOLIC SOCIAL TEACHING:
THE PRINCIPLES

Studying this tradition is a daunting task. There are many documents on the list, and each is fairly long. People interested in learning about official Catholic social thought often wonder: Where do I begin? Do I have to read them all? Is there one definitive text? How are all these documents related? The complexity of the tradition has been a hindrance to its accessibility. In 1998 the U.S. bishops acknowledged these concerns and set up a committee to address the issue of teaching the social tradition. William Byron, a leader of that committee, wrote:

One reason why the body of Catholic social teaching is underappreciated, under-communicated and not sufficiently understood is that the principles on which the doctrine is based are not clearly articulated and conveniently condensed. They are not "packaged" for catechetical purposes like the Ten Commandments and the seven sacraments . . . What are those Catholic social principles that are to be accepted as an essential part of the faith?[5]

Byron and the bishops solved that problem by coming up with a list of the seven themes they published in *Sharing Catholic Social Teaching: Challenges and Directions*. The text follows below.

The church's social teaching is a rich treasure of wisdom about building a just society and living lives of holiness amidst the challenges of modern society. It offers moral principles and coherent values that are badly needed in our time. In this time of widespread violence and diminished respect for human life and dignity in our country and around the world, the Gospel of life and the biblical call to justice need to be proclaimed and shared with new clarity, urgency, and energy.

Modern Catholic social teaching has been articulated through a tradition of papal, conciliar, and episcopal documents that explore and express the social demands of our faith . . . In these brief reflections, we wish to highlight several of the key themes that are at the heart of our Catholic social tradition. We hope they will serve as a starting point for those interested in exploring the Catholic social tradition more fully.

Life and Dignity of the Human Person: In a world warped by materialism and declining respect for human life, the Catholic Church proclaims that human life is sacred and that the dignity of the human person is the foundation of a moral vision for society. Our belief in the sanctity of human life and the inherent dignity of the human person is the foundation of all the principles of our social teaching. In our society, human life is under direct attack from abortion and assisted suicide. The value of human life is being threatened by increasing use of the death penalty. The dignity of life is undermined when the creation of human life is reduced to the manufacture of a product, as in human cloning or proposals for genetic engineering to create "perfect" human beings. We believe that every person is precious, that people are more important than things, and that the measure of every institution is whether it threatens or enhances the life and dignity of the human person.

Call to Family, Community, and Participation: In a global culture driven by excessive individualism, our tradition proclaims that the person is not only sacred but also social. How we organize our society—in economics and politics, in law and policy—directly affects human dignity and the capacity of individuals to grow in community. The family is the central social institution that must be supported and strengthened, not undermined. While our society often exalts individualism, the Catholic tradition teaches that human beings grow and achieve fulfillment in community. We believe people have a right and a duty to participate in society, seeking together the common good and well-being of all, especially the poor and vulnerable. Our church teaches that the role of government and other institutions is to protect human life and human dignity and promote the common good.

Rights and Responsibilities: In a world where some speak mostly of "rights" and others mostly of "responsibilities," the Catholic tradition teaches that human dignity can be protected and a healthy community can be achieved only if human rights are protected and responsibilities are met. Therefore, every person has a fundamental right to life and a right to those things required for human decency. Corresponding to these rights are duties and responsibilities—to one another, to our families, and to the larger society. While public debate in our nation is often divided between those who focus on personal responsibility and those who focus on social responsibilities, our tradition insists that both are necessary.

Option for the Poor and Vulnerable: In a world characterized by growing prosperity for some and pervasive poverty for others, Catholic teaching proclaims that a basic moral test is how our most vulnerable members are faring. In a society marred by deepening divisions between rich and poor, our tradition recalls the story of the Last Judgment (Mt 25:31–46) and instructs us to put the needs of the poor and vulnerable first.

The Dignity of Work and the Rights of Workers: In a marketplace where too often the quarterly bottom line takes precedence over the rights of workers, we believe that the economy must serve people, not the other way around. Work is more than a way to make a living; it is a form of continuing participation in God's creation. If the dignity of work is to be protected, then the basic rights of workers must be respected—the right to productive work, to decent and fair wages, to organize and join unions, to private property, and to economic initiative. Respecting these rights promotes an economy that protects human life, defends human rights, and advances the well-being of all.

Solidarity: Our culture is tempted to turn inward, becoming indifferent and sometimes isolationist in the face of international responsibilities. Catholic social teaching proclaims that we are our brothers' and sisters' keepers, wherever they live. We are one human family, whatever our national, racial, ethnic, economic, and ideological differences. Learning to practice the virtue of solidarity means learning that "loving our neighbor" has global dimensions in an interdependent world. This virtue is described by John Paul II as "a firm and persevering determination to commit oneself to the common good; that is to say to the good of all and of each individual, because we are all really responsible for all."

Care for God's Creation: On a planet conflicted over environmental issues, the Catholic tradition insists that we show our respect for the Creator by our stewardship of creation. Care for the earth is not just an Earth Day slogan, it is a requirement of our faith. We are called to protect people and the planet, living our faith in relationship with all of God's creation. This environmental challenge has fundamental moral and ethical dimensions that cannot be ignored.

This teaching is a complex and nuanced tradition with many other important elements. Principles like "subsidiarity" and the "common good" outline the advantages and limitations of markets, the responsibilities and limits of government, and the essential roles of voluntary associations . . . These principles build on the foundation of Catholic social teaching: the dignity of human life. This central Catholic principle requires that we measure every policy, every institution, and every action by whether it protects human life and enhances human dignity, especially for the poor and vulnerable.

These moral values and others outlined in various papal and episcopal documents are part of a systematic moral framework and a precious intellectual heritage that we call Catholic social teaching. The Scriptures say, "Without a vision the people perish" (Prv 29:18). As Catholics, we have an inspiring vision in our social teaching. In a world that hungers for a sense of meaning and moral direction, this teaching offers ethical criteria for action. In a society of rapid change and often confused moral values, this teaching offers consistent moral guidance for the future. For Catholics, this social teaching is a central part of our identity. In the words of John Paul II, it is "genuine doctrine."

The Pontifical Council for Justice and Peace in its 2004 *Compendium of the Social Doctrine of the Church* summarizes the principles and values of official Catholic social teaching somewhat differently than did the U.S. bishops. The council holds that there are four "permanent principles" of Catholic social doctrine: the dignity of the person, the common good, subsidiarity, and solidarity.

The first principle is the *dignity of the human person*. Humans are created in the image of God and have dignity that is expressed in many ways. Persons have both body and soul; they are by nature open to God, unique, and social. Persons have an essential equality and freedom. Because of their creation in God, all persons have rights that are "universal, inviolable, inalienable" (#153) as well as reciprocal duties.

The *common good* indicates "the sum total of social conditions which allow people, either as groups or as individuals, to reach their fulfillment more fully and more easily" (#164). The council notes, "God gave the earth to the whole human race for the sustenance of all its members, without excluding or favoring anyone" (#171). A fundamental implication of the common good is the principle of the universal destination of the earth's goods. "Everyone has the right to enjoy the conditions of social life" (#167). In the words of John Paul II, "The right to the common use of goods is the first principle of the whole ethical and social order and the characteristic principle of Christian social doctrine" (#172). There are two secondary principles of the common good. The first is the *right to private property,* and the second is the *fundamental option for the poor.* The Catholic tradition holds that "private property is an essential element of an authentically social and democratic economic policy, and it is the guarantee of a correct social order. The church's social doctrine requires that ownership of goods be equally accessible to all" (#176). The poor and marginalized "should be the focus of particular concern" (#182).

The third principle is *subsidiarity.* The word comes from a root word meaning "to help" or "to serve." The church recognizes that the primary relationships in society are family and small social groups. "This network of relationships strengthens the social fabric and constitutes the basis of a true community of persons, making possible the recognition of higher forms of social activity" (#185). The document quotes Pope Pius XI, who described subsidiarity as follows: "Just as it is gravely wrong to take from individuals what they can accomplish by their own initiative and industry and give it to the community, so also it is an injustice and at the same time a grave evil and disturbance of right order to assign to a greater and higher association what lesser and subordinate organizations can do. For every social activity ought of its very nature to furnish help to the members of the body social, and never destroy and absorb them" (#186). Subsidiarity demands, on the other hand, that in cases of injustice, the "higher" bodies must step in and aid those in distress. The principle serves to compel groups to take responsibility for their own well-being while at the same time limiting larger bodies, like the government, from undue interference. Yet when conditions are appropriate, the larger groups must act in behalf of the smaller. A secondary principle of subsidiarity is *participation.* All persons in society have the responsibility to contribute to and develop the communities that they belong to.

The final principle is *solidarity.* Catholic thought holds that there is an essential bond between all persons. This bond is seen in a particularly strong way with globalization in the contemporary world. The interdependence the church speaks of is, however, not merely based on technological or economic realities. The Pontifical Council for Justice and Peace writes, "The acceleration of interdependence between persons and peoples needs to be accompanied by equally intense efforts on the ethical-social plane in order to avoid the dangerous consequences of perpetrating injustice on a global scale" (#193). Solidarity is a virtue. In the words of Pope John Paul II, it is a "firm and persevering determination to commit oneself to the common good. That is to say, to the good of all and of each individual, because we are all really responsible for all" (#193).

To these four principles, the official Catholic social teaching adds four fundamental values: *truth, freedom, justice,* and *love.* The council concludes this discussion with what can be seen as a summary of the ministry of charity: "It is undoubtedly an act of love, the work of mercy by which one responds here and now to a real and impelling need of one's neighbor, but it is an equally indispensable act of love to strive to organize and structure society so that one's neighbor will not find himself in poverty" (#208).

THE PROBLEM WITH PRINCIPLES ALONE

The *Compendium of the Social Doctrine of the Church* notes that Catholic social teaching is "aimed at guiding people's behavior." It is "at the crossroads where Christian life and conscience come into contact with the real world. [It] is seen in the efforts of individuals, families, people involved in cultural and social life, as well as politicians and statesmen to give it a concrete form and application in history." The text continues by describing the three levels of the teaching, namely, "the foundational level of *motivations*; the *directive* level of norms for life in society; the *deliberative* level of consciences, called to mediate objective and general norms in concrete and particular social situations" (#73).

There are, then, three levels of Catholic social teaching. The first is to motivate people to care and to act. This is the level of the heart. The second is norms, that is to say, principles and themes to assist people in interpreting reality and to discern various courses of action. This is the rational level of the head. The third level is the challenge to people to link these norms to their everyday lives. This is the integrative level. These are three distinct activities. Too often the teaching of Catholic social teaching rests on the presentation on principles alone, without the heart and the integration. The goal of this book is to address all three levels. The remainder of this chapter includes descriptions of the ways the tradition tries to motivate and to appeal to people. The next chapter addresses the questions of choice, conscience, and integration into life.

When you read the various sources in this book, note how the author is trying to motivate you. What techniques or methods does the author use to get you to think or feel differently? How does the author reach you and make you want to act?. Some people are moved by stories and lives of real people. Some are moved by reason. Others are moved because they want to be obedient to authority. How about you? When you read these texts, pay attention to the principles stated and the reasons justifying the principles.

STUDYING CATHOLIC SOCIAL THOUGHT

A Universal Moral Voice

A helpful way to introduce reflection on the moral methodology of official and nonofficial Catholic social thought is through the work of Ernst Troeltsch. In his 1919 book titled *The Social Teachings of the Christian Churches*, Troeltsch argues that during the course of history Christians organized themselves in three distinct types or ways. He calls these three types church, sect, and mysticism. The Catholic Church is a church-type organization, and this directs its moral methodology.

In the *church* type, the Christian community is an organization of the "masses of people." It is the community of saints and sinners alike. The church type tends to have a strong institutional and hierarchical order. Being large and open, it tends also, when possible, to cooperate with the state. Most important, in terms of the interest of this book, church-type Christian organizations tend to teach not only their members but also the broader community. They teach universal principles with the intent of influencing individuals, groups, governments, and international organizations.

The *sect* type, on the other hand, organizes itself in small groups and communities. The sect type tends to require a more rigorous morality and spirituality, and thus it is not an organization of the masses. The sect type is composed of "saints." Members of sects tend to live apart from the world and be independent and critical of the state. If the church type tends to collaborate with the world, the sect type tends to distinguish itself from the world. The focus of the moral teaching of the sect type is developing its members. A sect type does not intend to teach people outside its membership.

The third type Troeltsch discusses is *mysticism*. In contrast to the church and sect types, mystics are contemplative. They seek the truth through inward paths, and they highlight personal religious experience. This type is basically indifferent to the state and to the world. The stress on the individual in mysticism leads Christians to a moral focus distinct from the other two types. Mystics tend to speak from their experience in relativistic or non-universal terms.

Using Troeltsch's typology, Catholicism sees itself in the church type. Catholic social thought seeks to reach the masses. What this means for morality and spirituality is that while Catholicism promotes personal growth, prayer, and religious experience, like mysticism, its mission is broader. The mission of the Catholic Church is also broader than that of the sect type. While the Catholic Church is committed to the good of the Catholic community, its mission includes building up the world community. As a church type, Catholicism promotes personal religious experience (like mysticism), the development of the person in the Catholic community (like the sect type), as well as the development of a more just society.

There are some groups and movements in social Catholicism that seem like Troeltsch's sect type. In this book we will read, for example, of Blessed Mother Teresa, a nun who lived in a community (a convent) with other women religious. We will also encounter Dorothy Day and the Catholic Worker movement. There are Catholic Worker "houses" all over the country that look like religious communities. What distinguishes these groups from sects in Troeltsch's sense is that these groups have missions that extend beyond themselves. These groups, in their own unique ways, seek to transform society.

The Authority Question, or Why Should I Follow This?

A fundamental issue behind any ethical teaching or writing is authority. People naturally ask the question, Why should I do this? The answer to this question is usually handled in one of two ways. The first type of response can be called authority from official position. The second type can be called authority based on a reasoning process. Take the example of a parent telling a child to clean her room. The daughter asks why. The parent can respond with an answer based on his or her "official" position. "Because I am your dad and I told you to clean your room." The parent can also respond through a reasoning process. "Because your room is messy; you have not cleaned it all summer, and I cannot see the floor."

Arguments from official positions are part of our general expectations in moral reflection. We naturally and rightly defer to persons in positions of authority. We trust their judgment, experience, and expertise. In the long run, however, arguments simply from position are not satisfying. We are creatures of intellect, and we desire reason. Like the child, we want to know why.

Catholic social thought uses both types of authority in its moral discourse. The pope and bishops are universally recognized as moral teachers. As such, their words must inform the Catholic conscience. If the pope makes a statement on war, for example, Catholics must take it very seriously. Note that no moral statement has ever been defined by the church as infallible. Other contributors in the tradition have authority from the way they lived their lives; the lives of the saints, for example, must inform the Catholic conscience. Blessed Mother Teresa or Dorothy Day or good people we know in our lives must inform our conscience.

The Catholic moral tradition characteristically, however, does not base its moral positions on arguments from the official position. This is an important point and a distinguishing feature of the tradition. Social Catholicism always answers the question why with forms of reasoned statements. It wants to convince people with reasons of the heart and of the mind.

Returning to Troeltsch's thinking, Catholicism fits the church type of Christian organization. The mystic speaks from deep personal experience. This experience grants authority for those who follow the mystic. The authority of moral ideas in the sect type depends upon their reference to particular religious sources. In the Catholic context, a justification of a moral position does not rest simply on the Bible or on the recognized position of the person in the organization. The moral methodology of the church type may very well include the experience or position of a leader or refer to a sacred text, but those alone are not sufficient to teach the broader community. The moral methodology of the church type is a basic appeal to *a common ground among all reasonable people*. It seeks to understand and articulate the universal human experience, and it does so through a variety of forms of moral reasoning and a variety of forms of moral discourse.

Forms of Moral Reasoning

It is the nature of Catholic morality in general and Catholic social thought in particular to be public. The intent of Catholic moral thought is to form and inform Catholics and non-Catholics alike. This is very different from the sect and mystic types of Christianity in that the audience directs the types of arguments presented.

Given that Catholic social thought addresses multiple audiences (members and nonmembers), the types of justifications it uses are multiple. At times the justification is explicitly *theological* or *biblical*. Passages from the Bible are quoted. This form of argumentation would appeal to Christians. At times the justification is explicitly based on the *tradition* of the Catholic Church. The positions of past popes or important theologians—for example, Thomas Aquinas—are quoted. This form of argumentation would appeal to Catholics. At times the justification is *philosophical*. This form of argumentation would appeal to the intellectual capacity of persons of all religious backgrounds. The tradition uses reason, strictly understood. At times the justification is based on *common human experience*. This form of argumentation appeals to all persons of good will. All people have experienced love or joy or struggles. There is common ground in these experiences. At times the justification is explicitly *pragmatic* (practical). This form of argumentation appeals to people's common sense, regardless of religious tradition. Thus certain forms of action have better outcomes than other forms of action.

This is the most important point about the moral methodology of the Catholic social tradition. Whether the justifications are biblical, theological, philosophical, experiential, or pragmatic, all are centered on what is universally recognized as the fundamental principle of Catholic social thought: every person has basic dignity, and every person has fundamental rights and responsibilities. This sense of the person is known through two sources: revelation and reason. That is to say, one comes to know that every person has basic dignity through religious sources, particularly the Bible, and through responsible and communal dialogue and reflection on one's experience of being a person.

The Variety of Forms of Moral Discourse

That the Catholic social tradition extends beyond the teaching of the Magisterium says much about the tradition. The authorities are all sorts of people. While we have popes and bishops who teach and inspire in their official roles, we also have laypeople, men and women, who contribute to the tradition in many ways. We have saints and prophets, theologians and activists. Just as there is a variety of roles that people play in this tradition, we also have a variety of ways in which the tradition is communicated. The following section describes the four forms of moral discourse found in the tradition: narrative, prophetic, ethical, and policy.[6]

The primary way of communicating Catholic social thought, indeed morality in general, is through looking at the lives of people who live it. Hearing stories about Blessed Mother Teresa or Dorothy Day or Archbishop Romero or any of the people listed earlier in this chapter challenges us to examine our commitment to the ministry of charity. The lives of these people, as well as the stories of the many socially active saints in the Catholic tradition, force us to reflect on the responsibility to live the faith in the midst of the world.

The basic form of moral discourse, how we learn and come to live morality, is *narrative*. Jesus clearly recognized the power of stories to teach and motivate. His parables—for example, the good Samaritan—continue two thousand years later to capture the moral imagination of people. Recall that he ends the story with the command, "Go and do likewise." Stories play a fundamental role in forming people's lives.

Catholic social thought is also *prophetic*. The term comes from the biblical idea of the prophet. A prophet is one who speaks for God. Prophets function as a conscience for the community. There are many people, both men and women, who are called prophets in the Bible. Prophetic moral discourse characteristically has two general features. First, prophets denounce. They tell the truth about current social conditions and indict the people for their religious or moral crimes. Prophets often use strong and passionate language to communicate their concerns. Read, for example, the books of Amos, Hosea, Micah, or Isaiah in the Old Testament. The second feature of prophetic discourse is hope. The prophets typically follow their denunciation with a hopeful announcement. If people change their ways, a brighter future will come. You will meet a few prophets and hear elements of prophetic discourse in the pages of this book.

By its very nature Catholic social thought engages people's minds and rationality. Yet it is not meant to be merely an academic endeavor. It is meant to engage the heart and to direct the lives of people. Catholic social thought directs answers to the two fundamental questions of morality: Who am I to be? (and why am I to be this kind of person?), and what am I to do? (and why should I do this?). Narrative and prophetic types of discourse appeal to the heart. They make their claims to our emotive aspect, for it is from that part of us that actions begin. They invite us to care. Yet they are not the only forms of moral discourse. For we need not only to care but also to act.

The third form of moral discourse is *ethical* discourse. Ethics is the practice of giving reasons for moral positions. Ethics clarifies and categorizes moral issues. Ethical discourse appeals to our intellectual capacity. It is thus the primary tool of philosophers and theologians writing about morality. As we have already seen, an important characteristic of Catholic social thought is that it gives reasons for moral positions. While the whole of social Catholicism includes all four forms of moral discourse, official Catholic social thought, while at times prophetic, tends to be primarily ethical discourse.

As a contribution to moral and social life, Catholic social thought is an interesting type of literature. We can think of it as something of a synthesis of usual forms of moral and political discourse. The two closest fields to Catholic social thought are political philosophy and political activism. In a sense, social Catholicism combines the two fields. The strength of standard political philosophy is that it is an intellectual endeavor. To use the category above, it is ethical discourse. It offers theories and justifications for political ideas. This form of discourse alone is not sufficient (indeed, any the four forms alone is not sufficient). One can read about justice or human rights or even the condition of the poor and not be motivated to do anything.

The other close field is political activism. Standard political activism, with its passion and direction, motivates people to be involved and to help solve problems. It often uses narrative and prophetic forms of moral discourse. This form of contribution, however, usually lacks a more comprehensive "big picture"—a theoretical framework. Catholic social thought aims both to offer people an intellectual foundation for social responsibility and to motivate them to be responsible.

Catholic social thought does not fit neatly into the usual categories that philosophers ascribe to moral theory. It is not simply consequentialist, but it does seek results and the betterment of human living conditions. It is not simply a theory of duties, but it does demand personal responsibility. It is not simply a human rights based theory, yet the church is one of the strongest international-rights-defending organizations in the world. It is not simply a virtue theory, although it demands personal conversion as well as social transformation. In the end, Catholic social thought defends the dignity of the person in all the ways that humans image God, calling on all people to direct their hearts and minds to make the world a better place through the recognition and affirmation of responsibilities and rights.

The final form of moral discourse, one that Catholic social thought directs but does not often directly participate in, is *policy*. Policy is concerned with what is possible given the realities of a social situation. It infuses moral ideas into practical situations. It is concerned with what works, and what works in one situation, country, or time period may not work in other situations, countries, or time periods. Governments, businesses, schools, and even families to a certain degree make policy to direct their actions.

The university where I teach has all sorts of policies addressing appropriate conduct. For example, we have policies on sexual harassment, cheating, sexual violence, and the use of alcohol. Policy can protect and encourage moral values as well as prohibit morally inappropriate behavior. As many people have noted, policies can indicate an institution's values. The director of Catholic Charities USA, Fr. Larry Snyder, has said on numerous occasions that "the federal budget is a moral document that serves to tell us where we place our priorities."

It is important to note that Catholic social thought is not a political program. It is not meant to provide a Catholic government. In the words of the *Compendium of Social Doctrine of the Church*, "The immediate purpose of the church's social doctrine is to propose the principles and values that can sustain a society worthy of the human person" (#580).

The tradition teaches in a universal voice. Note the list of principles: all persons have dignity, all persons have rights and responsibilities, all ought to care for the poor and vulnerable in our midst, work has dignity, all must commit to the common good and the care of the earth. While speaking in universals, the tradition expects all people to apply these principles within their particular circumstances. While it might criticize a particular policy, such as the federal budget, or support a certain policy, the church does not itself write policy for governments.

What, then, is the practical purpose of official Catholic teaching? In 1939 Claudia Carlen, who for many years researched the encyclicals, wrote, "Encyclicals are usually issued primarily for the purpose of guidance, admonition, or exhortation."[7] More recently, Kenneth Himes noted that encyclicals "attempt to speak to the broad audience of worldwide Catholicism and . . . the global audience of 'all people of good will.'" As such, "the teaching does not delve into the specifics of proposed solutions but functions more at the level of values and perspectives by which to frame the discussion of a problem and understand what is at stake."[8] Within the methodology of social Catholicism the application of the universal tradition is left to the people in particular contexts.

Two quotations from Pope Paul VI's *Octogesima adveniens* illustrate this method. Early in the document he wrote:

In the face of such widely varying situations it is difficult for us to utter a unified message and to put forward a solution that has universal validity. Such is not our ambition, nor is it our mission. It is up to the Christian communities to analyze with objectivity the situation that is proper to their own country, to shed on it the light of the Gospel's unalterable words and for action from the social teaching of the Church. (#4)

Later the pope calls on the conscience of individuals Christians:

It is to all Christians that we address a fresh and insistent call to action. Every person must be self-reflective and honestly examine oneself, to see what he or she has done up to now, and what he or she ought to do. It is not enough to recall principles, state intentions, point to crying injustice and utter prophetic denunciations; these words will lack real weight unless they are accompanied for each individual by a livelier awareness of personal responsibility and by effective action. (#48)[9]

THE CATHOLIC SOCIAL TRADITION, BROADLY UNDERSTOOD

The Catholic social tradition is broader than official Catholic social teaching. The social tradition includes the writings of theologians and philosophers on social issues. It includes the work of activists and policymakers as well as citizens involved in the ministry of charity who seek to live the tradition.

Significant Contributors to the Tradition

The following list is something of a "Who's Who" of nonofficial Catholic social thought. This section displays the fundamental richness of the tradition.[10] (An asterisk [*] indicates that the writings of the person are addressed in this book.)

St. Patrick (389–461). At age sixteen Patrick was kidnapped from his home in Britain and taken to Ireland, where he was forced to live as a slave. After six years he escaped, returned home, and studied for the priesthood. He returned to Ireland as a missionary and converted the Irish to Christianity. In his writings he condemns the practice of slavery (at least taking other Christians as slaves). Some commentators suggest that he is the first Christian writer to do so.

*St. Francis of Assisi** (1182–1226). Pope John Paul II declared St. Francis the patron of environmentalists. Francis is remembered for many things, including his famous "Canticle of Creation," in which he sings praise to his brothers, the sun, the wind, and fire; to his sisters, the moon and water; and to his mother, the earth. He was a friend to animals and to the poor, as well as a strong advocate for peace and nonviolence. The poem and song that begins "Make me an instrument of your peace," although actually written much later, is credited to Francis.[11]

St. Thomas Aquinas* (1225–74). St. Thomas is the most important systematic theologian in the Christian tradition. An Italian Dominican priest, he is known for his impressive *Summa theologiae*, a comprehensive integration of Christian theology, as well as his method of incorporating the philosophy of Aristotle into Christian thought. His teaching on natural law serves as a ground for Catholic moral theology, including Catholic social thought.

St. Catherine of Siena (1347–80). St. Catherine lived in "interesting" times. She experienced the Black Plague (one of the worst natural disasters in human history), the chaotic and violent times of fourteenth-century Europe, and a radically divided church (during her lifetime there were three popes—at the same time). Catherine, a deeply spiritual person, became a very public figure as she creatively responded to these struggles of her time.

St. Joan of Arc (1412–31). St. Joan is remembered most for her death. She was burned at the stake when she was nineteen. Her death (she was falsely found guilty of heresy by political enemies) mirrors her dramatic life. Joan responded to a spiritual call that she engage in the dominant political struggle of her day, namely, saving France from the English. She led troops into battle. Today she remains a political and national figure in France.

St. Angela Merici (1474–1540). St. Angela, born in Italy, was, as a young woman, moved by the poverty of her neighbors. After a life spent traveling and working with the poor, Angela organized a group of women to consecrate their lives to service of God through educating the poor. They chose a popular fourth-century martyr, St. Ursula, known as a protector of women, to be their patron. The group then came to be known as the Ursulines. This movement opened up new avenues and choices for women alongside the tradition routes of either marriage or a life in an enclosed convent. The Ursulines were one of many religious groups in the Catholic tradition whose mission was to serve the poor.

Bartolomé de Las Casas (1484–1566). At the time of the brutal Spanish conquest of the New World, Bartolomé was an ardent defender of the Native American peoples. He affirmed their human dignity and defended their rights in the face of genocide and slavery by his countrymen. Las Casas's writing on the rights of the native peoples serves as a very significant step in the history of ideas.

St. Louise de Marillac (1591–1660). After the death of her husband, Louise felt a call to give loving service to the poor. With the assistance of Vincent de Paul, she formed a community of women who became known as the Daughters of Charity. In the name of seeing Christ in the poor they founded hospitals, orphanages, and schools. They also cared for slaves and prisoners.

St. Martin de Porres (1579–1639). Pope John XXIII named St. Martin the patron of those who work for social justice. Martin, born in Lima, Peru, was the son of a Spanish nobleman and a woman of African descent. A social outcast, he became a person of undying compassion for the poor and marginalized, particularly Indians and African slaves. Trained in the medicine of his day, he cared for the sick and was known also to treat animals.

St. Vincent de Paul (1580–1660). Pope Leo XIII made St. Vincent the patron of organizations that help the poor. Vincent worked with slaves and helped to free many of them. He also worked with the sick. He is most remembered for organizing groups within parishes to feed and clothe the hungry. Along with his direct service to the poor, he organized the charitable efforts of those who were more well to do.

Francisco de Vitoria (1493–1546). Referred to as the founder of international law, Francisco defended the rights of native peoples in his philosophical treatises. His work is the forerunner of modern Catholic social thought, which uses the language of rights to defend the powerless in the face of injustice. Francisco de Vitoria's name is often associated with Francisco Suarez (1548–1617), another Catholic-rights theorist who built on Vitoria's work.

Mary Harris Jones (1830–1923). "Mother" Jones was a fiery leader of the American labor movement. For fifty years she participated in and led protests against child labor and actions for fair working conditions. She also pushed the church to play a larger role in addressing social injustice.

Wilhelm Emmanuel von Ketteler (1811–77). Ketteler was an outspoken critic of the prevailing economic conditions of the workers. As bishop of Mainz, Germany, he offered a social program based on the Catholic tradition. Pope Leo was greatly influenced by Ketteler's writings.

St. Thérèse of Lisieux (1873–97). St. Thérèse lived only twenty-four years, the last nine of them spent in a remote convent, yet she became a very popular saint. In her biography she wrote about "the little way—performing small, everyday actions and taking on daily sufferings out of love for God." Every minute of the day, she said, calls us to live in love. Through all our "little ways" we might effect a great change in the world. Thérèse died of tuberculosis.

Fribourg Union (1884–91). Fribourg Union was the name given to a group of Catholics, most of whom were laypeople, who met regularly to study social problems. They suggested concrete proposals that influenced the writing of *Rerum novarum.*

John Ryan* (1869–1945). Fr. Ryan, trained as an economist as well as a theologian, was the leading Catholic advocate for social justice in the early twentieth century. His books, such as *A Living Wage* and *Distributive Justice*, served as an intellectual foundation for Catholic activism. He was the first Catholic priest to give the invocation at a presidential inauguration (for Franklin D. Roosevelt in 1937).

John LaFarge (1880–1963). Fr. LaFarge, an American priest, was very active in the movement for racial justice. He published articles and books on racism, calling it a sin. He was an active supporter of the Federated

Colored Catholics and pushed the idea of interracialism (marriage between members of different races) to eliminate racial categories.

Jacques Maritain* (1882–1973). Maritain was the most important Catholic philosopher of the twentieth century. Born in France, he lived and taught for many years in the United States. He is remembered most for his interpretation of Thomas Aquinas for the modern world. Maritain's most enduring legacy may have been his involvement in the development of the understanding of human rights that came to be articulated in the 1948 United Nations Universal Declaration of Human Rights. Pope Paul VI recognized his contributions to the Catholic social tradition by citing his work in two footnotes (#17, 44) in the encyclical *Populorum progressio.*

Blessed Edith Stein (1891–1942). Stein was a German Jew and declared atheist who earned a doctorate in philosophy before she converted to Catholicism in 1921. She wanted to be a contemplative nun, but, on the advice of her spiritual advisers, she instead spent the next decade teaching. In 1933 she entered a Carmelite convent for a life of prayer. During this time the Nazis were advancing their campaign against the Jews. Indeed, she had to wear the Yellow Star of David on her religious habit while living in the convent. Her life of prayer was not an escape from the terrors of the Nazis. It was an act of empathy or solidarity with the suffering of her people. She was, in a sense, praying to take on their suffering. In 1942 the Nazis arrested all Jewish Catholics. Stein died in the gas chamber in Auschwitz.

St. Maximilian Kolbe (1894–1941). Kolbe was a Polish priest killed in Auschwitz. Arrested because he was a priest, he lived, as did so many others, in the brutally inhuman conditions of the camp for nearly two years. In an attempt to punish prisoners, the Nazis picked ten random men from a unit to be tortured and killed. Maximilian offered to go in place of another man and was then killed.

Catherine de Hueck Doherty (1896–1985). Born in Russia, Catherine moved to Canada in 1920 after the First World War. Ten years later she moved into an apartment in the slums of Toronto and created Friendship House, a place where the poor could find shelter and a meal. Seven years later she opened another Friendship House in Harlem, New York. There she included a dominant concern for racism. Friendship House became a place for interracial dialogue. In 1947 she returned to Canada and opened Madonna House, a place for spiritual reflection.

Dorothy Day* (1897–1980). There is no American more identified with Catholic social action than Dorothy Day. Day, and her colleague, Peter Maurin (1877–1949), founded the Catholic Worker Movement in 1933. The Catholic Worker, with its houses of hospitality (soup kitchens and homeless shelters), its newspaper, its farms, and its nonviolent social activism has had a dramatic impact on American Catholic social thought. At her death a commentator described Day as "the most influential, interesting and significant figure" in the history of American Catholicism.

John Courtney Murray* (1904–67). Fr. Murray was the most important American Catholic theologian of the twentieth century. His writings on religious freedom, separation of church and state, and pluralism had a dramatic effect on Catholic thinking about being American, Protestant America's view of Catholicism, and European Catholicism's view of the American political context. Murray was the primary author of the Vatican II document *Dignitatis humanae (Declaration on Religious Freedom)*. In 1960 he appeared on the cover of *Time* magazine.

Blessed Franz Jägerstätter (1907–43). Jägerstätter, an Austrian Catholic peasant, was beheaded by the Nazis for refusing to serve in Hitler's army. His friends and family, including his wife, as his parish priest, and the local bishop, encouraged him to follow orders and join the army in order to save his life. He believed joining the Nazis would be a mortal sin. He followed his conscience and faced the consequences.

Dom Hélder Câmara* (1909–99). Câmara was for twenty years a bishop in the archdiocese of Recife and Olinda, a very poor area of Brazil. He was known for his deep faith and his active life of service. Living under a brutal military dictatorship, he was a staunch defender of the poor, a promoter of human rights and democracy, and a tireless advocate of nonviolent action.

Blessed Mother Teresa* (1910–97). Born in Yugoslavia, Agnes Gonxha Bojaxhiu joined the Loreto sisters at the age of eighteen. In 1931 she took her first vows and the name Teresa. She spent the next twenty years teaching in her order's schools. In 1946, she had a "call within a call" to help the poor while living among them. For the next fifty years she worked with the poorest of the poor in Calcutta, India. By the time of her death, she had cared for an incalculable number of diseased, dying, and abandoned people. She was the recipient of many international awards, including the 1979 Nobel Peace Prize. She founded a religious order, the Missionaries of Charity, which now has over one hundred fifty communities around the world.

Thomas Merton (1915–68). Merton was a mystic, monk, poet, priest, and perhaps the most significant American Catholic writer of the twentieth century. In 1949 his biography *The Seven Storey Mountain* was a best seller. In his writing Merton linked faithfulness with, among other things, the issues of racism, war, and the environment. While inspiring faith-filled engagement in the world, he lived his adult life in the Trappist Abbey of Gethsemani in Kentucky.

Archbishop Oscar Romero* (1917–80). Romero was born in El Salvador in 1917; he was ordained in 1942 and became archbishop in 1977 during a bloody civil war. According to biographers, the most significant event in Romero's life occurred on March 12, 1977, the day his friend Fr. Rutilio Grande was murdered by soldiers. Before Grande's death, Romero supported the status quo in a society marked by so much injustice. After Grande's death, Romero became a dramatic prophet for peace and justice.

He was killed while saying Mass the day after he had preached a passionate sermon broadcast on the radio ordering soldiers to stop killing their Salvadoran brothers and sisters.

Daniel Berrigan (1921–). Fr. Berrigan is perhaps the most widely known Catholic peace activist in the United States. In 1969 he, along with eight other Catholics, entered the office of a U.S. Draft Board and burned draft files to protest the Vietnam War and the church's silence about it. The group came to be called the Catonsville Nine. In 1980 he and seven other Catholics entered a site where nuclear warheads were manufactured and took a hammer to the nose cones of the missiles to "beat the swords into plowshares" (Isa. 2:4), poured blood onto documents, and prayed. This group came to be called the Plowshares Eight. Berrigan is also an acclaimed poet and has for many years worked with terminally ill patients in New York.

Philip Berrigan (1923–2002). Like his brother Daniel, Philip Berrigan was a priest (he left after eighteen years) and a passionate activist for peace and justice. A veteran of World War II, his experience in the war directed his life. With his brother he was one of the Catonsville Nine and one of the Plowshares Eight. Philip Berrigan spent almost eleven years of his life in prison because of his peace activism.

Cesar Chavez (1927–93). Chavez was the most significant Latino American leader in American history. He committed his life to protecting and promoting the dignity of farm workers in California. His efforts were rooted in his Catholic faith and informed by the social encyclicals and the life of St. Francis of Assisi. Chavez gained national support in his work as he advocated a dramatic Christian nonviolent activism that included organizing workers into a union. He led strikes, boycotts, and pilgrimages (group walks with prayer and religious images to important destinations). Another element of his nonviolent approach was fasting; he denied himself food for long periods, twenty-five days on one occasion, to fortify himself and the movement, the United Farm Workers.

Gustavo Gutiérrez* (1928–). Fr. Gutiérrez is a Peruvian priest who was educated in Rome and worked for many years in the slums of Lima. His experience of the oppressive poverty there led him to the realization that poverty is not an accident of history. This caused him to reflect on the nature of theology. Gutiérrez's influential book *A Theology of Liberation* (1971), promoted a new way of doing theology, namely, from the vantage point of the poor. His theology calls on the poor to take control of their own liberation.

Helen Prejean (1939–). Sr. Prejean is the leading voice in the Catholic position on the death penalty. She is perhaps the leading anti-death-penalty advocate in the United States. Her work began simply when she wrote to a convicted murderer. She then served as a spiritual adviser to people on death row. These experiences compelled her to speak publicly about capital punishment. Her story is told in the book (made into a popular movie) *Dead Man Walking*.

Penny Lernoux (1940–89). Lernoux was an American journalist who lived and wrote in Latin America. Born a Catholic, she moved away from the church only to return after seeing the lived faith of Catholic missionaries (both laypeople and clerics) who worked with the poor. Her writings about the history and conditions of the suffering in Latin America had a profound impact on Christians around the world. She became a "voice for the voiceless" as her writing became her act of faith.

Jerzy Popieluszko (1947–84). Fr. Popieluszko was a chaplain for the outlawed Solidarity, a trade union federation, in Communist Poland during the 1980s. As the government repressed the workers and other Solidarity members, Popieluszko actively promoted their cause, linking the church to the sufferings of the people. The government harassed him and arrested him on several occasions. In a final act of intimidation, police beat him, tied ropes around him, and threw him into a reservoir to drown.

Lech Walesa (1943–). Like Popieluszko and Pope John Paul II, Walesa was deeply involved in the populist nonviolent movement that brought down the Communist government in Poland. Walesa worked in the Gdansk shipyard and became the leader of Solidarity. Solidarity was founded in 1980 by striking workers at the shipyard. A man of deep faith, he was continually harassed and imprisoned by the government. In 1980 *Time* magazine named him Man of the Year, and three years later he was awarded the Nobel Peace Prize. The Communist government would not allow him to leave the country to receive the award. The nonviolent pressure of Solidarity, rooted in Catholic spirituality, finally wore down the military regime and in 1989 a Solidarity member became the first noncommunist prime minister in Poland in four decades.

If Only St. Francis Were Alive Today

The people on the above list are recognized as leaders in the Catholic moral life. In particular ways they live or have lived exemplary lives. We can gain courage and insight by reading about them and following the path they open up for us. It would be a mistake, however, to think that working for peace and justice and caring for the poor is the job only of saints or moral superheroes. Borrowing words from Robert Ellsberg, these folks on the list

> realized the vocation for which all human beings were created and to which we are ultimately called. No one is called to be another St. Francis or St. Teresa. But there is a path to holiness that lies with our individual circumstances, that engages our own talents and temperaments, that contends

with out own strengths and weaknesses, that responds to the needs of our own neighbors and our particular moment in history.[12]

In most contexts I have experienced there have been "normal" people who have been moral beacons for me. Look around and you will find people committed within their particular lives to love, to justice, to peace, and to the common good. Finding them is a key to moral perseverance.

SOCIAL CATHOLICISM

As this chapter has suggested, the Catholic social tradition includes letters from popes, books from theologians, and works of love and justice (small and large) from activists. It includes contributions from teachers, philosophers, theologians, bishops, priests, nuns, activists, contemplatives, laypeople, politicians, citizens, martyrs, and saints. The topics addressed by the tradition include the whole range of economic, social, and political issues.[13] A detailed narrative of Catholic social thought would address the multiple interactions among theses voices. It would suggest how lay movements influenced particular popes and how encyclicals influenced social movements.[14] It would note the complex interaction between the "top down" elements of official teaching and the "bottom up" elements, that is, Catholics addressing particular problems in their social contexts. What the Pontifical Council for Justice and Peace says about official Catholic social teaching also applies to "non-official" contributions to Catholic social thought. Whether in an encyclical, a theological treatise, or a parish bulletin, Catholic social thought is, as the *Compendium of the Social Doctrine of the Church* puts it, "at the crossroads where Christian life and conscience come into contact with the real world" (#73).

Catholic social thought, in all its forms, stirs people to act. It offers reasons of the heart and of the mind to support action. It offers normative reflections and particular directions to address social problems. Catholic social thought is characteristically deliberative. It calls all people of good will to thought, discussion, and debate.[15]

Given the variety of sources and forms of this tradition, perhaps the phrase *Catholic social thought* is not sufficient to describe this essential element of Catholic life and culture. Theologian John Coleman prefers the term *social Catholicism*. He writes, "We need a more encompassing term to enfold both 'official' encyclical teaching (which cannot be simply privileged in ways that totally cut it off from unofficial thought and action) and the unofficial thought and movements."[16] Coleman is correct here, but perhaps even our description of what "counts" as social Catholicism or Catholic social thought must be broadened. Catholic social thought is part of the Catholic moral tradition as it is a part of the Catholic liturgical and aesthetic traditions.

That is to say, the Mass and the sacramental system of Catholicism inform the social outlook of Catholic culture.

Consider the following prayers from *The Sacramentary* (the official book, approved by the pope, that includes the prayers the priest says at various times during the Mass as well as prayers appropriate for particular liturgical seasons). Note how these prayers are meant to engender the social element of Catholic life. They link human unity, justice, and peace with God's will for humanity. Four liturgical prayers are quoted below.

Father, you have given all peoples one common origin, and your will is to gather them as one family in yourself. Fill the hearts of all people with the fire of your love and the desire to ensure justice for all their brothers and sisters. By sharing the good things you give us may we secure justice and equality for every human being, an end to all division, and a human society built on love and peace. We ask this through our Lord Jesus Christ, your Son, who lives and reigns with you and the Holy Spirit, one God, for ever and ever.

Lord, you guide all creation with fatherly care. As you have given all people one common origin, bring them together peacefully into one family and keep them united in love. We ask this through our Lord Jesus Christ, your Son, who lives and reigns with you and the Holy Spirit, one God, for ever and ever.

God of perfect peace, violence and cruelty can have no part with you. May those who are at peace with one another hold fast to the good will that unites them; may those who are enemies forget their hatred and be healed. We ask this through our Lord Jesus Christ, your Son, who lives and reigns with you and the Holy Spirit, one God, for ever and ever.

Lord, fill our hearts with the spirit of your charity, that we may please you by our thoughts, and love you in our brothers and sisters. We ask this through our Lord Jesus Christ, your Son, who lives and reigns with you and the Holy Spirit, one God, for ever and ever.[17]

Prayers, hymns, and homilies enable and nourish social Catholicism, as do art and images. Thus each chapter in this book begins and ends with a prayer.[18] Michael Schuck convincingly suggests that Catholic social thought is expressed not only in "written and spoken words but also in visual symbols." Catholic social thought includes "the socio-moral insights encoded in what faithful Catholics paint, sculpt, and build."[19] Music and art enkindle the sentiments that support social Catholicism. An image of the good Samaritan or singing "Make me an instrument of your peace" can help provide the grounding for one's entrance into social justice issues.

Social Catholicism presents a challenging vision of how things ought to be. It envisions a civilization of love, a culture of life. The tradition presents

> a vision of a world which reflects the Reign of God, and where justice, peace, truth, freedom and solidarity prevail. A world where the dignity of the human person, made in the image of God, is paramount. A world that does not know what exclusions, discrimination, violence, intolerance or dehumanizing poverty are, but rather a place where the goods of the earth are shared by all and creation is cherished for future generations. It is a place where all people, especially the poorest, marginalized, and oppressed, find hope and are empowered to come to the fullness of their humanity as part of the global community.[20]

Catholic social thought is not just a theory. It is not just about acting. It includes prayer, reflection, and contemplation. Its deepest roots lie in the spiritual practices of the faith. Its call is to the whole person and to each person's full life in the world.

SOME QUESTIONS FOR CONSIDERATION

1. Review the "Significant Contributors to the Tradition" section of the chapter and the principles of official Catholic social teaching. Which principles seem most reflected in the lives of these people? Why might this be the case?
2. Review the principles of Catholic social teaching in relation to the various forms of moral reasoning.
3. Review the varieties of forms of moral discourse. Give an example for each. Discuss the relationship among the four. Link them to the principles. Identify one, or more, which you feel most drawn toward.

Biblical Blessing
You shall say to them, "The Lord bless you and keep you;
the Lord make his face to shine upon you, and be gracious to you;
the Lord lift up his countenance upon you, and give you peace."
—Numbers 6:23–26

Chapter Two

Catholic Social Action

The Magnificat

My soul magnifies the Lord, and my spirit rejoices in God my Savior, for he has looked with favor on the lowliness of his servant. Surely, from now on all generations will call me blessed; for the Mighty One has done great things for me, and holy is his name. His mercy is for those who fear him from generation to generation. He has shown strength with his arm; he has scattered the proud in the thoughts of their hearts. He has brought down the powerful from their thrones, and lifted up the lowly; he has filled the hungry with good things, and sent the rich away empty. He has helped his servant Israel, in remembrance of his mercy, according to the promise he made to our ancestors, to Abraham and to his descendants forever.

—Luke 1:46–55

This chapter is the second of the two chapters that introduce social Catholicism. Chapter 1 was a chapter of lists. This chapter focuses on three issues: personalism, conscience, and vocation. *Personalism* is the theological foundation for Catholic social thought. Talking about it includes the motivational, directive, and deliberative levels addressed in the first chapter. *Conscience* and *vocation* explicitly address the deliberative or integrative levels of the tradition. They answer the two basic questions of morality: What am I to do? Who am I to be?

WHAT HOLDS THIS ALL TOGETHER?

As we saw in the last chapter, the Catholic social tradition (at least in the modern context) consists of many official documents written over nearly 125 years. It addresses a variety of issues and, depending on how one organizes the material, is summarized in up to a dozen different principles. The Catholic social tradition also includes the lives, actions, and writings of many thoughtful Catholics. It is sustained in and through prayer. It speaks in a variety of forms of discourse. It is universal in intent yet demands

32

interpretation in particular cultures. The tradition, moreover, uses several types of moral reasoning.

Given all these features, there is a variety of ways people study and explore the tradition.[1] Some people give detailed attention to the work of an individual contributor to the tradition. For example, one might explore the justification of private property in Pope Leo XIII's *Rerum novarum* or Dorothy Day's understanding of Christian nonviolence. Others are interested in how the thinking of one contributor relates to the thinking of another. For example, one could compare and contrast Pope Paul VI's understanding of development with Pope John XXIII's view of social order. A third area of study addresses the tradition as a whole and charts areas of development.[2]

An important question here concerns coherence and consistency: what holds this all together? We have seen the answer to this question already in Chapter 1. In the extract entitled "Catholic Social Teaching—Major Themes" it was noted that "the inherent dignity of the human person is the foundation of all the principles of our social teaching." And, as the *Compendium of Social Doctrine of the Church* states, "the immediate purpose of the Church's social doctrine is to propose the principles and values that can sustain a society worthy of the human person" (#580). The answer, then, is the human person, or more specifically, personalism.

Personalism: Attitudes and Actions Based on What It Means to Be a Person

A way to begin thinking about the meaning of the term *personalism* is to break it into its parts, *personal* and *ism*. The suffix *-ism* modifies the word *person* or *personal*. Think for a moment about the suffix *-ism*. We use it all the time, for example, Catholic*ism*, Protestant*ism*, pacif*ism*, sex*ism*, and terror*ism*. When we use these words we have a sense of how the *-ism* modifies the word it is attached to. In these examples *-ism* indicates a fundamental set of beliefs that a person or group holds. These beliefs guide the attitudes and actions of the persons or groups. These beliefs also direct how the persons or groups see and interpret the world.

The suffix itself is neither positive nor negative; we praise altruism and volunteerism but condemn racism. Think of the *-ism* as indicating a way of being and acting based on a set of beliefs expressed in the word attached to the *-ism*. Sexism, then, is a set of attitudes and actions that persons or groups may hold based on their (mistaken) views that men are superior to and meant to be dominant over women.

Personalism, then, is a philosophy, a way of looking at reality, based on an understanding of what it means to be a person. Generally speaking personalism holds that persons, that is to say, humans, are the center of moral reflection and indeed of morality.

The natural reaction to any moral position is to ask why. Why should I believe this? Why should persons be the center of moral reflection? We are asking ethical questions here. Ethics includes the practice of giving reasons for moral positions.

The previous chapter discussed the types of answers given to the question of authority—why should I believe this answer? In Catholic social teaching one might expect that the answer to this question might be based solely on the authority of the person. That is, one could say that the justification of personalism is simple—because the pope said it. This response, however, is not the answer that the popes themselves give. A characteristic of the tradition is that its ethics, its reason giving, is based on appealing to the mind (and, at times, the heart).

We must note that in this book when we speak of personalism, we mean a specific type of personalism. The personalism in this book might better be called Catholic personalism. There are and have been other sorts of personalism, religious and nonreligious. Catholic personalism shares essential elements with other sorts of personalism, but its biblical roots make it distinctive.

The Theological Grounding of Personalism

Catholic personalism is based on three fundamental theological ideas: creation, the incarnation, and the final end of humanity.

The most often quoted biblical passages in official Catholic social teaching are the first two chapters from Genesis, the creation stories. The popes and indeed most commentators in the tradition read these texts not so much as historical truth but as theological truth. Chapters 1 and 2 tell us something significant about the nature of God and the nature of persons. Briefly, on these pages we see that humans are individuals who, by their nature, are in relation to God, other persons, and the rest of creation. In these pages we see that humans are able to think and direct their actions by themselves. Humans have the ability to make rational choices, and they have free will. They are self-reflective.

Our call, our purpose, is to be responsible to God and for God in our relationships. That is the meaning of the phrase "created in the image of God." Genesis 3 indicates that we have the freedom to choose wrongly in our relationships to self, God, others, and nature. The basic features of the person, then, are that we are created in the image of God; we are able to act and choose with fundamental freedom; and we are in relation to ourselves, others, nature, and God. These human features indicate a foundational equality of all persons before God and in relation to one another.

The second biblical idea that serves as part of the foundation for personalism is the incarnation, that is, God taking human form in the person of

Jesus. The incarnation is a statement about God as well as a statement about humans and human nature. The incarnation confirms the status of human nature described in Genesis. When we reflect on our humanness we can see not only God's intentions for us and indeed all persons, but, given the incarnation, we can experience God in and through our relationships with others. This provides a very powerful motivation for our actions, for it commits us to see in others God through Jesus.

Second, because of the incarnation we have a substantive moral agenda in the life, teachings, and death of Jesus. Reflecting on who Jesus was, on his teachings and healings and interactions with others, as well as on his passion and death reveals a positive morality that is normative for Christians.

The third notion that serves as part of the foundation for personalism is the idea that all persons are created with a destiny to be in union with God. We share with others a common origin; common needs, freedoms, and relationships; and a common end.

The heart of social Catholicism, then, is the person.

Personalism and Human Experience

Personalism is deeply theological but outwardly very public. As described in the above paragraphs, it is expressed in universal and objective terms. Yet personalism recognizes the mystery of human nature and that persons are not static by nature. Reality, including the reality of persons, is dynamic and indeed evolutionary. Personalism, then, is at once grounded on theological ideas and open to non-theological understandings of the human condition. Personalism takes into account the data of the sciences as well as the experiences of communities. At any given time, our understanding may be limited, and so it must remain open to other sources of reflection on the human condition.

Indeed, the tradition has become more articulate about personhood over the years. Consider the thesis paragraph of Pope John XXIII's 1963 encyclical *Pacem in terris:*

Any well-regulated and productive society depends on the acceptance of one fundamental principle: each individual is truly a person. Humans are endowed with intelligence and free will. Because of this, all people have certain rights and duties. These rights and duties are universal and inviolable, and therefore inalienable. Since Christians consider human nature in accord with God's revelation, their evaluation of humankind is greatly increased. The blood of Jesus Christ redeems humans, and all people are children and friends of God, heirs to eternal glory.

Here we see a number of things. Note the fundamental principle, "each individual is truly a person." John describes this personhood in decidedly nonreligious or public language. Persons, he says, are "endowed with intelligence and free will." They have "certain rights and duties." Recall the discussion of *-isms*; the moral view follows from the descriptive foundation.

That persons have intelligence and free will is not a bad shorthand description of human nature. Persons, however, are more than this. We will see in the Vatican II texts and the writings that follow deeper and richer views of the person. Indeed, when we read Pope John Paul II we see the use of more experiential language in his personalism.

Personalism begins by calling persons to recognize their uniqueness and their basic humanity, their individuality and their fundamental relationship to others. It is initially subjective and internal. The other side of personalism (like a coin, it has two sides) calls persons to develop a keen sense of responsibility for their lives and for the lives of others. It also calls persons to recognize the uniqueness of every other human being and at the same time to see the basic humanity of every other person. Personalism has an objective, external side. The recognition of oneself and others as persons is the foundation of personalism. Catholic social thought makes sense when one sees this foundation.

The tradition holds that there are two fundamental principles of personalism. The first is that we are to treat all other humans as persons, with all respect and love that persons by their very nature are due. Minimally, all humans have a fundamental dignity that entitles them to a basic set of rights in society. On a deeper level, all persons ought to work toward creating the conditions in life for others to flourish. The second principle is that in order to fulfill ourselves as persons, we must give ourselves to others in a loving fashion. To experience ourselves as fully human, we must be responsive to and responsible for the needs of others. Pope John Paul II writes, "These two aspects, the affirmation of the person as a person and the sincere gift of self, not only do not exclude each other, they mutually confirm and complete each other."[3]

Here is the key to understanding personalism: to know it, we have to do it. It is like defining love. We cannot understand love unless we have been loved and have loved. In order to understand personalism, we have to see ourselves in a certain light—as a responsive and responsible person, created in the image of God. We are made for relationships with others.

WHAT DOES THIS MEAN FOR YOU?

Social Catholicism appeals to the personal conscience on a variety of levels. It calls us *to be* certain sorts of persons and it calls us *to do* certain

sorts of things. Recall that the methodology of the tradition demands con-
textual application of the principles. Catholic social thought is not a simple,
rule-based moral theology. That is to say, the tradition does not simply say:
"These are the rules. Do this, and do not do that." For morally serious
Catholics, it is much more difficult than that.

Pope John XXIII in his 1961 encyclical *Mater et magistra* offers a simple
outline of living the Catholic social tradition: "There are three stages that
should normally be followed in putting social principles into practice. First,
one reviews the concrete situation; secondly, one forms a judgment on it in
the light of the principles; thirdly, one decides what can and should be done
in these circumstances to implement the principles. These three stages are
expressed in the phrase: 'look, judge, act.'"

John XXIII is summarizing the characteristics of the virtue of prudence
as explained by Thomas Aquinas. Aquinas's insight into conscience, choice,
and action is worth considering today.

How to Make a Good Decision

Thomas wrote: "Prudence is right reason applied to action. Now there
are three such acts in prudence. The first act is to take good counsel. It is the
process of discovery or inquiry. The second act, an act of speculative reason, is to judge of what one has discovered. The third act regards practical
reason. It consists in applying the things discovered and judged to actions."[4]
In simple terms, prudence is "wisdom about human affairs."

The first stage in making a good decision is *inquiry*. Inquiry includes
personal discovery, observation, and taking counsel. Thomas writes that
one must "be ready to be taught by others." Instead of jumping to a judgment or acting in haste, Thomas demands "docility." The person with prudence has the habit of listening, of sitting still and hearing from those who
are experienced. What does one look for in this counsel? Prudence requires
memory of the past, a keen understanding of the present, and thoughtful
perception of future possibilities. Note that this stage of prudence, like the
other two, demands rigor of the heart and of the mind. We must be docile
to hear the counsel, and we must thoughtfully consider the counsel. The
person of prudence seeks wise and good counsel.

The second stage is *judgment*. After taking counsel and honestly studying
the situation, one must thoughtfully and earnestly pursue the truth in context. The person of prudence knows the appropriate moral principles that
relate to the issue. At this stage, the person comes to a decision about action
to be taken in the particular circumstance. This stage again requires both
rigor of the heart and of the mind. One must have a disposition marked by a
certain cautiousness and determined consideration of the consequences of
acting or not acting. One must have knowledge, insight, and perceptiveness.

Thomas notes that sometimes we judge rightly but fail to act. Thus we come to the third feature of prudence, what Thomas calls *command.* Our reason, he says, must command our mind, and we are to act in accord with our conscience. If rashness is opposed to inquiry and thoughtlessness is the foe of judgment, Thomas holds that unfaithfulness is the opposite of command. Persons who fail to act in a way that they think is the right way to act are unfaithful to themselves. We might say that they lack integrity or simply lack the will to act rightly.

The "look, judge, and act" process described by Pope John XXIII was described at that time (and before the pope wrote about it) as Catholic social action. The tradition of Catholic social thought expects persons to think clearly and carefully about the issues at hand *(look).* It expects that the principles of official Catholic social teaching be thoughtfully examined in order to gain knowledge and insight into the issue *(judge).* It also expects persons to follow through on their moral decisions *(act).* All of this is to say that the tradition expects persons to participate actively in the moral process. Social Catholicism ought to be thought of not as a series of distinct ideas and actions but as an integrated world view and set of moral attitudes. The U.S. bishops, speaking in the 1986 pastoral letter *Economic Justice for All,* point out that the purpose of Catholic social thought "is not merely to think differently, but also to act differently" (#25).

The fundamental term that captures what we are talking about here is *conscience.* Conscience is something that all of us know we have, yet it is something we have a very hard time defining. As theologian Richard Gula writes, "Trying to explain conscience is like trying to nail jello to the wall; just when you think you have pinned it down, part of it begins to slip away."[5] What follows is a brief outline of conscience.[6]

The word *conscience* comes from two words: *con,* which means "with," and *science,* which refers to "knowing or knowledge." The word *conscience* literally means "with knowledge." It is not merely intuition or impulse. We should think of conscience in two ways. Conscience is something *we have,* and it is something *we do.* It is a faculty, an inherent capability, we possess, and it is a process we ought to follow. We have all experienced having a conscience, that is, the need to think things through and the feeling that comes with doing the right thing or the wrong thing. But having a conscience does not mean we use it or use it well. Thus the current reflection on the process or steps of conscience, what Thomas calls prudence, Pope John calls "look, judge, act," and others call Catholic social action.

As described here, the three steps of conscience focus on the individual, but it is not individualist. It is demanding; it takes time. It is also natural; it is part of who we are. Most of us, however, do not take the time or give ourselves the space to listen to our heart and to dialogue with others. Too often we follow what is convenient for us and not what our conscience expects from us.[7]

Social Conscience

Let us look at Thomas's three stages in a contemporary context:

Look (Inquiry): In the first stage of Catholic social action the person or organization asks the question, What is going on? The initial step involves taking a hard, honest look at an issue. Here one needs to rely on sources that may not be explicitly theological or moral. For example, one needs to be familiar with relevant statistics or research from the sciences. The first stage in Catholic social action is to become familiar with the situation, to reflect, and to consult.[8] Pope John Paul II called this the "interior dialogue" (*Veritatis splendor*, #58). Indeed, in this stage a person is in dialogue with God.

"Looking" requires objectivity, yet we know that when Christians see hunger and oppression, they can never be "simply" objective. When they see poverty, when they see violations of human dignity, they cannot but be moved. This sensitivity to human suffering and need should motivate Christians to ask hard questions about the nature and causes of particular situations.

Judge (Judgment): What does one do with such information? One needs to do more than simply to feel bad about a situation. The second stage in Catholic social action is judgment. Pope John Paul II writes: "The judgment of conscience is a *practical judgment*, a judgment which makes known what a person must do or not do . . . It is a judgment which applies to a concrete situation the rational conviction that one must love and do good and avoid evil" (*Veritatis splendor*, #59).

Where does one begin? First, one describes the situation. This step always happens but is rarely reflected on. Often one "jumps" to a description of a situation without serious reflection. For example, it is easier to think that all homeless people are lazy than to explore who the homeless are. Moral reflection requires that one give a fair and honest account of the reality one is examining. In their encyclicals the popes spend a good deal of time describing the situation. Solutions follow from within the parameters of a description.

Catholic social action dictates thoughtful evaluation, careful description, and attentive response to situations of injustice. It includes discernment. This second stage means considering the context in relation to moral and religious ideas. If there is something "wrong," it seeks to explain why it is "wrong."

This second stage also includes reflection on responsibility. Responsibility is understood in two ways, namely, looking forward and looking backward. It includes a consideration of why the situation exists and who is responsible for it as well as a consideration of what we should do now and in the future to alleviate the injustice. All of this is to say that the Catholic tradition on social justice encourages and enables thoughtful reflection as well as determined decision-making.

Act (Command): By its very name, Catholic social action holds that Catholics have the moral and religious responsibility to renew the social order. In *Rerum novarum* Pope Leo XIII speaks of three forms of social action. The first level is individual action, what is commonly called charity. Leo XIII notes the responsibility of all to give alms and to help the poor. Second, he mentions institutional response to meet the needs of the poor. The church, he notes, has always responded to poverty on a scale larger than one to one. Throughout its history it has organized food distribution for the poor and has built schools, hospitals, orphanages, and other institutions to help the needy on a broad scale. Finally, and again this is Leo's contribution to Catholic social thought, he offers normative reflection on why the poor are poor. The third level analyzes political choices and accepted patterns of action in economic life. It then affirms or critiques these in order to address fundamental social issues. Social action includes thinking about the causes of poverty as well as direct action that meets the concrete needs of people. Leo XIII's contribution to the Catholic moral tradition is the recognition of the reality of this third level. His advocacy of this level marks a new stage in Catholic moral theology and the birth of what we have been referring to as official Catholic social thought. We will read more about this in the next chapter.

The tradition of Catholic social thought in its official and other forms is fundamentally about the protection and promotion of human dignity. It is at once theory and a program of advocacy. It is about being and doing, contemplation and action, feeling and thinking. It is a dramatic appeal to Christians to be Christians. Perhaps the best way to end an introduction to social Catholicism is with the first sentence of the Second Vatican Council's *Gaudium et spes*: "The joys and the hopes, the griefs and the anxieties of people, especially those who are poor or in any way afflicted, these are the joys and hopes, the griefs and anxieties of the followers of Christ."

THE VOCATION OF SOCIAL CATHOLICISM

Social Catholicism is a way of life, a way of looking at the world, a way of acting in the world. Looking, judging, acting is a life commitment. The best term to capture this idea is *vocation*.[9] Traditionally in Catholic theology, a vocation referred to a calling a person had (verified by the community) to be a priest or vowed religious, a nun, or a brother. While it is certainly true that some Catholics may feel called to the religious life, all Catholics ought to feel called to a life of discipleship. The term *vocation* has a broad and a narrow meaning. In the broad sense, it refers to the call all of us have as Christians. In the narrow sense, it refers to the more specific call a person might have to a certain life, lifestyle, or particular commitments.

In its official teaching the Catholic Church uses the term in both its broad and narrow senses. Regarding the former, the church is quite clear on the vocation of social Catholicism. According to the *Catechism of the Catholic Church*, it is the vocation of the Christians (particularly laypeople) "to seek the kingdom of God by engaging in temporal affairs and directing them according to God's will" (#898). Laypeople must "animate temporal realities with Christian commitment, by which they show that they are witnesses and agents of peace and justice" (#2442). "The vocation to eternal life does not suppress, but actually reinforces, a person's duty to put into action in this world the energies and means received from the Creator to serve justice and peace" (#2820).

As there are many forms of contribution to social Catholicism, there are many, many ways to live the call of social Catholicism. All Christians are called to live lives marked by love and justice. Some Christians are called to more particular lives and ministries of love and justice. The particular call, a vocation in the more narrow sense, occurs within the more general call, vocation in the broader sense. The next sections address the different spheres of responding to the call of social Catholicism, that is to say, different ways of considering the types of response to the social demands of Christian discipleship.

The point of the next three sections is not simply academic. The point is to invite you to consider to which one you are called.

The First Sphere: Works of Mercy, Works of Justice

All Christians have a vocational call to fundamental social responsibility. As Douglas Schuurman suggests, "True calling is experienced inside the ordinary, mundane world, not outside of it."[10] We are to respond to the needs of family, friends, neighbors, and fellow workers, indeed, all whom we meet. We are to be open to others and to respond to the moral demands of faith in our concrete and particular daily lives. We do simple acts of love and justice within all areas of social relationships. Again quoting Schuurman, "Vocation is first of all about serving God through serving the neighbor . . . The point is to love God and neighbor, and to take up the cross in the self-sacrificial paths defined by one's callings."[11]

Traditionally, Catholic theology has described the person-to-person sphere of social responsibility as the *works of mercy*. The corporal works of mercy are to feed the hungry, give drink to the thirsty, shelter the homeless, clothe the naked, visit the sick, visit those in prison, and bury the dead. The spiritual works of mercy are to convert the sinner, instruct the ignorant, counsel the doubtful, comfort the sorrowful, bear wrongs patiently, forgive injuries done to you, and pray for the living and the dead.

In more contemporary language personal works of mercy or works of justice are often described as charitable volunteerism. As the *Catechism of the Catholic Church* states, "Giving alms to the poor is a witness to fraternal charity: it is also a work of justice pleasing to God" (#2462). Christians, moved by their faith commitments, give their time and money to individuals and organizations; for example, they volunteer at local schools and mentor children; they serve meals at homeless shelters and visit the elderly; they give money to good causes. Works of mercy or works of justice today include thoughtful consumerism. As we shop, we support the companies that produce the products we buy. We ought to be mindful of what we buy and where we buy it. Contemporary works of mercy and justice include informed voting and care for the environment. Many Christians today are aware of excessive or wasteful uses of natural resources, so they "reduce, reuse, and recycle." They think about the impact their actions have on the air and the water. They think about the well-being of their global neighbors and work to ensure a livable world for their children's children.

We cannot do everything. We have many limitations. We cannot give to every charity that calls on the phone or sends letters in the mail. We cannot respond to every social issue. We cannot help every person in the world who needs help right now. We must make decisions; we must practice discernment. Simply put, we must act in ways we think appropriate for us.

This sphere, like the other two, includes personal prayer. Christians pray for the poor. They pray for peace. Christians pray to be open to hear the cry of the poor. They recognize the fundamental link between action and contemplation. Pope Benedict XVI, in his encyclical *Deus caritas est*, offers an extended reflection on the church's responsibility of charity in the follow quotations:

> With regard to the personnel who carry out the Church's charitable activity on the practical level, the essential has already been said: they must not be inspired by ideologies . . . but should rather be guided by the faith which works through love (cf. *Gal* 5:6). Consequently, more than anything, they must be persons moved by Christ's love, persons whose hearts Christ has conquered with his love, awakening within them a love of neighbor. The criterion inspiring their activity should be Saint Paul's statement in the *Second Letter to the Corinthians*: "the love of Christ urges us on" (5:14). (#33)

> Saint Paul, in his hymn to charity (cf. *1 Cor* 13), teaches us that it is always more than activity alone: "If I give away all I have, and if I deliver my body to be burned, but do not have love, I gain nothing" (v. 3). This hymn must be the *Magna Carta* of all ecclesial service; it sums up all the reflections on love . . . Practical activity will always be insufficient, unless it visibly expresses a love for others, a love nourished by an encounter with Christ. My deep personal sharing in the needs and sufferings of others becomes a sharing of my very self with them: if my gift is not to prove a source of humiliation, I must give to others not only something that is my own, but my very self; I must be personally present in my gift. (#34)

This proper way of serving others also leads to humility. The one who serves does not consider himself superior to the one served, however miserable his situation at the moment may be. Christ took the lowest place in the world—the Cross—and by this radical humility he redeemed us and constantly comes to our aid. Those who are in a position to help others will realize that in doing so they themselves receive help; being able to help others is no merit or achievement of their own. This duty is a grace. (#35)

Perhaps the most famous person-to-person Catholic social activist of the modern era was Blessed Mother Teresa (1910–97). For fifty years she worked with the poorest of the poor in Calcutta, caring for an incalculable number of diseased, dying, and abandoned people. The depth of the poverty and destitution of these people is hard for Americans to understand. In 1979 she was awarded the Nobel Peace Prize, an international recognition of her work and her spirituality. She founded a religious order, the Missionaries of Charity, which now has over one hundred fifty communities around the world. Blessed Teresa is known not for her words but for her actions, her simple yet dramatic acts of love. Below are some quotations from her that indicate the sense of her mission. Blessed Teresa was the living representation of a crucial aspect of the Catholic social tradition—direct love for the poor. She offers a powerful and enduring message to us about the essential nature of persons and essential responsibility of persons.

Love, to be true, must first be for our neighbor. This love will bring us to God.[12]

If sometimes our poor people have had to die of starvation, it is not because God didn't care for them, but because you and I didn't give, were not instruments of love in the hands of God, to give them that bread, to give them that clothing; because we did not recognize him, when once more Christ came in distressing disguise—in the hungry man, in the lonely man, in the homeless child, and seeking for shelter.

God has identified himself with the hungry, the sick, the naked, the homeless; hunger, not only for bread, but for love, for care, to be somebody to someone; nakedness, not of clothing only, but nakedness of that compassion that very few people give to the unknown; homelessness, not only just for a shelter made of stone, but that homelessness that comes from having no one to call your own.[13]

Our work . . . calls for us to see Jesus in everyone. He has told us that He is the hungry one. He is the naked one. He is the thirsty one. He is the one without a home. He is the one who is suffering. These are our treasures . . . They are Jesus. Each one is Jesus in His distressing disguise.[14]

Our purpose is to take God and His love to the poorest of the poor, irrespective of their ethnic origin or the faith that they profess. Our discernment of aid is not the belief but the necessity. We never try to convert those who receive to Christianity but in our work we bear witness to the love of God's presence and if Catholics, Protestants, Buddhists or agnostics become for this reason better men—simply better—we will be satisfied. Growing up in love they will be nearer to God and will find Him in His goodness.[15]

I believe in person to person contact. Every person is Christ for me and since there is only one Jesus, the person I am meeting is the one person in the world at the moment.[16]

If we pray we will believe. If we believe we will love. If we love we will serve. Only then can we put our love for God into living action through service of Christ in the distressing disguise of the poor.[17]

The final words quoted above summarize well this sphere of social Catholicism.

The Second Sphere: Public Expression, Personal Commitment

The distinction between the first sphere and the second sphere is the nature of the action and the level of commitment of the person. Here we move from the personal to the public, from direct action to education and awareness. We look to touch people and to influence their activities. In the first sphere we may boycott a product or a company because, let's say, it exploits poor workers or has an atrocious environmental record or produces morally problematic products. In the second sphere, we boycott and we let others know what we are doing. We write letters to the companies informing them of our moral deliberations on their practices or their product. We write letters to the editor or opinion pieces to local newspapers. We write letters to elected officials. In the first sphere we pray privately for persons or causes, in this stage we participate in public prayer for persons and causes.

In the second stage the social problem or the needs of the neighbor becomes "my" problem and "my" responsibility. The initial vocation of social Catholicism narrows as we feel called or compelled to address a particular issue in a more public manner. If the first sphere concerns our private, individual actions, this second sphere recognizes that we live and work within many social relationships and many social institutions. We are members of organizations, schools, churches, neighborhoods, companies, and so on. We work within these contexts for more just and caring relationships. We work to ensure better relations within these institutions and among social institutions. While always recognizing personal responsibility, in this sphere we are more public. We look for social and/or institutional change. Again, social Catholicism links prayer and contemplation, reflection and dialogue, with action and desired outcomes.

The Third Sphere: Social Analysis for Social Change

The third sphere of social Catholicism builds on the first two but includes a much deeper sense of commitment. It concerns not only action, personal and public, but also social involvement and social analysis. The best way to describe this sphere is to reflect on the "circle of praxis" developed by Joe Holland and Peter Henriot in their influential 1980 book *Social Analysis: Linking Faith and Justice* (revised and enlarged in 1983). Holland and Henriot suggest the circle of praxis as a modification of the look-judge-act model of Catholic action. They argue that the circle of praxis is an attempt to move reflections on social justice from the overly abstract and detached to a more involved and discerning activism. Since the publication of *Social Analysis*, many have commented on and contributed to Holland and Henriot's work. Indeed the circle of praxis (known also as the pastoral circle) has served as the organizing theme for many, many mission trips and immersion experiences over the years for students in Catholic colleges and universities. What follows is a summary of their work combined with reflections of others.

The circle of praxis is a process with four stages. The image of a circle is used to suggest a process of continued reflection and analysis. The first stage is immersion. Here one inserts oneself into the situation being considered in order to experience, as best one can, the conditions (for example, of poverty or injustice) firsthand. Thus, one may spend a week or two on a Native American reservation or in a Mexican American border town or at an Appalachian church. The second stage is social analysis. Here one describes and analyzes the situation. One researches the economic, political, and social conditions of the geographical area or of the people. These two stages are similar to the look step in the see-judge-act model.

The third stage, like the judge step in the earlier model, brings the Christian tradition to bear on the immersion experience and the social analysis. This stage, to be worked at with others, reflects on the Catholic social tradition and offers a normative analysis of the situation. The fourth stage, again worked on in deliberation and dialogue, considers appropriate responses in light of the first three steps. The responses might range from planning direct action to developing organizations devoted to enabling change.

The Catholic social tradition has had several characteristic responses at the third sphere.[18] Catholics have formed parallel institutions that provide services for people when government systems are problematic. Catholics have also developed organizations that advocate for the poor or marginalized in society. Such organizations speak for those whose voices are not heard in society, for example, immigrants and the unborn. They lobby governments and address other forces in communities. Catholics have also developed programs and institutions that serve to empower the poor. The Catholic Campaign for Human Development (CCHD) is an important example of an organization that strives to empower the poor. According to its executive director, the CCHD supports "thousands of community-based, self-help projects that are initiated and led by poor people themselves."[19] The CCHD's mission "is to confront the root causes and structure of poverty by funding local and regional self-help community-controlled projects."[20] Finally, Catholics have developed educational structures and programs to inform Catholics (including bishops, priests, and laypeople) about Catholic social thought and current social questions. Many dioceses and parishes, for example, have social justice committees.

The third and fourth stages in the circle of praxis capture the spirit of Pope Paul VI's words in his apostolic letter *Octogesima adveniens:* "It is up to the Christian communities to analyze with objectivity the situation that is proper to their own country, to shed on it the light of the Gospel's unalterable words and to draw principles of reflection, norms of judgment and directives for action from the social teaching of the Church . . . It is up to these Christian communities, with the help of the Holy Spirit, in communion with the bishops who hold responsibility and in dialogue with other Christian brethren and all people of goodwill, to discern the options and commitments which are called for in order to bring about the social, political, and economic changes. . . which should be promoted" (#3).

Concluding Comments on Vocation

Which sphere of social Catholicism do you feel most comfortable with, the first, second, or third? Which is a stretch for you? Which do you think you ought to pursue more than you do now? Recall the four forms of moral discourse described in Chapter 1: narrative, prophetic, ethical, and policy. Which do you feel most comfortable with? Which one do you think you ought to pursue more than you do now? These are vocational questions. Choosing ought to reflect your core ideas and values. You know when you are on the right track because there is a certain sense of "fit." This fit brings with it, in the words of Michael Himes, "a conviction that it is a good way to live life and spend one's energy and talent."[21]

Here is a final thought about vocation and Catholic social action. The tradition of social Catholicism provides tools for describing and understanding the world. This step, a normative description, is perhaps more important than providing solutions to the problems of the world. It is vital to the vocational call of social Catholicism for persons to describe social reality fairly, accurately, and honestly. For example, are the misfortunes of poor people in certain areas the result of bad luck or injustice? The descriptive answer is critical. Is polluted water the necessary result of industrialism or is it a sin? Do people naturally have human rights or do governments grant true rights?

A call that extends throughout the three spheres is to name things as they are and to influence the use of language in order to promote a more just society. The tradition not only invites people to change their opinion on issues but it seeks to alter the basis on which people's opinions are formed. It demands that we look with new eyes on old realities and think in different ways.[22]

IF YOU WERE A SLAVE, WOULD YOU BE AGAINST SLAVERY?

The previous section considered the vocation of social Catholicism. It suggested two ways of considering vocation, a general sense and a particular sense. The general sense of vocation is the call all Christians have to live lives of love and justice. The particular sense of vocation refers to specific life choices one makes in responding to God in one's life. The concluding paragraphs here address two important points about vocation, namely, that a true sense of vocation is both social and integrative.

John Neafsey is quite correct when he writes, "Vocation is not only about 'me' and my personal fulfillment, but about 'us' and the common good." Whether speaking of vocation in the general sense or specific sense, we should not think of a vocation as something that concerns only us and our life. True vocation, Neafsey continues, is "where our heart's desire comes together with what the world most needs from us. Authentic vocational discernment, therefore, seeks a proper balance between inward listening to our hearts and outward, socially engaged listening with our hearts to the realities of the world in which we live."[23] This, then, naturally points to the vocation of social Catholicism, regardless of the sphere of engagement one chooses to live within. When we combine the concerns of Pope Benedict XVI and Blessed Teresa we can understand more fully the social nature of vocation. The pope reminds us of the internal commitment we ought to have, and Mother Teresa reminds us of the social vision we ought to have. These two pillars, our interiority, that is to say, our commitment and motivation, coupled with our heightened sense of the other person, ought to direct our activity whether such activity is on the first, second, or third level of social Catholicism. As we shall see in the next chapter, Thomas Aquinas combines this internal focus with the external focus in his definition of justice.

The great sixteenth-century Spanish theologian Bartolomé de Las Casas (1484–1566) serves as an important guide for us today. Las Casas was an impassioned critic of his country's conquest of the Americas and particularly its treatment of the natives. What made his position so important was his moral method. He saw the natives as humans and took their experience seriously. Indeed, he challenged one of his opponents, a theologian who justified the Spanish conquests, on the grounds that the man had never been to the Indies and never met an Indian slave. Las Casas argued that if the man were an Indian, he would not tolerate slavery. In the words of Judge John Noonan:

> [Las Casas] worked more strenuously against slavery than any who pre-ceded him. No abolitionist—when abolitionists appeared centuries later—confronted the concrete evil of a slaveholding society with more passion and courage. To a moral challenge that seemed Sisyphean he brought what was essential to his task—experience, empathy, energy, and endur-ance. He put himself in the place of the oppressed. In the history of thought on slavery, Bartolomé de Las Casas towers over other men of his era and most men of other eras.[24]

Noonan's description of Las Casas's characteristic "experience, empa-thy, energy, and endurance" ought to empower us as we speak in moral narratives or in prophetic, ethical, or policy moral voices. These character-istics ought to enable us as we live and work within the three spheres of social action. The task of conscience, then, is to sensitize us to hear the cries of the poor, to experience and internalize their voices, and to judge what is required of us as individuals and as members of communities.[25]

The second concluding point on vocation is the integrating sense that vocation has for our lives. Vocation, again whether in the general or the particular sense, is not something we simply add to our lives. Vocation is not merely something a person does; it is something one is. Vocation is not a hobby, something to do in our spare time. Vocation is a unifying, inte-grating factor in our life. It is a source of meaning, identity, and affirma-tion. Social Catholicism directs us to see our vocation in life, regardless of our marital status or career choice, and to live lives marked by love and justice.

LIVING THE CALL IN COMMUNITY

Many organizations and resources promote and develop Catholic social thought and Catholic social action. Contact, research, join, support, and learn from these groups.[26]

Vatican Organizations

Caritas Internationalis is a confederation of 162 Catholic relief, develop-ment, and social service organizations working to build a better world, es-pecially for the poor and oppressed, in over 200 countries and territories.

Its mandate, based on Catholic social teaching, includes integral development, emergency relief, advocacy, peace building, respect for human rights, and support for proper stewardship of the planet's environment and resources. Caritas fights poverty, exclusion, intolerance, and discrimination; it empowers people to participate fully in all matters affecting their lives, and it advocates on their behalf at national and international forums.

The **Pontifical Council Cor Unum** expresses the care of the Catholic Church for the needy, encouraging human fellowship and making manifest the charity of Christ. It assists the pope and is his instrument for carrying out humanitarian actions.

The **Pontifical Council for Justice and Peace** promotes justice and peace in the world in the light of the gospel and of the social teaching of the church. It deepens the social doctrine of the church and attempts to make it widely known and applied. It researches justice and peace, the development of peoples, and violations of human rights.

Projects of the Bishops of the United States

The **Catholic Campaign for Human Development** is the domestic anti-poverty, social justice program of the U.S. Catholic bishops. Its mission is to address the root causes of poverty in America through promotion and support of community-controlled, self-help organizations and through transformative education.

Catholic Charities USA is the membership association of the Catholic Charities agencies and institutions nationwide that provide vital social services to people in need, regardless of their religious, social, or economic backgrounds. Catholic Charities USA supports and enhances the work of its membership by providing networking opportunities, national advocacy and media efforts, program development, training and technical assistance, and financial support. Catholic Charities USA is a member of Caritas Internationalis.

Catholic Relief Services is the official international relief and development agency of the U.S. Catholic community. It assists the poor and disadvantaged and works to alleviate human suffering, to promote development of all people, and to foster charity and justice throughout the world. Catholic Relief Services is committed to educating the people of the United States to fulfill their moral responsibilities toward their global brothers and sisters by helping the poor, working to remove the causes of poverty, and promoting social justice.

The **Department of Social Development and World Peace** is the national public-policy agency of the U.S. Catholic bishops. It helps bishops share the social teaching of the church, apply Catholic social teaching to major contemporary domestic and international issues that have significant moral and human dimensions, advocate effectively for the poor and vulnerable and for genuine justice and peace in the public-policy arena, and build the capacity of the church (national and diocesan) to act effectively in defense of human life, human dignity, human rights, and the pursuit of justice and peace.

Other Catholic Organizations

The Catholic Worker movement, grounded in a firm belief in the God-given dignity of every human person, includes over 185 Catholic Worker communities committed to nonviolence, voluntary poverty, prayer, and hospitality for the homeless, exiled, hungry, and forsaken. Catholic Worker members protest injustice, war, racism, and violence in all forms.

The Center for Concern envisions a world in which every person can survive, thrive, and contribute back to our communities, enhancing life for all who share the planet. Through research, analysis, networking, public education, and advocacy, the center works to advance more just, sustainable, and authentically human development for all, especially for the marginalized and those in poverty.

The Community of Sant' Egidio began in Rome in 1968. Today it is a movement of laypeople with more than fifty thousand members in seventy countries. It is dedicated to evangelization and charity. Sant' Egidio is a church public lay association characterized by prayer, the communication of the gospel, solidarity with the poor, dialogue and ecumenism, and work for peace.

The National Catholic Rural Life Conference supports rural people, family farms, and local businesses that promote sustainable community development.

Network, a national Catholic social justice lobby, educates, lobbies, and organizes to influence the formation of federal legislation to promote economic and social justice.

Pax Christi USA strives to create a world that reflects the peace of Christ by exploring, articulating, and witnessing to the call of Christian nonviolence. Pax Christi USA rejects war, preparations for war, and every form of violence and domination.

Salt of the Earth is an online resource for social justice issues published by Claretian Publications (which also published the monthly magazine *U.S. Catholic*).

The final word in this section belongs to Dorothy Day. She notes that one of the great dangers of our age is a sense of futility:

Young people say: What good can one person do? What is the sense of our small effort? They cannot see that we must lay one brick at a time, take one step at a time; we can be responsible only for the one action of the present moment. But we can beg for an increase of love in our hearts that will vitalize and transform all our individual actions, and know that God will take them and multiply them, as Jesus multiplied the loaves and fishes.[27]

SOME QUESTIONS FOR CONSIDERATION

1. Explain and give specific examples of the three steps in Catholic social action (what St. Thomas called prudence). Comment on each stage and on the process itself. Is it adequate? It is realistic? Is it missing anything? Support your thoughts with reasons.
2. Explain the three spheres of social Catholicism. Which one do you feel most comfortable with? What are the strengths and weaknesses of each? Support your thoughts with reasons.
3. Explain the notion of vocation. How does vocation relate to social Catholicism? What is your sense of vocation in response to the ideas presented in the chapter?

On True Fasting
Is not this the fast that I choose:
  to loose the bonds of injustice,
  to undo the thongs of the yoke;
to let the oppressed go free,
  and to break every yoke?
Is it not to share your bread with the hungry,
  and bring the homeless poor into your house,
when you see the naked, to cover them,
  and not to hide yourself from your own kin?
Then your light shall break forth like the dawn,
  and your healing shall spring up quickly;
your vindication shall go before you,
  the glory of the LORD shall be your rear guard.
Then you shall call, and the LORD will answer;
  you shall cry for help, and he will say, Here I am.

If you remove the yoke from among you,
  the pointing of the finger, the speaking of evil,
if you offer your food to the hungry
  and satisfy the needs of the afflicted,
then your light shall rise in the darkness
  and your gloom be like the noonday.

The Lord *will guide you continually,*
   and satisfy your needs in parched places,
   and make your bones strong;
and you shall be like a watered garden,
   like a spring of water,
   whose waters never fail.

                         —Isaiah 58:6–11

Chapter Three

About New Things

The Memorare
Remember, O most gracious Virgin Mary, that never was it known that anyone who fled to your protection, implored your help, or sought your intercession was left unaided. Inspired by this confidence, we fly unto you, O Virgin of virgins, our Mother. To you we come, before you we stand, sinful and sorrowful. O Mother of the Word Incarnate, despise not our petitions, but in your mercy hear and answer us. Amen.
—ATTRIBUTED TO ST. BERNARD OF CLAIRVAUX (1090–1153)

The focal point of this chapter is Pope Leo XIII's 1891 encyclical, *Rerum novarum*. The title literally means "about new things" or "about revolution." The English title generally given to it is *On the Condition of Labor*. This chapter begins with a short discussion of the context of *Rerum novarum*. Little did Pope Leo XIII know that by addressing the new and pressing social concerns of his day he would be initiating a new tradition in the Roman Catholic Church. *Rerum novarum*, "about new things," relies on some traditional thinking and theological method, namely, the work of the great medieval saint Thomas Aquinas. Before reading the encyclical we explore the foundation of modern Catholic social thought, that is, the social philosophy of St. Thomas. Understanding Thomas, particularly on the issues of law and justice, helps us understand the moral framework within which Leo XIII was working. After the section on *Rerum novarum* this chapter considers the work of Fr. John Ryan, an American priest who brought Leo XIII's ideas into the American context.

THOMAS AQUINAS:
A FOUNDATION OF CATHOLIC SOCIAL THOUGHT

When Pope Leo XIII wrote *Rerum novarum*, he responded to Catholic leaders both in Europe and in the United States who were looking for an official church position on the troubling issues of the day. Leo XIII's intellectual foundation for *Rerum novarum* was the theology of Thomas Aquinas.

Thomas, a medieval theologian (1224–74), is generally recognized as the most important systematic theologian in the Christian tradition. The influence of Thomas on contemporary Catholic social thought and indeed on contemporary Catholic moral theology in general cannot be overestimated. Pope Leo XIII was particularly interested in the thought of Thomas Aquinas; indeed, he used his office to encourage the revival of Thomistic theology and philosophy in Catholic schools.[1] *Rerum novarum* illustrates the pope's dependence on Thomas's work.[2]

There are at least three elements of Thomas's thinking that are vital to understanding the basis of Catholic social thought: law, justice, and moral action. The next section addresses Thomas's thinking in these areas.[3]

Thomas Aquinas on Law

We begin our study of the Catholic social tradition with an overview of Thomas Aquinas's "Treatise on Law" (*Summa theologica* I-II, Questions 90–108). Think of this as an introduction to the idea of law and the relationship between law and morality and law and justice. Some interesting questions arise here: What gives a law authority? Why should one feel morally compelled to obey or perhaps disobey a law? Should all moral evils be outlawed? Is the purpose of law to stop people from being bad or to encourage people to be good? Thomas addresses these questions, and indeed many others, in his "Treatise on Law."

In the following selections we read Thomas's definition of law and his understanding of the purpose of law. He states there are three types of law and addresses the question of moral and immoral human laws. As you read his work, think about his distinctions and ideas. Do they make sense for us today?

After reading these selections we can talk not only about the content of Thomas's philosophy of law but also about some characteristic features of his thinking. Some features of the way Thomas thinks and presents his views endure today in the Catholic social tradition. Notice, for example, the way he tries to convince the reader of his views. He does not quote the Bible or quote the popes. He does not use emotional language. Thomas's approach is rational. He uses logic and reason to demonstrate his position. It is clear that Thomas has confidence in human nature and human reason.

Another thing to notice about Thomas's thinking is his view of persons as social beings. We in the contemporary world tend to think of persons as individuals. We highlight our distinctiveness and difference from others. Thomas, on the other hand, notes our connectedness to others and to God. When persons are thought of as individuals, the primary moral category is rights. When persons are thought of as relational, the primary moral category is responsibility.

—Selections from Thomas on Law—

1. The Definition of Law

Law is an ordinance of reason for the common good, made by one who has care of the community, and promulgated (90.4).

2. Explaining the Definition

Ordinance of Reason: Law is a rule and measure of acts, whereby a man is induced to act or is restrained from acting. Now the rule and measure of human acts is reason, since it belongs to reason to direct to the end, which is the first principle in all matters of action. Consequently it follows that law is something pertaining to reason (90.1).

For the Common Good: A law, properly speaking, regards first and foremost the order to the common good (90.3).

Proper Authority: A private person cannot lead another to virtue efficaciously for he can only advise. If his advice is not taken, it has no coercive power, such as the law should have, in order to prove an efficacious inducement to virtue. But this coercive power is vested in the whole people or in some public personage, to whom it belongs to inflict penalties. As one man is a part of the household, so a household is a part of the state and the state is a perfect community. And therefore, as the good of one man is not the last end, but is ordained to the common good, so too the good of one household is ordained to the good of a single state, which is a perfect community (90.3).

Promulgated: In order for a law to obtain the binding force that is proper to a law, it must be applied to the people who are to be ruled by it. Promulgation is necessary for the law to obtain its force (90.4).

3. There Are Three Types of Law: Eternal, Natural, and Human

All things subject to God are ruled and measured by the eternal law. All things partake somewhat of the eternal law, in so far as, namely, from its being imprinted on them, they derive their respective inclinations to their proper acts and ends. Now among all others, humans are subject to God in the most excellent way, in so far as they partake in a share of God's providence. Humans have a share of the Eternal Reason; this participation in the eternal law by humans is called the natural law. The light of natural reason, whereby we discern what is good and what is evil, which is the function of the natural law, is nothing else than an imprint on us of God's will. It is therefore evident that the natural law is nothing else than our participation of the eternal law (91.2).

Every person acts for an end under the aspect of good. Consequently the first principle of practical reason is one founded on the notion of good, namely, that "good is that which all things seek after." Hence this is the first precept of law that "good is to be done and pursued, and evil is to be avoided." All other precepts of the natural law are based upon this: so that whatever the practical reason naturally apprehends as human good (or evil) belongs to the precepts of the natural law as something to be done or avoided (94.2).

Every human law has just so much of the nature of law, as it is derived from the law of nature. But if in any point it deflects from the law of nature, it is no longer a law but a perversion of law. The general principles of the natural law cannot be applied to all men in the same way on account of the great variety of human affairs: and hence arises the diversity of positive laws among various people (95.2).

4. The Purpose of Law

The proper effect of law is to lead people to their proper virtue: and since virtue is that which makes its subject good, it follows that the proper effect of law is to make those to whom it is given, good, either simply or in some particular respect. For if the intention of the lawgiver is fixed on true good, which is the common good regulated according to Divine justice, it follows that the effect of the law is to make people good simply . . . It is not always, however, through perfect goodness of virtue that one obeys the law, often it is through fear of punishment, and sometimes people obey law through the mere dictates of reason which is a beginning of virtue (92.1).

The purpose of human law is to lead people to virtue, not suddenly, but gradually. Law ought not lay upon the multitude of imperfect people the burdens of those who are already virtuous, namely, that they should abstain from all evil. Otherwise these imperfect ones, being unable to bear such precepts, would break out into yet greater evils (96.2).

Human law is framed for a number of human beings, the majority of whom are not perfect in virtue. Wherefore human laws do not forbid all vices, but only the more grievous vices, from which it is possible for the majority to abstain; and chiefly those that are to the hurt of others, without the prohibition of which human society could not be maintained: thus human law prohibits murder, theft and such like (96.2).

The goodness of any part is considered in comparison with the whole. Since every person is a part of society, it is impossible that a person be good, unless he or she is well proportionate to the common good. The common good cannot flourish, unless the citizens are virtuous, at least those whose business it is to govern (92.1).

Laws imposed on people should also be in keeping with their condition. As Isidore says, law should be "possible both according to nature, and according to the customs of the country" . . . The same is not possible to a child as to an adult; for this reason the law for children is not the same as for adults. Many things are permitted to children; if adults acted in such a manner they would be punished by law or at least be open to blame (96.2).

The natural law is a participation in us of the eternal law: while human law falls short of the eternal law . . . Wherefore, too, human law does not prohibit everything that is forbidden by the natural law (96.2).

5. Just and Unjust Laws

Laws framed by people are either just or unjust. If they are just, they have the power of binding in conscience, from the eternal law whence they are derived. Now laws are said to be just, both from the end and their form. They are just according to their end when they are ordained to the common good and when the lawmaker does not exceed his or her legitimate authority. They are just from their form when the burdens of the law laid on the subjects with an equality of proportion and a view to the common good (96.4).

Laws may be unjust in two ways. Unjust laws are contrary to human good or the Divine good. [An unjust law can be contrary to the human good either through its end, author or form.] Regarding its end as when an authority imposes on his or her subjects burdensome laws, conducive, not to the common good, but rather to his or her own cupidity or vainglory. Regarding its author, as when a person makes a law that goes beyond the power committed to him or her. Regarding the form, as when burdens are imposed unequally on the community, although with a view to the common good. The like are acts of violence rather than laws. . . . Wherefore such laws do not bind in conscience except perhaps in order to avoid scandal or disturbance (96.4).

A tyrannical law, through not being according to reason, is not a law, absolutely speaking, but rather a perversion of law (92.2).

Secondly, laws may be unjust through being opposed to the Divine good: such are the laws of tyrants inducing to idolatry, or to anything else contrary to the Divine law: and laws of this kind must nowise be observed (96.4).

6. The Moral Authority of Human Law

Every law is directed to the common good, and derives the force and nature of law accordingly . . . Now it happens often that the observance of some point of law conduces to the common weal in the majority of instances, and yet, in some cases, is very hurtful. Since then the lawgiver cannot have in view every single case, he shapes the law according to what happens most frequently, by directing his attention to the common good. Wherefore if a case arises wherein the observance of that law would be hurtful to the general welfare, it should not be observed (96.6).

Nevertheless it must be noted, that if the observance of the law according to the letter does not involve any sudden risk needing instant remedy, it is not competent for everyone to expound what is useful and what is not useful to the state: those alone can do this who are in authority, and who, on account of such like cases, have the power to dispense from the laws. If, however, the peril is so sudden as not to allow of the delay involved by referring the matter to authority, the mere necessity brings with it a dispensation, since necessity knows no law (96.6).

He who in a case of necessity acts beside the letter of the law, does not judge the law; but of a particular case in which he sees that the letter of the law is not to be observed (96.6).

Thomas Aquinas on Justice

The texts in this section are taken from Thomas's "Treatise on Justice" (*Summa theologica*, II-II, Questions 57–122). Note Thomas's rich description of justice. For him, and indeed for the Catholic tradition, justice refers both to the external actions of a person and to the internal characteristics of a person. Justice is about doing right actions as well as being the kind of person who is ready and willing to do the right thing. Justice includes thoughtful reflection on complex issues as well as a general attitude engendered in one's heart that opens one up to see the qualities of human relations. This is an important feature of Catholic social thought. Catholic social thought examines patterns of social life in light of the demands of justice, human rights, and a concern for the poor. It is, moreover, about the examination of the self. Catholic social thought includes the call to reflect, not only on poverty "out there," but also to reflect on poverty "inside" the self. Catholic social thought is about social order and personal morality. It is about development as a moral person as much as it is about a calling to work with those who are poor or in need.

—Selections from Thomas on Justice—

1. The Definition of Justice
[Justice] is a habit whereby a person renders to each one's due by a constant and perpetual will (58.1). Justice directs a person in relations with other people. Now this may happen in two ways: first in regard to his relations with individuals, secondly in regard to his relations with others in general, in so far as a person who serves a community, serves all those who are included in that community. Accordingly justice in its proper acceptation can be directed to another in both these senses (58.5).

2. The First Type of Justice: General Justice

Now it is evident that all who are included in a community, stand in relation to that community as parts to a whole; while a part, as such, belongs to a whole, so that whatever is the good of a part can be directed to the good of the whole . . . Justice which is in this way styled general is called "legal justice" is referable to the common good, because thereby people are in harmony with the law that directs the acts of all the virtues to the common good (58.5).

[Legal justice] stands foremost among all the moral virtues, for the common good transcends the individual good of one person. In this sense Aristotle declares (*Ethic.* v, 1) that "the most excellent of the virtues would seem to be justice, and more glorious than either the evening or the morning star" (58.12).

3. The Second Type of Justice: Particular Justice and Its Two Types

Particular justice is directed to the private individual who is compared to the community as a part to the whole. Now a twofold order may be considered in relation to the part. In the first place there is the order of one part to another, to which corresponds the order of one private individual to another. This order is directed by commutative justice, which is concerned about the mutual dealings between two persons (61.1).

In the second place there is the order of the whole towards the parts, to which corresponds the order of that which belongs to the community in relation to each single person. This order is directed by distributive justice, which distributes common goods proportionately. Hence there are two species of justice, distributive and commutative (61.1).

Distributive Justice: The act of distributing the goods of the community (so that each one receives that which, in a way, is his own) belongs to none but those who exercise authority over those goods; and yet distributive justice is also in the subjects to whom those goods are distributed in so far as they are contented by a just distribution (61.1).

In distributive justice something is given to a private individual, in so far as what belongs to the whole is due to the part, and in a quantity that is proportionate to the importance of the position of that part in respect of the whole. Consequently in distributive justice a person receives all the more of the common goods, according as he holds a more prominent position in the community (61.2).

Hence in distributive justice the mean is observed, not according to equality between thing and thing, but according to proportion between things and persons: in such a way that even as one person surpasses another, so that which is given to one person surpasses that which is allotted to another. Hence Aristotle says (*Ethic.* v, 3, 4) that the mean in the latter case follows "geometrical proportion," wherein equality depends not on quantity but on proportion (61.2).

Commutative Justice: On the other hand in commutations something
is paid to an individual on account of something of his that has been
received, as may be seen chiefly in selling and buying, where the notion
of commutation is found primarily. Hence it is necessary to equalize thing
with thing, so that the one person should pay back to the other just so
much as he has become richer out of that which belonged to the other.
The result of this will be equality according to the "arithmetical mean"
which is gauged according to equal excess in quantity (61.2).

4. Justice and Equality

Equality is the general form of justice, as it is in distributive and commutative justice. In general justice however we find equality of geometrical proportion, whereas in the particular justice [distributive and
commutative] we find equality of arithmetical proportion. Hence in
distributive justice a person's station is considered in itself, whereas in
commutative justice it is considered in so far as it causes a diversity of
things (61.2).

RERUM NOVARUM

The Context of *Rerum Novarum*

May 15, 1891, is recognized as the birth date of official Catholic social
thought. Catholic social thought is a body of moral teaching on social issues officially promulgated by the church (popes, councils, bishops) through
formal and authoritative statements (encyclicals, pastoral letters, and documents written by councils of bishops). *Rerum novarum* began a new trajectory in church teaching. Leo XIII's now-famous defense of workers' rights
was published during the chaotic times of developing industrialism and a
century after the violent days that marked the French Revolution. While
innovative, the encyclical was built on a solid theological tradition and the
long history of the church's active concern for the poor.

Leo XIII perceived that the causes of poverty and destitution in his day
were the dramatic changes in the patterns of social interaction that had
swept through Europe. *Rerum novarum* offers a strong critique of the economic and social status quo of his day, namely, early capitalism. The encyclical offers an equally strong critique of the solution offered by some people
of his day, namely, early socialism. Leo XIII presents an alternative view of
business and government as protectors of the poor, a view that includes the
traditional call of Christian charity.

The first sentence of *Rerum novarum* illustrates the social context Leo XIII addresses: "The spirit of revolutionary change, which has long disturbed the nations of the world, has passed from politics to economic life." This spirit of change is, according to Leo XIII, most destructive. He is referring to the revolution and violence that tore through Europe in the century preceding the publication of his encyclical. These bloody revolutions had a dramatic impact on the structure of European society and on the church. Leo XIII's immediate predecessors suffered greatly during these times, when huge numbers of priests and nuns were killed and as vast areas of church property were confiscated. In the years before Leo XIII became pope, the church experienced a dramatic reduction in temporal as well as spiritual power and authority. Two popes were kidnapped and imprisoned. One of them, Pope Pius VI, died a prisoner in 1799. These revolutionary changes, although historically diverse, came to be known and condemned by the church as liberalism.

Leo XIII believed that liberalism was spreading from politics to economics. He saw this in the social consequences of the Industrial Revolution: the appalling working conditions in factories and mines, the brutally long working hours demanded by employers, the exploitation of children, extremely low wages paid to laborers, and their terrible living conditions. Leo XIII seems to think that the solution offered by the socialists was also a result of the spread of liberalism.[4] *Rerum novarum*, then, is Leo XIII's response to the dramatic social and moral conditions brought on by the political and industrial revolutions.

Imagine a time when there were no minimum-wage laws, no child-labor laws, no forty-hour work week, no overtime pay, no workers' compensation or insurance, no retirement plans or accounts, no Social Security plan, no laws about safety in the work place. Factory laborers spent twelve to fifteen hours a day at work, with a rare day off, yet made barely enough money to support their families. In this text we see Leo XIII arguing against the two dominant voices of his day: capitalism, which he saw as the cause of the social problems; and socialism, which he saw as an inappropriate solution to the problems.

According to the capitalism of his day, often called laissez-faire capitalism, government does not have any competence in economic matters. Therefore, it is not appropriate for government to interfere with the working of the free market. The market sets wages, working conditions, hours of work, and who can work. Leo XIII rejected this theory, arguing instead for a strong but limited role for the state in economic affairs.

Leo XIII also argued strongly against at least four fundamental concepts of the socialism of his day: class conflict, religion, private property, and the role of the state. These ideas find their source in the writings of Karl Marx. Marx believed that capitalism is based on a class conflict; that is, the rich and poor are fundamentally at odds. Indeed, the rich are rich because they keep the poor poor. He thus encouraged the poor to take matters into their own hands and forcibly to seize control of the means of production—factories and farms. Leo XIII held an organic view of society. He believed that a society is like a body and, like a body, has many parts. Some parts play more important roles than others. The brain and lungs, for example, are more important than the toes and fingers. The parts do, however, work in harmony. So it is with society. There are rich and poor, and they are to live in a complementary, not oppressive or violent or hateful relationship.

Marx rejected religion as an ideology, a lie perpetrated by the rich to keep the poor in their place. He claimed that religion "is the opium of the people."[5] The rich could afford such pleasures as opium to take their minds off the troubles of this world. The poor, on the other hand, had religion to dull their minds and take their focus off of their sufferings as they looked forward to their reward in heaven. Marx's communist society would be atheistic. Leo XIII, on the other hand, held that religion, that is to say Catholicism, is part of the solution for a just society.

Central to Marxism is the rejection of private property in favor of communal ownership or control. The irony we see in *Rerum novarum* is that the model of capitalism Leo XIII addressed was based on the concept of private property, but wages were so low and the working conditions so restrictive that workers could never earn enough to own property. Leo XIII argues, then, against both systems, which in very different ways worked against private ownership of property.

The final issue of socialism that Leo XIII addresses is the role of government. If the capitalism of his day presented a government too distant from people's lives, the communism of his day presented a view of government too intrusive in people's lives.

While *Rerum novarum* was written over a century ago, in a very different context than our own, it remains a classic text. It has a certain timelessness; it asks fundamental questions and offers responses that transcend historical particularities. It continues over time to provoke discussion and to invite interpretation. Elements of the text remain relevant to present conditions. Leo XIII addresses many questions that are a part of current political conversation. What is a moral work place? What conditions are necessary for a moral economy? How do social groups relate? Are they marked by cooperation and cohesion or by tension and conflict? What role should religion play in political discussions? Leo XIII also addresses the meaning and justification of private ownership of property, the concept of a just wage, and the role of government in the economy. While much of *Rerum novarum* applies to the present, it is also a product of its own time, offering now-dated social analysis and solutions to social problems.

Rerum Novarum (abridged and edited)
Pope Leo XIII, May 15, 1891

INTRODUCTION: ON THE CONDITION OF WORKERS

The spirit of revolutionary change, which has long disturbed the nations of the world, has passed from politics to economic life. The elements of this conflict are unmistakable. The immense growth in industry and great discoveries in science have fundamentally altered the relations between workers and employers. For a few individuals this has meant enormous fortunes but for the masses it has resulted in utter poverty. This conflict has caused workers to become more unified and self-reliant. It also has encouraged general moral deterioration.

These problems are difficult to resolve. It is not easy to define the relative rights and mutual duties of the rich and of the poor, of capital and of labor. In our world, moreover, there are people who are eager to take advantage of the many differences of opinion and stir up the people to revolt.

Some remedy must be found soon. The working class is treated so unjustly that many of them live in miserable and wretched conditions. Since the ancient workers' guilds were abolished in the last century people now lack protection in the work place. As public authority set aside religion, workers have been surrendered, isolated and helpless, to the hardheartedness of employers and the greed of unchecked competition. This evil has been increased by rapacious usury, although traditionally condemned by the Church, currently practiced by covetous and grasping people. Most business decisions, including hiring and firing practices and trade policy, are concentrated in the hands of few. All of this is to say that today a small number of very rich people have burdened the teeming masses of the working poor with conditions that are not much better than slavery.

1. UNDERSTANDING THE PROBLEM

THE PRINCIPLE OF PRIVATE PROPERTY

As a remedy for these social evils, socialists prey on the envy of the poor toward the rich. They maintain that the solution to these problems is to do away with private possession of goods and make the goods of individuals common to all. They believe that government should then administer the common property. This equal share in wealth will then be the cure for the present evil. This solution is unjust on a number of grounds: it would hurt workers, rob the lawful of their possessions and inject government into an area that is not its own.

Justification from the Purpose of Work: The reason a person engages in remunerative labor is to obtain property. A person who works for pay does so for the purpose of receiving in return what is necessary for the satisfaction of his or her needs. The workers also to have the right to use pay as they see fit. Thus, if workers live within their means, save some money, and invest in land, the land becomes their wages under another form. Thus, workers would be able to use such land as they would use their wages. Ownership necessarily includes the ability to choose use, whether in wages or property.

Justification based on Human Nature: Like all life in God's creation, humans have the fundamental instincts of self-preservation and propagation. Unlike plants and animals, humans have a mind. This is a distinguishing human feature. We have choice; we are the masters of our own acts. We must make decisions for our future welfare. Thus humans can possess the fruits of the earth as well as the earth itself. The fact that God has given the earth for the use and enjoyment of the whole human race does not prohibit private ownership of property. That God has granted the earth to all humanity does not mean people can use the earth as they please. Human authority must place limits on private property. Moreover, the earth, even though apportioned among private owners, ceases not thereby to minister to the needs of all. Those who do not own land contribute their labor; hence, it may truly be said that all human subsistence is derived either from labor on one's own land, or from some paid work on the land.

Justification from the Transformative Character of Work: There is more proof that private ownership is in accord with the law of nature. When people work, that is to say, when they turn the activity of their mind and the strength of their body toward procuring the fruits of nature, they make a part of that which they work on their own. When people work, they leave an impression of themselves, their personality on the object of labor. Justice demands that people should possess that which they have worked on. That is to say, workers have a right to keep a portion of what they work on as their own.

When a person works on something, he transforms it. Consider working the land, it begins wild and barren. Once it is worked, once it is tilled and cultivated through toil and skill, it is utterly changed. It is now fruitful and productive. It is impossible to separate the parts in this process. How can it be just that the fruit of a person's own sweat and labor can be possessed and enjoyed by another? As effects follow their cause, so is it just and right that the results of labor belong to the laborers.

Justification from the Established Social Practice through the Ages: Human societies throughout time have held that private ownership was in conformity with human nature and most conducive to peace and tranquility in human existence.

Justification based on the Protection of Family: The justification of individual rights is even stronger when considered in the context of a person's social and domestic obligations. Consider the family. No human law can abolish the natural and original right of marriage, nor in any way limit the chief and principal purpose of marriage ordained by God's authority from the beginning: "Increase and multiply" (Gen. 1:28). The family is the "society" of one's house, a society very small, but still a true society. Indeed the society of the family is prior to any other society, including the nation. The family has rights and duties that are quite independent of these larger communities.

It is a most sacred law of nature that parents must meet the basic needs of their children. There is no other way to do this than through the means of private ownership of property, which parents can pass on to children through inheritance. A family then has rights to the pursuit of its freedom and well-being. As a rule, government should not intrude into family life. However, if a family finds itself in a desperate situation, its needs are to be met through public aid. In like manner, if there is a great disturbance of mutual rights within a family, public authority must intervene. Such intervention does not rob citizens of their rights; in fact such intervention justly and properly safeguards and strengthens rights.

The first and most fundamental principle, therefore, in the work to alleviate the terrible conditions of the working poor must be the defense of private property. This being established, we proceed to consider the remedy for the contemporary social order.

THE HUMAN CONDITION

Some people mistakenly wish to reduce all members of society to one level. The truth is that there naturally exist significant differences among people; these differences include capacity, skill, health, strength, and fortune. Such inequality is not a disadvantage either to individuals or to the community. Social and public life can only be maintained by means of various parts.

Likewise, pain and hardship are part of the human condition. There are those who pretend this is not so and aim to delude others. Nothing is more useful than to look at the world as it really is, and at the same time to seek a remedy elsewhere for its troubles.

2. RESOLUTION OF THE PROBLEM

It is a fundamental error to hold that one social class is by nature hostile to another social class, that is to say, it is wrong to suggest that by nature the wealthy and the workers live in mutual conflict. Just as there are different parts of the human body and the body has a symmetry and balance, so society is ordained by nature with two classes who are meant to dwell in harmony and agreement. Each class needs the other. Capital cannot do without labor; labor cannot do without capital.

MUTUAL RIGHTS AND DUTIES

The Responsibility of Workers: Workers must fully and faithfully perform the work that has been freely and equitably agreed upon. They must never injure the property, nor outrage the person, of an employer. They must never resort to violence in defending their own cause, nor engage in riot or disorder. They must have nothing to do with persons of evil principles, who work with artful promises of great results, and excite foolish hopes that usually end in useless regrets and grievous loss.

The Responsibility of Employers: The wealthy owners and employers must not look upon their workers as their bondsmen. They must respect the human dignity of every worker as a person and a Christian. They must keep in mind that physical labor is honorable as it enables a person to earn a living in an upright manner. They must know that it is shameful and inhuman to use workers as objects for their own personal gain. They must be aware that justice demands that the good of a worker's soul must be kept in mind. The employer must ensure that workers have time for religious duties. The employer must ensure that the worker not be exposed to corrupting influences and dangerous occasions. The employer must ensure that workers not be led away to neglect their homes and families, or to squander their earnings. Furthermore, the employer must never make people work beyond their strength, or employ them in work unsuited to their sex and age.

The principal duty of every employer is to give every worker what is just. Doubtless, before deciding whether wages are fair, many things have to be considered. Wealthy owners and all employers must be mindful that forcing the poor into unjust conditions for their own selfish gain and profit is condemned by all laws, human and divine. To defraud anyone of wages is a great crime that cries to the avenging anger of Heaven. "Listen! The wages of the laborers who mowed your fields, which you kept back by fraud, cry out, and the cries of the harvesters have reached the ears of the Lord of hosts" (James 5:4). Finally, the rich must religiously refrain from cutting down the workers' earnings, whether by force, by fraud, or by usurious dealing. The vulnerability of workers demands proportionate protection. If these moral rules were obeyed, would there be any social strife today?

HOW ARE WE TO USE POSSESSIONS?

The Church aims higher than simply ending social strife. The Church works to bring the social classes together in friendship. The great truth, the truth on which Christian dogma rests, is that when we have given up this present life, we shall really begin to live. God has not created us for the perishable and transitory things of earth, but for things heavenly and everlasting. God has given us this world as a place of exile, and not as our abiding place. As for riches and the other things that people call good and desirable, whether we have them in abundance, or are lacking in them—so far as eternal happiness is concerned—it makes no difference; the only important thing is to use them properly.

The rich are warned that money and possessions do not bring freedom from sorrow and they are of no benefit for eternal happiness, indeed riches are obstacles (Matt. 19:23–24). All must know that in the end, they will be asked to give a strict accounting of their lives. They must know the principle of proper use of wealth. It is one thing to have the right to own money and another to appropriately use money. Private ownership is the natural right of humans. As St. Thomas says, "It is lawful for a man to hold private property; and it is also necessary for the carrying on of human existence." But if the question were asked: How must one's possessions be used? The Church replies without hesitation. Again in the words of St. Thomas, "Man should not consider his material possessions as his own, but as common to all, so as to share them without hesitation when others are in need" (*Summa theologiae*, IIa-IIae, q. 64, art. 2). No one is commanded to give to others from what he or she needs to live. No one is commanded to give away what is reasonably required to keep one's self or one's family becomingly in life. But when these conditions are met, when one's standing in life is considered, it becomes a duty to give to the poor out of what remains. This is a duty, not of justice (save in extreme cases), but of Christian charity.

To sum up: Whoever has received a large share of temporal blessings has received them for a purpose. The person must use these blessings for personal development. At the same time he or she must use them, as a steward of God, for the benefit of others.

The poor must know that in the eyes of God, poverty is no disgrace and that there is dignity in work. Indeed God seems inclined to those who suffer misfortune; for Jesus Christ calls the poor "blessed"(Matt. 5: 3); He lovingly invites those in labor and grief to come to Him for solace (Matt. 11:28); and He displays tender love toward the lowly and the oppressed. These reflections cannot fail to keep down the pride of the well to do, and to give heart to the unfortunate. The rich will thus be moved to generosity and the poor will become moderate in their desires. True nobility lies in one's moral qualities, that is, in virtue. All people, no matter how rich or how poor, equally share the capacity for virtue and such virtue will be rewarded with everlasting happiness.

If Christian morality were to prevail, the rich and poor would be united in friendship and in love. If Christian morality were followed people would come to experience each other as children of the same God. This is the Gospel message. If society were penetrated by these ideas would not strife quickly cease?

3. THE CHURCH AND THE POOR

If human society is to be healed, it must return to Christian life and Christian institutions. The Church responds directly to the needs of the poor and works to relieve poverty through its many organizations. The Church has always provided aid for the needy and called on Christians to support charity. She has established religious congregations and institutions for help and mercy, so that hardly any kind of suffering has not gone unmet.

It cannot be doubted, however, that to relieve the problems now facing us, more than the Church is needed. All sectors of society must act and act in unison. We now turn to consider the role government ought to play in these matters.

4. THE RESPONSIBILITY OF GOVERNMENT

THE PROMOTION OF THE COMMON GOOD

The primary duty of government is to ensure that its laws and institutions, its general character and means of administration, realize public well-being and private prosperity. A society prospers and thrives through moral rule, well-regulated family life, respect for religion and justice, the moderation and fair imposition of public taxes, the progress of the arts and of trade, the abundant yield of the land, and indeed everything which makes the citizens better and happier. Public officials serve the common good by serving every class in society while at the same time directly promoting the interests of the poor. In fact, the more that is done for the benefit of the working classes through the laws of the country, the less need will there be to seek special means to relieve their suffering.

There is another and deeper consideration which must not be lost sight of. The poor are citizens equally as the rich; they are real parts of the commonwealth. It need hardly be said that the poor are in every city a large majority of the population. Justice demands that each person be given his or her due; thus those in public authority must provide for the welfare and the comfort of the working classes. Among the many and grave duties of rulers, the first and chief is to act with distributive justice toward every class.

All citizens, without exception, ought to contribute to the common good, yet it should not be supposed that all are able to contribute in the same extent. Justice, therefore, demands that the interests of the working classes should be carefully watched over by the government. Such a policy would enable the working classes, whose labors greatly contribute to the wealth of the community, to share in the benefits they create. This includes being housed, clothed, and enabled to support life.

INDICATORS OF THE GOOD SOCIETY

A government must not absorb the individual or the family; both should be allowed freedom consistent with the common good and the interest of others. Whenever the general interest of any particular class suffers, or is threatened with harm, which can in no other way be met or prevented, the public authority must become involved. It is in the interest of the community and individuals that peace and good order be maintained; that all things should be carried on in accordance with God's laws and those of nature; that the discipline of family life should be observed and that religion should be obeyed; that a high standard of morality should prevail, both in public and private life; that justice should be held sacred and that no one should injure another with impunity; that the members of the commonwealth develop the capability of guarding and defending their country.

GOVERNMENT ACTION

There are many situations where government action must be invoked: Strikes that cause disturbance to the public peace; working conditions causing family ties or religious duties to be relaxed or that mixing the sexes presents dangerous occasions for evil; or if employers laid burdens upon their workmen which are unjust, or if employers degrade workers with conditions repugnant to their dignity as human beings; finally, if employers endanger the health of workers by excessive labor, or by work unsuited to sex or age. The limits of government intervention must be determined by the nature of the occasion, the principle being that the law must not undertake more, nor proceed further, than is required for the remedy of the evil or the removal of the mischief.

PROTECTION OF THE SOCIAL ORDER

All rights must be religiously respected, yet when there is question of defending the rights of individuals, the poor have a claim to special consideration. The richer class have many ways of shielding themselves, and stand less in need of help from the government; whereas the mass of the poor have no resources of their own to fall back upon. The must chiefly depend upon the assistance of government. And it is for this reason that wage earners, since they mostly belong to the mass of the needy, should be specially cared for and protected by the government.

Workers strike for many reasons, for example they are forced to work long hours, or the work is too physically demanding or because they consider their wages insufficient. Strikes should be prevented by public measures because they can injure both the workers and the owners. Strikes may also harm trade and the general public good. On occasion strikes have caused violence and social disorder. The laws should forestall and prevent such troubles from arising; they should lend their influence and authority to the removal of the causes that lead to conflicts between employers and employed.

PROTECTION OF WORKERS

The worker, too, has interests that should be protected by the government; and first of all, there are spiritual interests. Workers have the obligation not to work on Sunday and holy days.

We must protect workers from the cruelty of greedy employers who use humans as mere instruments for money making. It is neither just nor human to grind workers down with excessive labor so as to stupefy their minds and wear out their bodies. Human power has physical limitations. A person's strength is developed and increased by use and exercise, but only on condition of due intermission and proper rest. Daily labor, therefore, should be so regulated so as not to be protracted over longer hours than strength admits. How many and how long the intervals of rest should be must depend on the nature of the work, on circumstances of time and place, and on the health and strength of the worker. Those who work in mines and quarries, for example, and extract coal, stone and metals from the bowels of the earth, should have shorter hours as their labor is more severe and trying to health. Then, again, the season of the year should be taken into account; for not infrequently a kind of labor is easy at one time which at another is intolerable or exceedingly difficult. Finally, work that is quite suitable for a strong man cannot rightly be required from a woman or a child.

In regard to children, great care should be taken not to place them in workshops and factories until their bodies and minds are sufficiently developed. For, just as very rough weather destroys the buds of spring, so does too early an experience of life's hard toil blight the young promise of a child's faculties, and render any true education impossible. Women are not suited for certain occupations; a woman is by nature fitted for work in the home, and it is that which is best adapted at once to preserve her modesty and to promote the good bringing up of children and the well-being of the family. As a general principle it may be laid down that a worker ought to have leisure and rest proportionate to the wear and tear of one's strength, for waste of strength must be repaired by cessation from hard work. In all agreements between employers and employees there should be allowed proper rest for soul and body.

MORAL REQUIREMENT OF THE JUST WAGE

We now approach a subject of great importance. One in which right thinking is absolutely necessary. Some people hold that wages are regulated only by free consent. Thus when an employer pays the agreed upon wage, he or she has fulfilled his obligation to the worker. The only way injustice might occur would be if the employer refused to pay the whole of the wages, or if the worker did not complete the work agreed upon. Then, and only then, should public authorities intervene, namely, to see that each obtains his or her due.

No fair-minded person can completely agree with this position. It is incomplete. This position ignores important considerations. To labor is to exert oneself for the sake of procuring what is necessary for the various purposes of life, and chief of all for self-preservation. Hence, a person's labor necessarily has two characteristics. First of all, labor is personal. The exertion of power belongs to the worker. Such ability was given to the worker to pursue personal good. Secondly, one's labor is necessary. One cannot live without the results of work. Self-preservation is a basic law of nature. If we consider labor merely as personal, it would be within the worker's right to accept any wage whatsoever. Just as one is free to work or not to work, so one is free to accept a small wage or even none at all. But when we consider the fact that work is also necessary for one to live, our conclusion is altogether different.

The personal and necessary aspects of work are separable in theory but not in practice. We all have the fundamental duty to preserve our lives. To neglect this duty is a moral crime. It necessarily follows that each of us has a natural right to procure what is required in order to live. The poor can procure that in no other way than by what they can earn through their work.

Workers and employers should make free agreements on wages and other matters. In doing so, however, they must rest such agreements on a law of justice, namely, that wages must be sufficient to support a worker in reasonable comfort. If through necessity or fear of a worse evil a worker accepts harder conditions because an employer will give no better, he or she is made the victim of force and injustice. While governments can intervene to resolve unjust and unsafe working conditions, it is better that government supported organizations or boards be created to safeguard the interests of workers.

SOCIAL BENEFITS OF JUST-WAGE POLICY

There are great social benefits to just wages. If workers can earn enough to live comfortably and be able to support their families, they will be able to save some money and secure some property. We have seen that the problem of our day, this great labor question, will not resolved except through the principle that private ownership must be held sacred and inviolable. Public policy should favor ownership and enable as many as possible to become owners.

Three excellent results will follow from this. First of all, property will certainly become more equitably divided. Today our cities are divided by a wide chasm into two social classes. On the one side there are those who hold power and wealth. This side controls all the labor and trade, manipulates all the sources of supply, and has a dominant influence in governments. On the other side there is the needy and powerless multitude, sick and sore in spirit and ever ready to cause conflict. If working people can be encouraged to look forward to obtaining a share in the land, the consequence will be that the gulf between vast wealth and sheer poverty will be bridged over, and the respective classes will be brought nearer to one another.

Second, people work harder when they work on things that are their own. This would add to the production of the land and to the wealth of the community. Third, this would decrease immigration. If people had the means of living a tolerable and happy life, they would cling to the country in which they were born.

These important benefits, however, can be reckoned on only provided that a person's means be not drained and exhausted by excessive taxation. The right to possess private property is derived from nature, not from people. It would be unjust of a government if under the name of taxation it were to deprive the private owner of more than is fair.

5. THE PERSONAL RESPONSIBILITY OF WORKERS

MORAL JUSTIFICATION OF WORKERS' ASSOCIATIONS

Finally, workers themselves may effect change. They may, for example, work with employers to create organizations that help those in need, especially to care for workers in times of sickness and in death and to care for widows and orphans. They also can create institutions for the welfare of children. The most important form of organizations is the workers' union. History attests to the excellent results brought about by the workers' guilds of olden times. It is wrong for governments to absolutely prohibit private societies. To enter into a "society" of this kind is the natural right of every person. Government has the duty to protect such rights. If it were to forbid its citizens to form associations this would contradict the principle of its own existence, namely, the natural tendency of persons to dwell in society.

RECOGNITION OF PEOPLE MAKING A DIFFERENCE

There are many Catholics who have worked to better the conditions of the working class. They have taken up the cause of the workers and have worked to infuse a spirit of equity into the mutual relations of employers and employed. These people have kept the laws of the Gospel in the minds of both the rich and poor. They deserve much praise. The bishops have often promoted workers' associations. They have supported many clergy members to work for the spiritual interest of the members of such associations. Many well-to-do Catholics have cast their lot with the wage earners and have spent large sums in founding and widely spreading benefit and insurance societies. These activities have greatly benefited the community. Such associations provide hope for the future. Governments must watch over but not interfere with organizations. To conclude, workers' associations should be so organized and governed so as to promote the most suitable means for helping each individual member better his or her condition in body, soul, and property. These associations ought to look to God and encourage religious practices.

The pressing question of our day concerns the condition of the workers. The resolution of this problem is in the interest of all members of society. Christian workers will be able to resolve the problems with ease if they form associations, choose wise guides, and follow on the path of their forefathers, a path that produces great advantage for them and for the common good.

If this were the case there would be much more ground for hope and for recalling the sense of duty in workers who have given up their faith. Many workers today feel that they have been fooled by empty promises and deceived by false pretexts. They know that their grasping employers too often treat them with great inhumanity and hardly care for them outside the profit their labor brings. If they belong to a union, it is probably one that promotes the sense of conflict that often accompanies poverty. Broken in spirit and worn down in body, how many of them would gladly free themselves from such terrible bondage! Yet they are afraid to take a step. To these people, Catholic associations are of incalculable service, by helping them out of their difficulties, inviting them to companionship and receiving the returning wanderers to a haven where they may securely find repose.

CONCLUSION: COMMON RESPONSIBILITY

Every person must immediately respond to the problems of workers within his or her ability lest the danger grow beyond remedy. Political authorities must use the laws and institutions of their countries to respond to these problems. Employers and wealthy owners must always remember their moral duties. The working class, whose interests are at stake, should make every lawful and proper effort to relieve their distress. In the end, however, it must be recalled that only religion can destroy evil at its root. Thus the primary task is to re-establish Christian morals. Without this, any plan or program, even those developed by the wisest people, will fail.

SOCIAL JUSTICE AND *RERUM NOVARUM*

Notice that in the last paragraph of *Rerum novarum* Pope Leo XIII calls on all people to respond to these pressing issues. He notes that political authorities, employers, and the workers themselves must do what they can in their particular situations to relieve the distress that disrupts society. No one sector of society alone can solve this problem. It is a problem of *social* justice.

Justice is a dominant theme in this encyclical. We can see the influence of Thomas Aquinas on Leo XIII's thought here. Yet the pope does not simply repeat Thomas. His agenda is formed by concern for the poor of his day, those whom he identifies as non-owning workers. *Rerum novarum* demands the protection of the dignity of these poor and vulnerable people. This concern moves Leo XIII's understanding of justice a few steps from Thomas's view of justice. This is not to say that Thomas was not concerned about the poor. As G. K. Chesterton stated in a biography of Thomas, "He had from the first that full and final test of truly orthodox Catholicity; the impetuous, impatient, intolerant passion for the poor; and even that readiness to be rather a nuisance to the rich, out of a hunger to feed the hungry."[6] Chesterton, in this moving sentence, touches on the foundation of Catholic

social thought while writing on the life of Thomas. An essential feature of
Catholicism from its very origins in the life of Jesus until today is an "impetuous, impatient, intolerant passion for the poor."

Justice, for Thomas, includes internal and external aspects. We see both
evident in *Rerum novarum*. Leo XIII calls for personal conversion and social action. Thomas also speaks of justice in terms of equality, equality of
geometrical proportion and equality of arithmetical proportion. Another
way of thinking about this distinction is that justice can be understood as
strict equality or as proportionate equality (fairness). At times justice calls
for strict equality. For example, in justice professors must treat all their
students with equal dignity. They may, however, give some students higher
grades than others. They must grade based on an objective standard of fairness. At times justice requires equality; at other times it requires fairness.

Pope Leo XIII is not arguing for equal pay for employers and employees.
Justice does not demand equality in this sense. He is arguing, rather, for
fairness in pay. Justice demands that employers pay employees a fair wage
based both on their effort and labor and on the moral requirements of self-
preservation and protection of the family. Yet Leo XIII's understanding of
justice is deeper than equality and fairness. Justice, for Leo XIII, and indeed
the whole tradition of Catholic social thought, requires that people and
institutions in society address the needs of people who are without voice or
power or authority. Put simply, justice demands active concern for the poor.
The working definition of justice, then—in Leo XIII and, as we shall see, in
the whole of the Catholic social tradition—is giving one what is due with a
constant and perpetual will. What is due is determined by consideration of
three moral norms: equality, fairness, and active concern for the poor.

FR. JOHN A. RYAN: *RERUM NOVARUM* IN AMERICA

The person most often recognized for bringing *Rerum novarum* to the
forefront of American Catholic life is Fr. John A. Ryan (1869–1945). Fr.
Ryan was an influential theologian (he was also trained as an economist)
and public advocate for just social policy. His two most important books
are *A Living Wage* (1906) and *Distributive Justice* (1916). Ryan was active
on national and local levels working to pass wage laws and other social
welfare issues. The following excerpts are from *A Living Wage*.[7] Note how
he develops the theme of a living wage from *Rerum novarum*. One can also
see here his roots in Thomas Aquinas's natural law theology.

The thesis to be maintained in this volume is that the laborer's claim to a
Living Wage is of the nature of a right. This right is personal, not merely
social: that is to say, it belongs to the individual as individual, and not as
member of society; it is the laborer's personal prerogative, not his share

of social good; and its primary end is the welfare of the laborer, not that of society. Again, it is a natural, not a positive right, for it is born with the individual, derived from his rational nature, not conferred upon him by a positive enactment. (43)

A right in the moral sense of the term may be defined as an inviolable moral claim to some personal good. When this claim is created, as it sometimes is, by civil authority it is a positive or legal right; when it is derived from man's rational nature it is a natural right. All rights are moral means whereby the possessor of them is enabled to reach some end. Natural rights are the moral means or opportunities by which the individual attains the end appointed to him by nature. For the present it is sufficient to say that this end is a right and reasonable life. (44)

The life of the individual person is so sacred that, as long as the right thereto has not been forfeited by the perverse conduct of the subject himself, it may not be subordinated to the welfare of any other individual or any number of individuals. (45)

With respect to their natural rights, all men are equal, because all are equal in the rational nature from which such rights are derived: By nature every man is a person, that is, a rational, self-active, and independent being. Every man is rational because he is endowed with the faculties of reason and will. His will impels him to seek the good, the end, of his being, and his reason enables him to find and adjust means to this end. Every man is self-active, inasmuch as he is master of his own faculties and able in all the essentials of conduct to direct his own actions. Every man is independent in the sense that he is morally complete in himself, is not a part of any other man, nor inferior to any man, either in the essential qualities of his being or in the end toward which he is morally bound to move. In short, every individual is an "end in himself," and has a personality of his own to develop through the exercise of his own faculties. (46)

Men are equal as regards the number of their natural rights. The most important of these are the rights to life, to liberty, to property, to a livelihood, to marriage, to religious worship, to intellectual and moral education. These inhere in all men without distinction of person, but they have not necessarily the same extension, or content, in all. (47)

Since, therefore, the individual is obliged to live a moral and reasonable life in the manner just described, the means to this end, i.e., natural rights, are so necessary and so sacred that all other persons than the one in whom they reside are morally restrained from interfering with or ignoring them. The dignity of personality imposes upon the individual the duty of self-perfection; he cannot fulfill this duty adequately unless he is endowed with natural rights. Such is the immediate basis of natural rights and the proximate source of their sacredness; their ultimate source is to be found in the Reason and Will of God, who has decreed that men shall pursue self-perfection and that they shall not arbitrarily deprive one another of the means essential to this purpose. (50)

The Catholic view is that the individual's natural rights are derived from and determined by his nature, that is to say, his essential constitution, relations and end. They are also said to proceed from the natural law, which is simply that portion of God's eternal law that applies to actions of human beings. (62)

The doctrine of natural rights . . . insists that the individual is endowed by nature, or rather, by God, with the rights that are requisite to a reasonable development of his personality, and that these rights are, within due limits, sacred against the power even of the State; but it insists that no individual's rights extend so far as to prevent the State from adjusting the conflicting claims of individuals and safeguarding the just welfare of all its citizens. In other words, man's natural rights must not be so widely interpreted that the strong, and the cunning, and the unscrupulous will be able, under the pretext of individual liberty, to exploit and overreach the weak, and simple, and honest majority. (64)

The true formula is, that the individual has a right to all things that are essential to the reasonable development of his personality, consistently with the rights of others and the complete observance of the moral law. Where this rule is enforced the rights of all individuals, and of society as well, are amply and reasonably protected. (65)

"The minimum of the material conditions of decent and reasonable living" comprises, for the adult male, the means of supporting a family. To this much of the world's goods he has a natural right which is valid "against the members of the industrial community in which he lives." In the case of the laborer this claim must be formulated in terms of wages. The laborer has a right to a family Living Wage because this is the only way in which he can exercise his right to the means of maintaining a family, and he has a right to these means because they are an essential condition of normal life. (118)

The right to the means of maintaining a family, therefore, is not finally derived from the duty of maintaining it—from the needs of the family—

but from the laborer's dignity, from his own essential needs. True it is that if the support of wife and children did not in the normal order of things fall upon the husband and father, he would not have a right to the additional remuneration required for this purpose; but this merely shows that the duty is the occasion, or condition, not the ultimate cause of the right. The right to the conditions of being the head of a family, which is obvious, implies the right to a family Living Wage because nature and reason have decreed that the family should be supported by its head. (119)

Moreover, the right to a family Living Wage belongs to every adult male laborer, whether he intends to marry or not; for rights are to be interpreted according to the average conditions of human life, and these suppose the laborer to become the head of a family . . . Hence it is sufficiently accurate to say that the family that ought to serve as a standard of measurement in the matter of decent remuneration for the adult male laborer, is one having four or five children. (120–22)

SOME QUESTIONS FOR CONSIDERATION

1. As in Pope Leo XIII's day, people today are questioning the role of government in economics and the social order. What are Leo XIII's principles for government involvement? Do you think they are applicable today?
2. Pope Leo XIII gives several reasons to justify private ownership of property. Given your experience as an owner—or your hopes to be one—evaluate his argument.
3. Compare Pope Leo XIII's and/or Fr. Ryan's arguments for a living wage with wage laws and practices today (for example, living-wage ordinances and minimum-wage laws).
4. Based on Thomas Aquinas, Pope Leo XIII, and Fr. Ryan, what does the term *justice* mean in the Catholic tradition?
5. While parts of Pope Leo XIII's thought are classic, some elements of *Rerum novarum* seem out of date. What issues in the text do you think are bound to nineteenth-century thinking? What reasons would you give to counter Leo XIII's thinking? Why should others agree with your view and not with Leo XIII's view?
6. Review the principles of Catholic social thought from the first chapter—the dignity of the human person, the common good, subsidiarity, and solidarity—and describe how they are expressed in the chapter.
7. Using the "look, judge, and act" model, discuss what Pope Leo XIII sees in the world, what his judgment is, and what actions he determines are appropriate.

8. How do the authors of the selections in this chapter defend and support their positions? Review the discussion of moral arguments from
Chapter 1. Do the authors argue from authority or do they use theological, biblical, philosophical, common sense, and pragmatic arguments?

9. Review the three spheres of Catholic social action: works of mercy
and justice, public expression and personal commitment, and social
analysis for social change. How do the readings in this chapter express these spheres?

10. What is personalism? How is it supported in this chapter?

11. Discuss the four forms of moral discourse—narrative, prophetic, ethical, and policy—and how they are expressed in this chapter.

Prayer to St. Joseph, Patron of Workers

*St. Joseph, Patron of Workers, help us to respect the dignity of all
workers. Help us to learn about and to care about workers who do not
have fair wages, just benefits, safe working environments. Help us to
raise our voices for justice for workers. Help us to ask our government
and our representatives to develop policies that create jobs with dignity.*

*You taught your son the value of work and the joy of work well done.
Teach us these lessons. Guide us in our own work and in the work of
justice we are all called to participate in. Renew our strength and commitment each day as we face the work ahead as we labor for the common
good of all. Amen.*

—JANE DEREN

Chapter Four

Personalism and Human Rights

Papal Prayer for Peace
   *Let us pray with deep fervor for the peace that Jesus came to bring.
May he banish all things that endanger peace. May he transform us into
witnesses of truth, justice and love. May he enlighten our leaders so that
they may always work to promote the common good and that they always protect and defend the gift of peace. May Christ inflame our hearts
and minds so we are able to break the barriers that divide us, so that we
are able to strengthen bonds of mutual love, so that we are able to sincerely understand one another, and so that we are able to forgive those
who have done us wrong. Through his power and inspiration we pray
that we all come to recognize one another as children of God. We pray
that the peace we all long for, the peace that Jesus came to bring, may
blossom forth and reign forever among us.*
                           —ADAPTED FROM POPE JOHN XXIII, *PACEM IN TERRIS*

The central text of this chapter is Pope John XXIII's 1963 encyclical *Pacem in terris (Peace on Earth)*. As the title indicates, the primary concern of the encyclical is peace in the world. The fundamental moral principles presented by John to support peace are human rights, which he says are "universal, inviolable and inalienable" claims people have. Underlying these rights is an understanding of the human person rooted in the Bible and expressed in the thinking of Thomas Aquinas. In the middle of the twentieth century, particularly with the work of the philosopher Jacques Maritain, this view of the person in Catholic social thought began to be called personalism. This chapter looks at the development of personalism as well as *Pacem in terris*.

This chapter also addresses significant developments in Catholic social thought in the United States. It looks at the contributions of the great theologian John Courtney Murray within the cultural context of Catholics in America. The final section considers the life, work, and legacy of Dorothy Day, described as "the most influential, interesting and significant person" in the history of American Catholicism.[1]

THE PERSONALIST PHILOSOPHY OF JACQUES MARITAIN

Rerum novarum was Pope Leo XIII's response to the liberalism that he saw spreading from the political sphere into economic life. Like many others of his time, Leo used the term *liberalism* to cover the ideas behind the many changes that challenged traditional society during the eighteenth and nineteenth centuries.[2] Eventually, the term came to be more clearly defined. *Liberalism*, now a political philosophy with which Americans are very familiar, is a way of thinking about life in society that gives priority to the autonomy of the individual (in contrast to communism). That is, this liberalism, sometimes called classic liberalism, espouses individual freedom in politics and in economics and thus suggests that social relations are primarily the result of free choice rather than natural conditions. Liberalism is agnostic about the idea of a universal good or end for human life. Since its priority is individual choice, it cannot offer an objective view of the human good; that remains for individuals or groups to figure out. Liberalism is also agnostic about religion. It is not in favor of it or against it. It does, however, hold that the realm of religion is personal not social.

We live in a liberal democracy. We have the Bill of Rights with its many protections for individual freedoms. We do not have a state-sponsored religion. We are not a Christian nation in the literal sense of the term. In this liberal democracy we have several different political parties and views. Both liberals and conservatives in our country espouse liberal values (in the classic sense).

Pope Leo and his predecessors rejected liberalism. For example, in 1864 Pope Leo's immediate predecessor, Pius IX, wrote that it is "insanity" to hold that

> liberty of conscience and worship is each man's personal right, which ought to be legally proclaimed and asserted in every rightly constituted society; and that a right resides in the citizens to an absolute liberty, which should be restrained by no authority whether ecclesiastical or civil, whereby they may be able openly and publicly to manifest and declare any of their ideas whatever, either by word of mouth, by the press, or in any other way. (*Quanta cura*, #3)

Pope John XXIII and his successors, on the other hand, conditionally accept this new emphasis on freedom. Yet their view of freedom is not simply individual freedom of choice. The Catholic encounter with liberalism, and its promotion of freedom, caused a renewed consideration of the theoretical foundation of Catholic social thought, namely, the work of Thomas Aquinas.

We saw in an earlier chapter that Thomas Aquinas had a strong notion of the social character of humans. In the twentieth century Catholic theologians and philosophers developed Thomas's notion into what has become known as personalism. Indeed, it would not be incorrect to say that the fundamental idea underlying contemporary Catholic social thought is personalism. A most important development of this notion came from Jacques Maritain (1882–1973).

Maritain was the most important Catholic philosopher of the twentieth century. Born in France, he lived and taught for many years in the United States. Maritain is remembered most for his interpretation of Thomas Aquinas for the modern world. His most enduring legacy may be his involvement in the development of the understanding of rights that came to be articulated in the 1948 United Nations Universal Declaration of Human Rights (see the section below).[3] He argued that human rights were justified by the philosophical principles of Thomas Aquinas.

Reflecting on the growth and development of Catholic social thought, it is Maritain's understanding of the human person that is so significant. Maritain held that human nature possesses two substantial elements. Everyone is at once an individual and a person. As an *individual*, the human is a part of the greater whole of society, and as such, individuals must be ordered to the whole of society. But humans are more than individuals. They are *persons* in relation to God. As a person the human has a transcendent character. For Maritain, this is the deepest dimension of being.[4] The transcendent character of human nature, he states, "surpasses and is superior to all temporal societies."[5] Society, through its organizational and governing body, can make certain claims on us as individuals. Yet we have an essence, a moral dignity, that gives us rights over society. For Maritain, and indeed for Catholic thought generally, governments have a specific and limited purpose, namely, to serve persons in the common good. Governments do not grant rights to individuals as much as they have to recognize rights already present in them.[6]

Maritain uses this personalist philosophy to justify not only human rights, but also democracy and the related principle of religious pluralism. Commentator Thomas Bokenkotter suggests that for Maritain democracy is not simply a political enterprise. It requires a solid, structured moral foundation. "Belief in the dignity of the human person and in human rights, human equality, freedom, law, mutual respect and tolerance, the unity of humankind and the ideal of peace, is essential for the survival of democracy."[7] Maritain's work, cited by Pope Paul VI in his encyclical *Populorum progressio* (1967), helps develop the foundation for Catholic social thought in the latter half of the twentieth century.

The following is Maritain's description of the common good, a critical theme in Catholic social thought. The quotation captures the depth of his understanding of the human and of human life in society.

That which constitutes the common good of political society is not only: the collection of public commodities and services—the roads, ports, schools, etc., which the organization of common life presupposes; a sound fiscal condition of the state and its military power; the body of just laws, good customs and wise institutions, which provide the nation with its structure; the heritage of its great historical remembrances, its symbols and its glories, its living traditions and cultural treasures. The common good includes all of these and something much more besides—something more profound, more concrete and more human. For it includes also, and above all, the whole sum itself of these. This sum that is quite different from a simple collection of juxtaposed units. It includes the sum or sociological integration of all the civic conscience, political virtues and sense of right and liberty, of all the activity, material prosperity and spiritual riches, of unconsciously operative hereditary wisdom, of moral rectitude, justice, friendship, happiness, virtue and heroism in the individual lives of its members. For these things all are, in a certain measure, communicable and so revert to each member, helping him to perfect his life and liberty of person. They all constitute the good human life of the multitude.[8]

THE UNITED NATIONS

The United Nations officially came into existence in 1945.[9] The Catholic Church has always been a strong supporter of the organization. In *Pacem in terris*, for example, Pope John XXIII affirms the work of the U.N., particularly its Universal Declaration of Human Rights. Paul VI and John Paul II made public appearances at the U.N. and gave memorable speeches to the General Assembly. Indeed, the church is an active member of the organization as a permanent observer. As a permanent observer the church has full rights in the U.N. except that it cannot vote. Popes have historically looked to the U.N. for leadership in global issues.

The following is an excerpt from the Universal Declaration of Human Rights adopted by the United Nations in 1948. The declaration includes a preamble and thirty articles. The preamble introduces the document and presents a set of justifications for what follows. Each article articulates a basic human right or a set of human rights. The extract below includes the preamble and the first five articles. There is a strong correlation between this text and *Pacem in terris,* which follows later in this chapter.[10] Catholic legal scholar Mary Ann Glendon notes that the papal encyclicals and the work of Catholic philosophers and theologians helped form and advance the international human rights movement.[11]

—Preamble—

Whereas recognition of the inherent dignity and of the equal and inalienable rights of all members of the human family is the foundation of freedom, justice and peace in the world,

Whereas disregard and contempt for human rights have resulted in barbarous acts which have outraged the conscience of mankind, and the advent of a world in which human beings shall enjoy freedom of speech and belief and freedom from fear and want has been proclaimed as the highest aspiration of the common people,

Whereas it is essential, if man is not to be compelled to have recourse, as a last resort, to rebellion against tyranny and oppression, that human rights should be protected by the rule of law,

Whereas it is essential to promote the development of friendly relations between nations,

Whereas the peoples of the United Nations have in the Charter reaffirmed their faith in fundamental human rights, in the dignity and worth of the human person and in the equal rights of men and women and have determined to promote social progress and better standards of life in larger freedom,

Whereas Member States have pledged themselves to achieve, in cooperation with the United Nations, the promotion of universal respect for and observance of human rights and fundamental freedoms,

Whereas a common understanding of these rights and freedoms is of the greatest importance for the full realization of this pledge,

Now, Therefore THE GENERAL ASSEMBLY proclaims THIS UNIVERSAL DECLARATION OF HUMAN RIGHTS as a common standard of achievement for all peoples and all nations, to the end that every individual and every organ of society, keeping this Declaration constantly in mind, shall strive by teaching and education to promote respect for these rights and freedoms and by progressive measures, national and international, to secure their universal and effective recognition and observance, both among the peoples of Member States themselves and among the peoples of territories under their jurisdiction.

Article 1: All human beings are born free and equal in dignity and rights. They are endowed with reason and conscience and should act towards one another in a spirit of brotherhood.

Article 2: Everyone is entitled to all the rights and freedoms set forth in this Declaration, without distinction of any kind, such as race, color, sex, language, religion, political or other opinion, national or social origin, property, birth or other status. Furthermore, no distinction shall be made on the basis of the political, jurisdictional or international status of the country or territory to which a person belongs, whether it be independent, trust, non-self-governing or under any other limitation of sovereignty.

Article 3: Everyone has the right to life, liberty and security of person.

Article 4: No one shall be held in slavery or servitude; slavery and the slave trade shall be prohibited in all their forms.

Article 5: No one shall be subjected to torture or to cruel, inhuman or degrading treatment or punishment.

CATHOLIC AND AMERICAN

"We hold these truths to be self-evident." So begins the second paragraph of the Declaration of Independence, dated July 4, 1776. The signers of this history-changing document thought they were presenting universal truth when they stated that "all men are created equal" and that all have "certain unalienable Rights," primarily the rights to "Life, Liberty and the pursuit of Happiness." The signers of the Declaration of Independence also held that governments derive their authority from the governed (rather than from God or from the military power of the rulers). The consequence of this principle is that when a government is "destructive of these ends, it is the Right of the People to alter or to abolish it." These were radical ideas. They challenged long-held views about authority, power, and the social order. They also challenged long-held views of the Roman Catholic Church on authority, power, and social order. Tension between "being Roman Catholic" and "being American" flared up several times during our history. This chapter briefly looks at two instances, the *nativism* and *Americanism* controversies.

Nativism

In the early nineteenth century a popular anti-Catholic movement known as nativism erupted in the United States. Nativism refers to strong public sentiment favoring the native population (in this context, white American Protestants) over immigrants (in this context, European, particularly Irish, Catholics). According to historian Lawrence McCaffrey, in 1789 there were about thirty thousand Catholics in America. By 1860 there were nearly three million, many of whom were recent Irish immigrants.[12] The influx of immigrants posed a dramatic challenge to traditional Protestant America. Many people believed that Catholics were superstitious, given their views of sacraments and saints, and were anti-intellectual, given the roles priests, bishops, and the pope played in their lives. At times nativism was written into state laws. McCaffrey notes, for instance, that in several states Catholics were not recognized as full citizens until well into the 1800s. North Carolina did not repeal anti-Catholic legislation until 1835.[13] Anti-Catholic nativism was also expressed in books and magazines. Violence against Catholics was not infrequent during these times.

In the mid 1800s nativism was encapsulated in a political party called the Know Nothings. The party's motto was "Americans must rule Americans." Historian Jay Dolan notes, "Its members even had to take an oath that they would not vote for any foreigners, Roman Catholic in particular. By 1854, four years after its founding, the Know Nothing party had over one million members. It had elected eight governors, more than one hundred congressmen, and the mayors of Boston, Chicago, and Philadelphia, as well as thousands of lesser officials throughout the United States."[14]

Perhaps there were "reasons" for the prejudice and discrimination against Catholics—not unlike the "reasons" people today might give for prejudice and discrimination. From the middle decades of the 1800s into the twentieth century, Catholics made up a disproportionate number of the poor in American cities. Indeed, Catholic children formed the largest group of children sent to reformatories. Scholars Dorothy Brown and Elizabeth McKeown describe these striking conditions in their book *The Poor Belong to Us: Catholic Charities and American Welfare:* "In a formal statement in 1866, the entire body of Catholic bishops of the United States admitted that Catholic delinquency has assumed alarming proportions. 'It is a melancholy fact, and a very humiliating avowal for us to make,' they [the bishops] confessed, 'that a very large portions of the vicious and idle youth of our principal cities are the children of Catholic parents.'"[15]

People often forget that the Ku Klux Klan in the early days of the twentieth century was a nativist-inspired organization designed to intimidate Catholics—thus the burning cross—as well as Jews and African Americans. While direct action and violence against Catholics subsided in the twentieth century, there remained among some sectors of Protestant American a lingering skepticism about Catholics. They wondered if Catholics, with their allegiance to the pope, could be true Americans.

The American Protestant suspicion of Catholicism became very public in 1960 when the Democratic Party nominated Senator John F. Kennedy, a Catholic, for president. In September of that year Kennedy made a famous and often cited speech to a group of Protestant ministers in Houston, Texas. Since then, his words have often been used as a standard for thinking about how a politician's faith (usually a Catholic politician) should influence his or her political decision-making. Some commentators think that Kennedy went too far in separating his public life from the church. The following is an excerpt from Kennedy's speech. What do you think?

But because I am a Catholic, and no Catholic has ever been elected President, the real issues in this campaign have been obscured—perhaps deliberately, in some quarters less responsible than this. So it is apparently necessary for me to state once again—not what kind of church I believe in, for that should be important only to me—but what kind of America I believe in.

I believe in an America where the separation of church and state is absolute—where no Catholic prelate [bishop] would tell the President (should he be Catholic) how to act, and no Protestant minister would tell his parishioners for whom to vote—where no church or church school is granted any public funds or political preference—and where no man is denied public office merely because his religion differs from the President who might appoint him or the people who might elect him.

I believe in an America that is officially neither Catholic, Protestant nor Jewish—where no public official either requests or accepts instructions on public policy from the Pope, the National Council of Churches or any other ecclesiastical source—where no religious body seeks to impose its will directly or indirectly upon the general populace or the public acts of its officials—and where religious liberty is so indivisible that an act against one church is treated as an act against all . . .

But let me stress again that these are my views—for contrary to common newspaper usage, I am not the Catholic candidate for President. I am the Democratic Party's candidate for President who happens also to be a Catholic. I do not speak for my church on public matters—and the church does not speak for me.

Whatever issue may come before me as President—on birth control, divorce, censorship, gambling or any other subject—I will make my decision in accordance with these views, in accordance with what my conscience tells me to be the national interest, and without regard to outside religious pressures or dictates. And no power or threat of punishment could cause me to decide otherwise . . .

But I do not intend to apologize for these views to my critics of either Catholic or Protestant faith—nor do I intend to disavow either my views or my church in order to win this election.[16]

Americanism

Can one be a good American and a good Catholic? This question arose in another and very different context during the final years of the nineteenth century. This time the tension was not from outside the church but it was from within the church. The essential feature of this tension was the problem of accommodation. Should American Catholics accommodate their practices and views to American life and culture? On one side of the debate were bishops and laypeople who believed that Catholics should be part of the so-called melting pot American society. These folks worked to harmonize Catholic and American values. For example, they supported separation of church and state as well as freedom of religion. They had a much more tolerant view of Protestants than other Catholics.

A leading advocate for "American" Catholicism was Archbishop John Ireland of St. Paul, Minnesota. Ireland, born in 1838, was bishop from 1888 until his death in 1918. He argued that the church must adapt to American culture. In his words, "to conquer the new world to Christ, the church . . . must herself be new, adapting herself in manner of life and in method of action to the conditions of the new order, thus proving herself, while ever ancient, to be ever new, as truth from heaven is and ever must be."[17]

On the other side were bishops and laypeople who argued that the church could not change and that Catholics should maintain and affirm their ethnic and cultural identity. Two quotations from Pope Leo XIII express the position against "American" Catholicism. Responding in 1895 to the American form of government, the pope wrote: "It would be very erroneous to draw the conclusion that in America is to be sought the type of the most desirable status of the Church, or that is would be universally lawful or expedient for State and Church, to be, as in America, dissevered and divorced."[18] Four years later Leo wrote an apostolic letter to Cardinal James Gibbons of Baltimore, one of the members of the more conservative group that condemned forms of Americanism. Church historian Jay Dolan comments, "For Leo XIII, the idea of an American Catholicism was fundamentally flawed. Roman Catholicism was one and the same throughout the world and did not allow for any cultural adaptation. To suggest otherwise was heresy."[19]

While the Americanist controversy was relatively short lived, it nonetheless illustrated a tension that exists within Catholicism. There are those in the church who find strength and comfort within traditional elements of church practice and are thus cautious of accepting change, concerned that the essentials of the faith may be lost. On the other hand, there are those in the church who are concerned that elements within the tradition must develop and grow, given new contexts, so that the tradition itself may flourish.

John Courtney Murray

In the 1950s and early 1960s Catholic theologian John Courtney Murray (1904–67) led a national Catholic conversation on the "American Proposition" and its relationship to the Catholic intellectual tradition. His work, particularly his 1960 book *We Hold These Truths*, received wide notice. Indeed, his picture appeared on the cover of *Time* magazine in December of that year. Murray, recognized by many as the most important American Catholic theologian of the twentieth century, worked to ease the lingering nativist concerns in America as well as the Americanist concerns in Rome. After John F. Kennedy became president, *Newsweek* magazine noted, "Murray demonstrated in theory what John F. Kennedy demonstrated in practice: that Americanism and Roman Catholicism need no longer fear each other."[20] Indeed, Murray aimed to move the relationship from fear to leadership. For him, Catholicism could serve America by helping people understand the natural-law basis of democracy; that is, Catholicism could help Americans understand what it means to be American. It should be noted here that Kennedy had no such agenda. Historian Arthur Schlesinger notes that while "one could not doubt his devotion to his Church," Kennedy was not interested in demonstrating the relevance of Catholic doctrine to the modern world.[21]

Several short excerpts from Fr. Murray's writings are included in this section.[22] The excerpts start with his view of natural law. Murray's foundational link between Catholicism and American political life is natural law. He argues that it is through natural law that we can best understand the basic presuppositions of American life, namely, the truths we hold in common. From natural law we consider briefly the relationship between morality and law as well as the importance of civil society.

Natural Law

In the following quotations we see Murray defending the rationality of natural-law theory, a foundation of Catholic moral thought we saw expressed in the earlier chapters of this book.

> The doctrine of natural law has no Roman Catholic presuppositions. Its only presupposition is threefold: that man is intelligent; that reality is intelligible; and that reality, as grasped by intelligence, imposes on the will the obligation that it be obeyed in its demands for action or abstention. Even these statements are not properly "presuppositions," since they are susceptible of verification.[23]

> History does not alter the basic structure of human nature, nor affect the substance of the elementary human experiences, nor open before man wholly new destinies. Therefore, history cannot alter the natural law, insofar as a natural law is constituted by the ethical a priori, by the primary principles of the moral reason, and by their immediate derivatives. But history does change what I have called the human reality. It evokes situations that never happened before. It calls into being relationships that had not existed. It involves human life in an increasing multitude of institutions of all kinds, which proliferate in response to new human needs and desires, as well as in consequence of the creative possibilities that are inexhaustibly resident in human freedom.[24]

Law and Morality

The relationship between law or social policy and morality is a topic that always invites debate. As we saw earlier, when we read Thomas Aquinas, law and social policy must reflect the moral law. Yet the relationship is, as Thomas recognized, complex. While law must reflect morality and morality must influence policy, not all elements of morality must be encoded in law. Murray's description of law is telling. He writes, for example, that policy is "the meeting place of the world of power and the world of morality, in which there takes place the concrete reconciliation of the duty of success that rests upon the statesman and the duty of justice that rests upon the civilized nations that he serves."[25] Murray at once recognizes this balance and recognizes the importance of the moral basis of democracy:

> There can be no such thing as governmental neutrality in questions concerning the moral bases of society. Such neutrality would, as I have just said, be as impossible as it would be immoral. The official attitude in such questions must be partisan; government must take a side. Concretely, it must positively favor the human heritage against those who would dissipate it by the corrosion of doubt, denial, or cynicism. This is its obvious duty to the society of which it is the agent; this, at the very least, is a matter of vital political self-interest.[26]

The moral aspirations of law are minimal. Law seeks to establish and maintain only that minimum of actualized morality that is necessary for the healthy functioning of the social order. It does not look to what is morally desirable, or attempt to remove every moral taint from the atmosphere of society. It enforces only what is minimally acceptable, and in this sense socially necessary. Beyond this, society must look to other institutions for the elevation and maintenance of its moral standards— that is, to the church, the home, the school, and the whole network of voluntary associations that concern themselves with public morality in one or another aspect. Law and morality are indeed related, even though differentiated. That is, the premises of law are ultimately found in the moral law. And human legislation does look to the moralization of society. But, mindful of its own nature and mode of action, it must not moralize excessively; otherwise it tends to defeat even its own more modest aims, by bringing itself into contempt.

Therefore the law, mindful of its nature, is required to be tolerant of many evils that morality condemns. A moral condemnation regards only the evil itself, in itself. A legal ban on an evil must consider what St. Thomas calls its own "possibility." That is, will the ban be obeyed, at least by the generality? Is it enforceable against the disobedient? Is it prudent to undertake the enforcement of this or that ban, in view of the possibility of harmful effects in other areas of social life? Is the instrumentality of coercive law a good means for the eradication of this or that social vice? And, since a means is not a good means if it fails to work in most cases, what are the lessons of experience in the matter? What is the prudent view of results—the long view or the short view? These are the questions that jurisprudence must answer, in order that legislation may be drawn with requisite craftsmanship.[27]

Bill of Rights and the First Amendment to the Constitution

Murray spent a good deal of time reflecting on the Bill of Rights, particularly the First Amendment to the Constitution. (Indeed, some have nicknamed him the First Amendment Theologian.) He defended the First Amendment against some Catholic theologians in Europe, arguing that such a law limiting the role of government in religion does not necessarily make a society secular. Indeed, he holds that in a pluralistic society such a law is morally necessary to keep the social peace. Before reading a few of his thoughts, it is helpful to review the First Amendment: "Congress shall make no law respecting an establishment of religion, or prohibiting the free exercise thereof; or abridging the freedom of speech, or of the press; or the right of the people peaceably to assemble, and to petition the Government for a redress of grievances." Note how Murray relates the Bill of Rights to natural law in the following quotations:

> The philosophy of the Bill of Rights was also tributary to the tradition of natural law, to the idea that man has certain original responsibilities precisely as man, antecedent to his status as citizen. These responsibilities are creative of rights that inhere in man antecedent to any act of government; therefore they are not granted by government and they cannot be surrendered to government. They are as inalienable as they are inherent. Their proximate source is in nature, and in history insofar as history bears witness to the nature of man; their ultimate source, as the Declaration of Independence states, is in God, the Creator of nature and the Master of history.[28]

> From the standpoint both of history and of contemporary social reality the only tenable position is that the first two articles of the First Amendment are not articles of faith but articles of peace. Like the rest of the Constitution these provisions are the work of lawyers, not of theologians or even of political theorists. They are not true dogma but only good law. That is praise enough. This, I take it, is the Catholic view.
>
> If history makes one thing clear it is that these clauses were the twin children of social necessity, the necessity of creating a social environment, protected by law, in which men of differing religious faiths might live together in peace.[29]

> The American Catholic is on good ground when he refuses to make an ideological idol out of religious freedom and separation of church and state, when he refuses to "believe" in them as articles of faith. He takes the highest ground available in this matter of the relations between religion and government when he asserts that his commitment to the religion clauses of the Constitution is a moral commitment to them as articles of peace in a pluralist society.[30]

Civil Society

Active and informed citizens are an essential feature of a healthy democracy. Yet a healthy democracy does not rest simply on the activities of individuals alone; it also depends on the existence of intermediary groups within the community. A healthy democracy needs a healthy civil society. The term *civil society* refers to the activity and interaction between and within the great variety of nongovernmental and nonbusiness associations and organizations within society. Members the civil society include churches, neighborhood groups, nonprofit agencies, professional associations, as well as the many other groups organized around a particular feature of social life (again, independent of government and business). Civil society suggests how these many groups function in society. That is to say, within a democracy there exists an ethos of shared values (the truths we hold in common) such as toleration, respect, and mutual rights that enable these diverse groups to exist together. Murray recognized this fact. The first chapter of *We Hold These Truths* is "E Pluribus Unum," the first motto of the United States. This motto, which still appears on U.S. currency, means "out of many, one."

> This is the "great society," whose scope is as broad as civilization itself, of which civil society is at once the product and the vehicle. The term designates the total complex of organized human relationships on the temporal plane, which arise either by necessity of nature or by free choice of will, in view of the cooperative achievement of partial human goods by particular associations or institutions. The internal structure of civil society is based upon the principle of social pluralism, which asserts that there are a variety of distinct individual and social ends, either given in human nature or left to human freedom, which are to be achieved by cooperative association. Each of these ends is the root of a responsibility, and therefore of an original right and function. Hence there arises the principle of the subsidiary function as the first structural principle of society. But the whole society also has the function of preserving and developing itself as a whole. There is a good-of-the-whole, a common good, the social good, pluralist in structure but still somehow one.[31]

Loss of the Sense of the Sacred

Murray, a strong supporter of the American Proposition, was not without criticism of American culture. While he was an "ardent defender of the free enterprise system,"[32] he was very critical of the role that materialism plays in American culture:

> [American culture] presents itself as something of a monster . . . Its most striking characteristic is its profound materialism. It had, in fact, one dominating ideal: the conquest of the material world, with the aid of

science, a conquest that has made one promise: a more abundant life for the ordinary man and woman, the abundance being ultimately in physical comfort . . . It has given its citizens everything to live for and nothing to die for. And its achievement may be summed up thus: it has gained a continent and lost its own soul. Say rather that it has lived so much on the surface that it has lost contact with it soul.[33]

Murray was a strong defender of both the First Amendment and the idea of "minimal law," yet at the same time he was a dramatic proponent of the necessity of religion in public life:

Contemporary democratic ideology . . . does not deny God. But it surely ignores him. Surely this ignorance is being installed at the center of the democratic idea, as a fatal corruption. Ignorance of God has acquired status in public law; it is woven into the national mores; it is socially accredited in institutions. The man ignorant of God has become a social type; and his ignorance is socially transmitted by a multitude of social mechanisms; not least perhaps by the central institution of public education. The democracy that owed its origins to spiritual insight now trusts its future to spiritual ignorance . . . How shall the freedom of the spirit be born of spiritual ignorance? How shall the Great Hope not turn into a great deception, if it is divorced from its dynamic inspiration?[34]

PACEM IN TERRIS

There are many comparisons to be made between Pope Leo XIII's *Rerum novarum* and Pope John XXIII's *Pacem in terris*. In many ways Pope John's openness to the world and his optimism expressed in *Pacem in terris* could not be more different from Pope Leo's deep concern "about new things." The subject matter of the two encyclicals also differs. Leo was concerned about workers, the moral work place, and the moral economic order, given the dramatic changes brought about during the Industrial Revolution. John's concern was global social relations. He looked out on a world threatened by war, indeed on the edge of nuclear war. He experienced the horrors of the two "world" wars. *Rerum novarum* and *Pacem in terris* do, however, share some common ground. John continued and reinterpreted the natural-law foundation found in Leo. That is to say, the starting point of John's encyclical is the nature of the human person and the consequent moral requirements for the social and political orders.

Perhaps the most striking comparison to be made between *Rerum novarum* and *Pacem in terris* is the role that rights language plays in each encyclical. A right is a legitimate moral claim that one has (usually) on the government. Leo names several rights, primarily the right to a just wage, and the right to have and use property. He also notes that people have the rights to marry, to participate in society, and to form organizations. These moral claims are made to protect persons in the face of powerful governments and businesses. *Pacem in terris* greatly expands this list of rights and at the same time puts rights language front and center in Catholic social thought.

Pacem in terris was written at a most interesting time in history. Consider the context.

- In 1959 Pope John called for a universal council of the Catholic Church. The Second Vatican Council brought together the bishops of the world and met each fall from 1962 to 1965.
- In the early 1960s the conflict in Vietnam was growing. On three separate occasions in 1963 Vietnamese Buddhist monks caught the world's attention as they set themselves on fire in public places in protest of the political situation.
- In 1961 the Berlin Wall (the dominant symbol of the Cold War) was built.
- In 1962 Pope John was named Man of the Year by *Time* magazine. He was the first pope to receive such recognition (Pope John Paul II was named Man of the Year in 1994).
- The same week in 1963 that John issued *Pacem in terris*, Martin Luther King, Jr., wrote his famous "Letter from the Birmingham Jail."
- Four months later Dr. King led the civil rights march on Washington, where some 250,000 to 400,000 people heard his "I Have a Dream" speech.

The immediate event that motivated Pope John to write *Pacem in terris* was the threat of nuclear war, more specifically, a series of events that occurred primarily in October 1962 known as the Cuban Missile Crisis.[35] At that time the Soviet Union was placing missiles in Cuba, missiles that could easily and quickly reach the United States. President John F. Kennedy ordered a blockade of the island. Soviet Premier Nikita Khrushchev responded by threatening to use the weapons against the United States if it invaded Cuba. After a tense two weeks, often referred to as Fourteen Days in October, the Soviets backed down.

Looking back at this event some forty years later, historian Arthur Schlesinger wrote: "It is not an exaggeration to say that it was the most dangerous moment in all human history. Never before had two contending powers possessed between them the technical capacity to blow up the world. The world is very lucky that the two rival states were led by two men passionately determined to avoid nuclear war."[36]

Six months later *Pacem in terris* was published. John sent advance copies to both Kennedy and Khrushchev. Pope John died less than two months later. President Kennedy was assassinated in November of that year. Khrushchev was out of power within the year.

Theologian Roger Ruston points out that in *Pacem in terris* Pope John frequently uses the phrase "the universal common good." Ruston writes: "John's primary concern is 'human solidarity,' not the conversion of the whole world to Christianity. This is a huge break with the past . . . The papacy now sees itself working in conjunction with the U.N. and the rest of the world community, the majority of whom are not Catholics, or Christians, for the sake of the common good."[37]

Pacem in terris was written during troubled times, yet the reader cannot but be impressed by the optimism and the faith that pervade the document.

Pacem in Terris (abridged and edited) Pope John XXIII, April 11, 1963

INTRODUCTION: DIVINE ORDER AND THE HUMAN HEART

Peace on earth, something people throughout history have longed for and sought after, can only be established and guaranteed if the divinely established order is observed.

A marvelous order reigns in the world and in the forces of nature. It is within our nature as persons to comprehend this order and work to harness the forces of nature for universal good. God created us "in His own image and likeness"(Gen. 1:26), endowed us with intelligence and freedom, and made us lord of creation.

In striking contrast to the perfect order of the universe, however, is the disunity between individuals and among nations. The Creator has imprinted on the human heart an order that can be understood through the individual conscience. God has written the moral law and indeed the laws between peoples and governments into human nature.

These laws clearly indicate how we ought to relate to others in society. They also indicate how relationships between members of a society and public officials ought to be conducted. They show too what principles must govern international relations and govern the relation of individuals and nations to the global community. Since humans have common interests it is imperative that a global community of nations be established.

1. PERSONAL RIGHTS, PERSONAL RESPONSIBILITY

Any well-regulated and productive society depends on the acceptance of one fundamental principle: that each individual is truly a person. Humans are endowed with intelligence and free will. Because of this, all people have certain rights and duties. These rights and duties are universal and inviolable, and therefore inalienable. Since Christians consider human nature in accord with God's revelation, their evaluation of humankind is greatly increased. The blood of Jesus Christ redeems humans, and all people are children and friends of God, heirs to eternal glory.

EVERY PERSON HAS FUNDAMENTAL RIGHTS

The Right to a Life with Dignity: Every person has the right to life. Every person has the right to bodily integrity and to the means necessary for the proper development of life, namely, food, clothing, shelter, medical care, rest, and, finally, the necessary social services. In consequence, every person has the right to be looked after in the event of ill health; disability stemming from work; widowhood; old age; enforced unemployment; or when deprived of the means of livelihood.

Rights Pertaining to Moral and Cultural Values: Every person has the right to be respected. Every person has a right to a good name. Every person has a right to freedom in investigating the truth, and—within the limits of the moral order and the common good—to freedom of speech and publication, and to freedom to pursue whatever profession he or she may choose. Every person has the right, also, to be accurately informed about public events. Every person has the natural right to share in the benefits of culture, and hence to receive a good general education, and a technical or professional training consistent with the degree of educational development in his or her own country.

The Right to Worship God According to One's Conscience: Every person has the right to worship God according to the dictates of individual conscience, and to profess faith both privately and publicly.

The Right to Choose Freely One's State in Life: Every person has the right to choose the kind of life that appeals to him or her. Every person has the right to found a family, where men and women enjoy equal rights and duties, or to embrace the priesthood or the religious life. The family, founded upon marriage freely contracted, one and indissoluble, must be regarded as the natural, primary cell of human society. The interests of the family, therefore, must be taken seriously into consideration in social and economic affairs, as well as in faith and morals. Each of these spheres has an impact on the strength of family and its ability to fulfill its mission. Parents have the primary right to support and educate their children.

Economic Rights: Every person has the inherent right to be given the opportunity to work, and to be allowed the exercise of personal initiative in work. Working conditions must not harm physical health, the morals of workers, or impair the normal development of young people. Women must be accorded such conditions of work as are consistent with their needs and responsibilities as wives and mothers. Each worker is entitled to a just wage. This must be especially emphasized. The amount a worker receives must be sufficient, in proportion to available funds, to allow the family a standard of living consistent with human dignity. Every person has the right to the private ownership of property, including that of productive goods. With this right comes a social obligation.

The Right of Meeting and Association: Humans are social by nature. Consequently all persons have the right to meet and to form associations. They have the right to organize associations as they see fit. They have also the right to exercise their own initiative and act on their own responsibility within these associations.

The Right to Emigrate and Immigrate: Every human being has the right to freedom of movement and of residence within the confines of his or her own country. When there are just reasons in favor of it, every person must be permitted to immigrate to other countries and take up residence there. The fact that people are citizens of a particular country does not deprive them of membership in the human family, the global community.

Political Rights: Every person has the right to take an active part in public life, and to make a personal contribution to the common good. Every person is entitled to the legal protection of his or her rights. Such protection must be effective, unbiased, and strictly just.

EVERY PERSON HAS FUNDAMENTAL RESPONSIBILITIES

These natural rights are inseparably connected to many duties. Rights and duties find their origin, their sustenance, and their indestructibility from the natural law, which in conferring the one imposes the other. Thus the right to live involves the duty to preserve one's life; the right to a decent standard of living, the duty to live life in an appropriate manner; the right to be free to seek out the truth, the duty to devote oneself to the search for truth.

Reciprocity of Rights and Duties Between Persons: Personal rights correspond to duties in others. All must recognize and respect the rights of others. Every human right is justified on the natural law; this confers its respective duty. People who claim their rights and ignore their duties are people who build with one hand and destroy with the other.

Mutual Collaboration: Since people are by their very nature social, they live together and work for each other's good. A well-ordered society depends on the mutual recognition of rights and duties.

An Attitude of Responsibility: Human society cannot be based on force. Human dignity requires that persons be free and that they be able to act responsibly. Every person must act on his or her own initiative, conviction, and sense of responsibility, not under the threat of external coercion.

Social Life in Truth, Justice, Charity and Freedom: Human society must be based on truth if it is to be considered well ordered, creative, and consonant with human dignity. Justice must guide human society. Justice is based on the respect of rights and the fulfillment of duties. Human society must be animated by love so persons can feel the needs of others. Through love persons are moved to share their goods with others, and to work to create a world expressing intellectual and spiritual values. Human society thrives on freedom, and thus uses means consistent with the dignity of its individual members, who, being endowed with reason, assume responsibility for their own actions and the common good.

CHARACTERISTICS OF THE PRESENT DAY

There are three things that characterize our age. First, workers have gradually gained ground in economic and social life. Workers all over the world are demanding that they will not be treated as objects devoid of intelligence and freedom. Workers today insist on being treated as human beings.

Secondly, women are now playing a more significant role in political life. This development is happening more rapidly in historically Christian nations. Women expect the rights and duties that belong to them as human persons.

Finally, this age is evolving with new social and political lines. Most nations have either attained political independence or are on the way to attaining it. Soon no nation will rule over another. No nations will be subject to an alien power. Today, the conviction is widespread that all persons are equal in natural dignity. There is simply no justification for racial discrimination.

2. PERSONS AND PUBLIC AUTHORITY

MORAL AUTHORITY

A society, if it is to be well ordered and prosperous, must be governed by public authorities who responsibly promote the common good. Such authority, however, has moral limits. True authority rests on moral force. Public authorities should appeal to individual conscience, that is to say, to the duty every person has to contribute to the common good. Legitimate governments are founded on the moral order. Any laws or decrees passed contravening the moral order, and hence God's will, have no binding force in conscience.

All people, indeed all groups within society, must make their own unique contribution to the common good. Governments have a primary responsibility toward the common good, indeed that is their very reason for existence. In working for the common good public authorities must understand both the particular context of their communities and the objective demands of human dignity. For on one hand, the common good of a community includes the realization of cultural features indicative to a particular community. On the other hand, the common good essentially refers to human nature and the dignity of the human person.

PROMOTION OF THE COMMON GOOD

Every citizen has a share in the common good, yet the common good cannot be identified with the interests of any class or group. Public authorities, however, must give special attention to the poor and marginalized members of society since they are less able to defend their rights. The common good includes all those social conditions that favor the full development of human personality.

The common good is best safeguarded when personal rights and duties are guaranteed. The chief concern of government must therefore be to ensure that these rights are recognized, respected, defended and promoted, and that each individual is enabled to perform his or her duties more easily. Any government that refuses to recognize human rights or acts in violation of them fails its duty; its decrees are fully lacking in binding force.

Governments must give considerable attention to the social and economic progress of their citizens. They must develop the essential services to ensure this. Such services include roads, transportation and communications systems, clean drinking water, housing, medical care, ample facilities for the practice of religion, and aids to recreation. Governments promote insurance systems in the case of misfortune. Governments must make efforts to develop employment opportunities and ensure workers are paid just wages. Each nation ought to have a legal system in conformity to the principles of justice.

The common good is best promoted when public officials exhibit certain character traits. Officials should have a clear idea of the nature and limits of their own authority. They ought to be competent, have perseverance and be persons with integrity. They must have the ability both to recognize what is needed in a given situation and to act appropriately, promptly and effectively. Civic leaders must recognize that all people have the right to take an active role in government and thus they ought to have frequent contact and dialogue with citizens to promote the common good

3. INTERNATIONAL RELATIONS

The natural law that governs the life and conduct of individuals must also regulate the relations of political communities with one another. Nations also have rights and duties. International relationships, therefore, must likewise be harmonized with the dictates of truth, justice, willing cooperation, and freedom.

BUILT ON THE FOUNDATION OF TRUTH

The first point to be settled is that mutual ties between nations must be governed by truth. Truth calls for the elimination of every trace of racial discrimination, and the consequent recognition of the inviolable principle that all States are by nature equal in dignity. Each of them accordingly has the right to exist, to develop, and to possess the necessary means and accept a primary responsibility for its own development.

Some nations may have attained a superior degree of scientific, cultural and economic development. But that does not entitle them to exert unjust political domination over other nations. It means that they have to make a greater contribution to the common cause of social progress.

REGULATED BY JUSTICE

Justice must regulate international relations. This necessitates both the recognition of their mutual rights, and, at the same time, the fulfillment of their respective duties. States have the right to existence, to self-development, and to the means necessary to achieve this. They have the right to play the leading part in their own development, and the right to their good name and due honors. When differences arise, they must be settled in a truly human way, not by armed force or by deceit or trickery. Justice is more fully served when the conditions of minority groups are improved.

SOLIDARITY AMONG NATIONS

Active Cooperation: Truth and justice must regulate international relations. Nations must take positive steps to collaborate and pool their resources. While public authorities must protect the common good of their nations, that common good cannot be divorced from the common good of the entire human family. Thus, in pursuing their own interests, societies must join plans and forces whenever the efforts of particular nations alone cannot achieve the desired goal.

Political Refugees: The Church reaches out particularly to refugees. It is with bitter anguish that we speak for these suffering people exiled from their homelands for political reasons. Their numbers and sufferings are great. Repressive governments reverse the right order of society and indeed reject their fundamental purpose, namely, to recognize the freedom of citizens and protect their rights.

Refugees are persons. Thus all their rights must be recognized. Refugees cannot lose these rights simply because they are deprived of citizenship. A person has the right to enter a country so as to provide more fittingly for self and family. Nations should accept such immigrants and help them to integrate into their societies.

War and Preparation for War in the Modern World: The enormous production and stockpiling of armaments in the world is deeply distressing. This practice demands an incredible amount of intellectual and material resources. This at once burdens people of those countries and deprives poor countries of the help they need for their economic and social development.

In the modern world people seem to believe that the only way to ensure peace is through stockpiling weapons. When one country increases its military strength, others immediately acquire more weapons. When one country produces weapons of mass destruction, others consider themselves justified in producing the same.

Consequently people live in the grip of constant fear. They are afraid that at any moment the impending storm may break upon them with horrific violence.

People have good reason to fear. While it is difficult to believe that anyone would initiate the appalling slaughter and destruction that war would bring in its wake, there is no denying that it could happen. Moreover, even though the monstrous power of modern weapons does indeed act as a deterrent, there is reason to fear that the very testing of nuclear devices for war purposes can, if continued, lead to serious danger for various forms of life on earth.

Hence justice, right reason, and the recognition of human dignity cry out for a cessation of the arms race. Nations must reduce their stockpiles of weapons. Nuclear weapons must be banned. A general agreement must be reached on a suitable, effective and controlled disarmament program.

Unless the process of disarmament be thoroughgoing and complete, that is to say, that it reach the very souls of people, it will be impossible to stop the arms race or to reduce armaments, not to mention Our goal of abolishing nuclear weapons. All people must sincerely co-operate in this. This requires a dramatic change in thinking. The world must come to the realization that true and lasting peace among nations cannot consist in the possession of an equal supply of armaments but only in mutual trust. We are confident that this can be achieved.

We beg and beseech all people, and above all the rulers of nations, to spare no pain or effort to ensure that public affairs follow a course in keeping with human dignity. The warning of Pope Pius XII still rings in our ears, "Nothing is lost by peace; everything may be lost by war."

ADVANCING LIBERTY

International relations must be regulated by the principle of freedom. No country has the right to take any action that would constitute an unjust oppression of other countries or an unwarranted interference in their affairs. All people are united by their common origin and fellowship, their redemption by Christ, and their supernatural destiny. Thus the more wealthy nations ought to be of assistance to those countries in the process of economic development.

We look forward to the time in the very near future when the poorer nations attain the degree of economic development that enables their citizens to live in conditions more in keeping with their human dignity. At the same time We insist on the need for helping these peoples in a way that guarantees the preservation of their own freedom. People must be conscious that they themselves ought to play a major role in their own economic and social development. Wealthy nations must reject policies of domination and have basic respect for the countries they assist.

SIGNS OF THE TIMES

People nowadays are becoming more and more convinced that disputes that arise between nations must be resolved by negotiation and agreement not by recourse to arms. The reason for this is practical. The destructive force of modern weapons terrifies people. Given the immense destructive capacity of modern weapons, it no longer makes sense to maintain that war is the appropriate way to restore violations of justice. Unfortunately fear reigns supreme among nations. They spend enormous amounts of money on weapons, they say, to deter others from attacking them.

We are hopeful that through establishing dialogue and a policy of negotiation nations will come to recognize the natural ties that bind them together as persons. We are hopeful, too, that they will come to a stronger realization of the most profound truth of our common nature. Namely, that love, not fear, must characterize interpersonal and international relationships. Love unites people together in all sorts of ways, from such union countless blessings can flow.

4. THE GLOBAL COMMUNITY OF PERSONS

Recent progress in science and technology has had a profound influence on human life. There has been phenomenal growth in relationships at all levels including growing economic interdependence between nations. National economies are becoming so interdependent that a kind of world economy is being born from the simultaneous integration of the economies of individual nations. It is now the case that a country's social progress, order, security and peace are necessarily linked with the social progress, order, security and peace of every other country.

The world has changed. In the past nations were able to work for the universal common good through diplomatic channels, meetings and discussions, treaties and agreements; by using the ways and means suggested by the natural law, the law of nations, or international law. In the modern world, however, the problems of world peace and security pose very serious, complex and urgent questions about the universal common good. Individual nations themselves do not have the authority to address these concerns. Contemporary political structures are not adequate to promote the universal common good.

Today the moral order demands the establishment of some such general form of public authority with power and global organization. This authority cannot be imposed by force. It must be set up with the consent of all nations. If its work is to be effective, it must operate with fairness, absolute impartiality, and with dedication to the common good of all peoples. The mission of such an organization must be the recognition, respect, safeguarding and promotion of the rights of the human person.

The same principle of subsidiarity that governs the relations between public authorities and individuals, families and intermediate societies in a single nation, must also apply to the relations between the public authority of the world community and the public authorities of each political community. The special function of this universal authority must be to evaluate and find a solution to economic, social, political and cultural problems that affect the universal common good. These are problems that, because of their extreme gravity, vastness and urgency, must be considered too difficult for the rulers of individual nations to solve with any degree of success.

But it is not part of the duty of universal authority to limit the sphere of action of the public authority of individual nations, or to arrogate any of their functions to itself. On the contrary, its essential purpose is to create world conditions in which the public authorities of each nation, its citizens and intermediate groups, can carry out their tasks, fulfill their duties and claim their rights with greater security.

The United Nations Organization has the special aim of maintaining and strengthening peace between nations, and of encouraging and assisting friendly relations between them, based on the principles of equality, mutual respect, and extensive cooperation in every field of human endeavor.

The Universal Declaration of Human Rights passed by the United Nations General Assembly on December 10, 1948, provides a clear proof of the far-sightedness of this organization. The preamble of this declaration affirms that the genuine recognition and complete observance of all the rights and freedoms outlined in the declaration is a goal to be sought by all peoples and all nations.

We think the document should be considered a step in the right direction, an approach toward the establishment of a juridical and political ordering of the world community. It is a solemn recognition of the personal dignity of every human being; an assertion of everyone's right to be free to seek out the truth, to follow moral principles, discharge the duties imposed by justice, and lead a fully human life.

It is therefore Our earnest wish that the United Nations Organization may be able progressively to adapt its structure and methods of operation to the magnitude and nobility of its tasks. May the day be not long delayed when every human being can find in this organization an effective safeguard of personal rights. These rights, which are derived directly from one's dignity as a human person, are universal, inviolable and inalienable. This is all the more desirable in that people today are taking an ever more active part in the public life of their own nations, and in doing so they are showing an increased interest in the affairs of all peoples. They are becoming more and more conscious of being living members of the universal human family.

5. PASTORAL EXHORTATIONS

Christians must take an active part in public life, and work together for the benefit of their local communities and for the whole human race. It is vitally necessary for them to endeavor, in the light of Christian faith, and with love as their guide, to ensure that every institution, whether economic, social, cultural or political, facilitate human development.

We understand how difficult it is to relate the objective requirements of justice to concrete situations. We would remind all who work for social change that growth is gradual. It takes time and effort to improve human institutions.

We who, in spite of Our inadequacy, are nevertheless the vicar of Him whom the prophet announced as the Prince of Peace, conceive of it as Our duty to devote all Our thoughts and care and energy to further this common good of all humanity. Yet peace is but an empty word if it does not rest upon that order which Our hope prevailed upon Us to set forth in outline in this encyclical. It is an order that is founded on truth, built up on justice, nurtured and animated by charity, and brought into effect under the auspices of freedom.

CONCLUSION: A PRAYER FOR PEACE

Let us pray with deep fervor for the peace that Jesus came to bring. May He banish all things that endanger peace. May He transform us into witnesses of truth, justice and love. May He enlighten our leaders so that they may always work to promote the common good and that they always protect and defend the gift of peace. May Christ inflame our hearts and minds so we are able to break the barriers that divide us, so that we are able to strengthen bonds of mutual love, so that we are able to sincerely understand one another, and so that we are able to forgive those who have done us wrong. Through His power and inspiration we pray that we all come to recognize one another as children of God. We pray that the peace we all long for, the peace that Jesus came to bring, may blossom forth and reign forever among us.

DOROTHY DAY AND PETER MAURIN: PERSONALISM IN PRACTICE

There is no American more identified with Catholic social thought and action than Dorothy Day (1897–1980). Day and her colleague Peter Maurin (1877–1949) founded the Catholic Worker movement in 1933. The Catholic Worker, with its houses of hospitality (soup kitchens and homeless shelters), its newspaper, its farms, and its social activism has had an incredible impact on American Catholicism and how we understand Catholic social thought. Day's life, told so movingly in her autobiography, *The Long Loneliness,* was marked by several significant events. She was raised in a home without any direct involvement in religion or faith. Indeed, as a young woman Day rejected religion as nothing more than an institution that supported the social status quo. Yet she was greatly moved by human suffering, particularly the suffering caused by terrible working conditions and poverty. In the following quotation she reflects on the time before she became Catholic. This section suggests her deep concern for the poor, her moral vision, and her early suspicion of religion.[38]

> There was a great question in my mind. Why was so much done in remedying social evils instead of avoiding them in the first place? There were day nurseries for children, for instance, but why didn't fathers get money enough to take care of their families so that mothers would not have to go out to work? There were hospitals to take care of the sick and infirm, and of course doctors were doing much to prevent sickness, but what of occupational diseases, and the diseases that came from not enough food for the mother and children? What of the disabled workers who received no compensation but only charity for the remainder of their lives?
>
> Disabled men, without arms and legs, blind men, consumptive men, exhausted men with all the manhood drained from them by industrialism; farmers gaunt and harried with debt; mothers weighed down with children at their skirts, in their arms, in their wombs, children ailing and rickety—all this long procession of desperate people called to me. Where were the saints to try to change the social order, not just to minister to the slaves but to do away with slavery?[39]

In the early 1930s, after the birth of her daughter, Day gave serious consideration to becoming a Catholic. Eventually, both she and her baby were baptized. The following quotation suggests her ambiguity about the church. She loved the church, she said, but she was frustrated by the actions and attitudes of some of it officials. They did not seem to live the message of the gospel:

> I love the Church for Christ made visible. Not for itself, because it was so often a scandal to me. Romano Guardini said the Church is the Cross on which Christ was crucified; one could not separate Christ from His Cross, and one must live in a state of permanent dissatisfaction with the Church. The scandal of businesslike priests, of collective wealth, the lack of the sense of responsibility for the poor, the worker, the Negro, the Mexican, the Filipino, and even the oppression of these, and the consenting to the oppression of them by our industrialist-capitalist order, these made me feel often that priests were more like Cain than Abel. "Am I my brother's keeper?" they seemed to say in respect to the social order. There was plenty of charity but too little justice.[40]

The Catholic Worker is a movement of laypeople, independent from yet faithful to official church authority. The movement is dedicated to following

Jesus' commandment to love. In a letter to an interested person, Day described the community at the Catholic Worker this way:

> I explained that we were not a community of saints but a rather slipshod group of individuals who were trying to work out certain principles, the chief of which was an analysis of man's freedom and what it implied. We could not put people out on the street, I said, because they acted irrationally and hatefully. We were trying to overcome hatred with love, to understand the forces that made men what they are, to learn something of their backgrounds, their education, to change them, if possible, from lions into lambs. It was a practice in loving, a learning to love, a paying of the cost of love.[41]

The Catholic Worker espouses the traditional corporal and spiritual works of mercy. Day explains:

> We were to reach the people by practicing the works of mercy, which meant feeding the hungry, clothing the naked, visiting the prisoner, sheltering the harborless, and so on. We were to do this by being poor ourselves, giving everything we had; then others would give, too. Voluntary poverty and the works of mercy were the things he stressed above all. This was the core of his message. It had such appeal that it inspired us to action, action which certainly kept us busy and got us into all kinds of trouble besides.[42]

Coupled with this direct concern for people, the Catholic Worker also addresses broader social questions. Throughout its existence members have supported workers and workers' rights, and protested war and violence. The personalism of the Catholic Worker calls upon each and every person to take responsibility for others. Every parish, for example, should have a soup kitchen, homeless shelter, or home for the poor. The following quotation suggests the skepticism Day has that government will be able to take on these responsibilities that all persons have:

> The city, the state, we even have nicknamed them Holy Mother the City, Holy Mother the State, have taken on a large role in sheltering the homeless: But the ideal is for every family to have a Christ room, as the early fathers of the Church called it. The prophets of Israel certainly emphasized hospitality. It seems to me that in the future the family, the ideal family, will always try to care for one more. If every family that professed to follow Scriptural teaching whether Jew, Protestant, or Catholic, were to do this, there would be no need for huge institutions, houses of dead storage where human beings waste away in loneliness and despair.

Responsibility must return to the parish with a hospice and a center for
mutual aid, to the group, to the family, to the individual.[43]

Recognizing the dramatic social ills caused by economic systems and
war, Day still locates the problem at the personal level: "The greatest challenge of the day is: how to bring about a revolution of the heart, a revolution which has to start with each one of us? When we begin to take the
lowest place, to wash the feet of others, to love our brothers with that
burning love, that passion, which led to the Cross, then we can truly say,
'Now I have begun.'"[44]

Day's faith inspired her to be active in the world, yet it demanded that
her activism be nonviolent. She rejected war outright. The following powerful quotation was written immediately after the United States dropped
the atomic bomb on Japan.

Mr. Truman was jubilant. President Truman. True man; what a strange
name, come to think of it. We refer to Jesus Christ as true God and true
Man. Truman is a true man of his time in that he was jubilant. He was
not a son of God, brother of Christ, brother of the Japanese, jubilating as
he did. He went from table to table . . . telling the great news. We have
killed 318,000 Japanese. That is, we hope we have killed them. It is to be
hoped they are vaporized, our Japanese brothers, scattered, men, wom-
en, and babies, to the four winds, over the seven seas. Perhaps we will
breathe their dust into our nostrils, feel them in the fog of New York in
our faces, feel them in the rain on the hills of Easton. "We have spent
two billion on the greatest scientific gamble in history and won," said
President Truman jubilantly.

The papers list the scientists (the murderers) who are credited with
perfecting this new weapon. Scientists, army officers, great universities
(Catholic included), and captains of industry—all are given credit lines
in the press for their work of preparing the bomb, and other bombs, the
President assures us, are in production now.

We are making the bombs. This new great force will be used for good
the scientists assured us. And then they wiped out a city of 318,000. This
was good. The President was jubilant. Today's paper with its columns of
description of the new era, the atomic era, which this colossal slaughter of the innocents has ushered in, is filled with stories covering every
conceivable phase of the new discovery. Picture of the towns and the
industrial plants where the parts are made are spread across the pages. In
the forefront of the town of Oak Ridge, Tennessee, a chapel, a large,
comfortable-looking chapel benignly settled beside the plant. And the
scientists making the first tests in the desert prayed, one newspaper account said.

Yes, God is still in the picture. God is not mocked. God permits these things. We have to remember it. We are held in God's hands, all of us, and President Truman too, and these scientists who have created death, but will use it for good. He, God, holds our life and our happiness, our sanity and our health; our lives are in His hands. He is our Creator. Creator.[45]

Peter Maurin (1877–1949), Day's colleague and co-founder of the Catholic Worker, was a French-born peasant philosopher. Maurin provided much inspiration and intellectual backing for the Catholic Worker. Maurin died on the fifty-eighth anniversary of the promulgation of *Rerum novarum*. He is perhaps most remembered for his "Easy Essays," which in short and dramatic fashion capture the philosophy of the Catholic Worker.

—Better or Better Off?—

The world would be better off, if people tried to become better. And people would become better if they stopped trying to be better off.

For when everybody tries to become better off, nobody is better off. But when everybody tries to become better, everybody is better off.

Everybody would be rich if nobody tried to be richer. And nobody would be poor if everybody tried to be the poorest.

And everybody would be what he ought to be if everybody tried to be what he wants the other fellow to be.[46]

THE AIMS AND MEANS OF THE CATHOLIC WORKER

"The Aims and Means of the Catholic Worker" originally appeared in the *Catholic Worker* in 1987 (seven years after Day's death). It is a testimony to the commitment of the Catholic Worker movement. It also indicates areas where many American Catholics disagree with the Catholic Worker. Note the statement's criticism of capitalism and consumerism. Note also its commitment to nonviolence and voluntary poverty. Many Catholics supported its soup kitchens, but some of them, and many others, could not agree with its strong rejection of war.

The aim of the Catholic Worker movement is to live in accordance with the justice and charity of Jesus Christ. Our sources are the Hebrew and Greek Scriptures as handed down in the teachings of the Roman Catholic Church, with our inspiration coming from the lives of the saints, "men and women outstanding in holiness, living witnesses to Your unchanging love" (Eucharistic Prayer).

This aim requires us to begin living in a different way. We recall the words of our founders, Dorothy Day who said, "God meant things to be much easier than we have made them," and Peter Maurin who wanted to build a society "where it is easier for people to be good."

When we examine our society, which is generally called capitalist (because of its methods of producing and controlling wealth) and is bourgeois (because of prevailing concern for acquisition and material interests, and its emphasis on respectability and mediocrity), we find it far from God's justice.

In economics, private and state capitalism bring about an unjust distribution of wealth, for the profit motive guides decisions. Those in power live off the sweat of others' brows, while those without power are robbed of a just return for their work. Usury (the charging of interest above administrative costs) is a major contributor to the wrongdoing intrinsic to this system. We note, especially, how the world debt crisis leads poor countries into greater deprivation and a dependency from which there is no foreseeable escape. Here at home, the number of hungry and homeless and unemployed people rises in the midst of increasing affluence.

In labor, human need is no longer the reason for human work. Instead, the unbridled expansion of technology, necessary to capitalism and viewed as "progress," holds sway. Jobs are concentrated in productivity and administration for a "high-tech," war-related, consumer society of disposable goods, so that laborers are trapped in work that does not contribute to human welfare. Furthermore, as jobs become more specialized, many people are excluded from meaningful work or are alienated from the products of their labor. Even in farming, agribusiness has replaced agriculture, and, in all areas, moral restraints are run over roughshod, and a disregard for the laws of nature now threatens the very planet.

In politics, the state functions to control and regulate life. Its power has burgeoned hand in hand with growth in technology, so that military, scientific and corporate interests get the highest priority when concrete political policies are formulated. Because of the sheer size of institutions, we tend towards government by bureaucracy—that is, government by nobody. Bureaucracy, in all areas of life, is not only impersonal, but also makes accountability, and, therefore, an effective political forum for redressing grievances, next to impossible.

In morals, relations between people are corrupted by distorted images of the human person. Class, race and sex often determine personal worth and position within society, leading to structures that foster oppression. Capitalism further divides society by pitting owners against workers in perpetual conflict over wealth and its control. Those who do not "produce" are abandoned, and left, at best, to be "processed" through institutions. Spiritual destitution is rampant, manifested in isolation, madness, promiscuity and violence.

The arms race stands as a clear sign of the direction and spirit of our age. It has extended the domain of destruction and the fear of annihilation, and denies the basic right to life. There is a direct connection between the arms race and destitution. "The arms race is an utterly treacherous trap, and one which injures the poor to an intolerable degree" (Vatican II).

In contrast to what we see around us, as well as within ourselves, stands St. Thomas Aquinas' doctrine of the Common Good, a vision of a society where the good of each member is bound to the good of the whole in the service of God.

To this end, we advocate:

Personalism, a philosophy which regards the freedom and dignity of each person as the basis, focus and goal of all metaphysics and morals. In following such wisdom, we move away from a self-centered individualism toward the good of the other. This is to be done by taking personal responsibility for changing conditions, rather than looking to the state or other institutions to provide impersonal "charity." We pray for a Church renewed by this philosophy and for a time when all those who feel excluded from participation are welcomed with love, drawn by the gentle personalism Peter Maurin taught.

A decentralized society, in contrast to the present bigness of government, industry, education, health care and agriculture. We encourage efforts such as family farms, rural and urban land trusts, worker ownership and management of small factories, homesteading projects, food, housing and other cooperatives—any effort in which money can once more become merely a medium of exchange, and human beings are no longer commodities.

A "green revolution," so that it is possible to rediscover the proper meaning of our labor and/or true bonds with the land; a distributist communitarianism, self-sufficient through farming, crafting and appropriate technology; a radically new society where people will rely on the fruits of their own toil and labor; associations of mutuality, and a sense of fairness to resolve conflicts.

We believe this needed personal and social transformation should be pursued by the means Jesus revealed in His sacrificial love. With Christ as our Exemplar, by prayer and communion with His Body and Blood, we strive for practices of

Nonviolence. "Blessed are the peacemakers, for they shall be called children of God." (Matt. 5:9) Only through nonviolent action can a personalist revolution come about, one in which one evil will not be replaced simply by another. Thus, we oppose the deliberate taking of human life for any reason, and see every oppression as blasphemy. Jesus taught us to take suffering upon ourselves rather than inflict it upon others, and He calls us to fight against violence with the spiritual weapons of prayer, fasting and noncooperation with evil. Refusal to pay taxes for war, to register for conscription, to comply with any unjust legislation; participation in nonviolent strikes and boycotts, protests or vigils; withdrawal of support for dominant systems, corporate funding or usurious practices are all excellent means to establish peace.

The works of mercy (as found in Matt. 25:31–46) are at the heart of the Gospel and they are clear mandates for our response to "the least of our brothers and sisters." Houses of hospitality are centers for learning to do the acts of love, so that the poor can receive what is, in justice, theirs, the second coat in our closet, the spare room in our home, a place at our table. Anything beyond what we immediately need belongs to those who go without.

Manual labor, in a society that rejects it as undignified and inferior. "Besides inducing cooperation, besides overcoming barriers and establishing the spirit of sister and brotherhood (besides just getting things done), manual labor enables us to use our bodies as well as our hands, our minds." (Dorothy Day) The Benedictine motto *Ora et Labora* reminds us that the work of human hands is a gift for the edification of the world and the glory of God.

Voluntary poverty. "The mystery of poverty is that by sharing in it, making ourselves poor in giving to others, we increase our knowledge and belief in love." (Dorothy Day) By embracing voluntary poverty, that is, by casting our lot freely with those whose impoverishment is not a choice, we would ask for the grace to abandon ourselves to the love of God. It would put us on the path to incarnate the Church's "preferential option for the poor."

We must be prepared to accept seeming failure with these aims, for sacrifice and suffering are part of the Christian life. Success, as the world determines it, is not the final criterion for judgments. The most important thing is the love of Jesus Christ and how to live His truth.[47]

SOME QUESTIONS FOR CONSIDERATION

1. Using the ideas of Jacques Maritain and Pope John XXIII, explain the concept of the common good. Is it a helpful concept for current political discussions?
2. Philosophers and others have often debated the concept of human rights. Using Maritain's and John XXIII's thinking, explain what a human right is and how human rights are justified.
3. Analyze the views on war presented by Pope John XXIII in *Pacem in terris* and by Dorothy Day and the Catholic Worker movement.

4. The foundation of Catholic social ethics is *personalism*. Using Maritain, John XXIII, and Dorothy Day and the Catholic Worker movement, explain what is meant by that term.

5. Poverty is referred to in several ways in this chapter. How can one reject poverty as evil and at the same time advocate voluntary poverty?

6. Reflect on contemporary tension between being a Catholic and being an American. Compare *Pacem in terris* with the general social practices of the United States. Comment on Murray's understandings of natural law, law and morality, and civil society in relation to those practices.

7. Consider President Kennedy's address on faith and the public life in relation to *Pacem in terris*.

8. Review the principles of Catholic social thought from the first chapter—the dignity of the human person, the common good, subsidiarity, and solidarity—and describe how they are expressed in the chapter.

9. Using the "look, judge, and act" model, discuss what Pope John XXIII sees in the world, what his judgment is, and what actions he determines to be appropriate.

10. How do the authors of the selections in this chapter defend and support their positions? Review the discussion of moral arguments from the first chapter. Do the authors argue from authority, or do they use theological, biblical, philosophical, common sense, and or pragmatic arguments?

11. Review the three spheres of Catholic social action: works of mercy and justice, public expression and personal commitment, and social analysis for social change. How do the readings in this chapter express these spheres?

12. Discuss the four forms of moral discourse—narrative, prophetic, ethical, and policy—and how they are expressed in this chapter.

Prayer from the Sacramentary

Father, you have given all peoples one common origin, and your will is to gather them as one family in yourself. Fill the hearts of all people with the fire of your love and the desire to ensure justice for all their brothers and sisters. By sharing the good things you give us may we secure justice and equality for every human being, an end to all division, and a human society built on love and peace. We ask this through our Lord Jesus Christ, your Son, who lives and reigns with you and the Holy Spirit, one God, for ever and ever.

Chapter Five

Christ's Love Impels Us

Opening Prayer of the Second Vatican Council
    We are here before You, O Holy Spirit, conscious of our innumerable sins, but united in a special way in Your Holy Name. Come and abide with us. Deign to penetrate our hearts. Be the guide of our actions, indicate the path we should take, and show us what we must do so that, with Your help, our work may be all things pleasing to You. May you be our only inspiration and the overseer of our intentions, for You alone possess a glorious name together with the Father and Son. May You, who are infinite justice, never permit that we be disturbers of justice. Let not our ignorance induce us to evil, nor flattery sway us, nor moral and material interest corrupt us. But unite our hearts to You alone, and do it strongly, so that, with the gift of Your grace, we may be one in You and may in nothing depart from the truth. Thus, united in Your name, may we in our every action follow the dictates of Your mercy and justice, so that today and always our judgments may not be alien to You and in eternity we may obtain the unending reward of our actions.[1]
    —ATTRIBUTED TO ST. ISIDORE OF SEVILLE (560–636)

In January 1959, Pope John XXIII unexpectedly called for a meeting of the world's bishops, an ecumenical council. It would be the first such council in some ninety years. In attendance were approximately twenty-six hundred bishops as well as many nonvoting experts and observers from most major Christian denominations.[2] This council, which came to be called the Second Vatican Council (or Vatican II), dramatically shaped the Catholic Church. It met at the Vatican each fall from 1962 to 1965 and issued sixteen documents. Most of the documents concerned internal church matters. In this chapter we read selections from the four documents that deal with the church in relation to the world.

The first selection is from *Gaudium et spes (The Pastoral Constitution of the Church in the Modern World)*. It addresses the nature of the human person, community, and human action. The second section in this chapter contains shorter selections from three influential documents from the council. The first two concern the question regarding Christianity in relation to other religions. They are *Nostra aetate (The Declaration on the Relation of the Church to Non-Christian Religions)* and *Lumen gentium (The Dogmatic Constitution on the Church)*. The third document, *Dignitatis humanae (Declaration on Religious Freedom)*, centers on the question of religious freedom.

The third section of this chapter is Pope Paul VI's encyclical *Populorum progressio (On the Development of People)*. Paul directed the council after John died in 1963. This document, written two years after the council, addresses a crucial topic of the day, namely, defining and defending development programs. As Allan Deck narrates, "The United Nations declared this [the 1960s] the 'Decade of Development,' a period of economic expansion, industrialization, and international trade previously unknown in human history with repercussions in every corner of the globe."[3] In the encyclical the pope challenges simplistic views of what development ought to mean. The essential question raised here is the nature of what it means to live a fully human life. The solution includes the necessary material conditions to live with dignity as well as a set of moral expectations of persons in relation to others in the world.

A final note of introduction: Nine days after Vatican II began, the council fathers released a document about their work. The document was a surprise on two accounts. First, observers were not expecting such a message, and second, in a very uncharacteristic move, the council fathers addressed the message to all people. This was the first time in the history of the church that an ecumenical council addressed all people and not just Catholics (*Pacem in terris* would do the same some four months later).[4] "Message to Humanity" is a helpful introduction to the work and intention of the council. Walter Abbott comments, "These opening words of the Council look to renewal of the Catholic Church, to compassionate dialogue with modern men, to peace, to social justice, to whatever concerns the dignity of man and the unity of mankind. The message shows awareness of the world's problems and a keen desire to help."[5] The opening message of the Second Vatican Council to the world follows.

Message to Humanity (abridged and edited) 1962

FROM THE FATHERS OF THE COUNCIL TO ALL PEOPLE:

We take great pleasure in sending to all people and nations a message concerning that well-being, love, and peace which were brought into the world by Christ Jesus, the Son of the living God, and entrusted to the Church. In this assembly, under the guidance of the Holy Spirit, we wish to inquire how we ought to renew ourselves, so that we may be found increasingly faithful to the gospel of Christ.

The faith, hope, and the love of Christ impel us to serve our brothers and sisters, thereby patterning ourselves after the example of the Divine Teacher, who "came not to be served but to serve." Hence, the Church too was not born to dominate but to serve.

Coming together in unity from every nation under the sun, we carry in our hearts the hardships, the bodily and mental distress, the sorrows, longings, and hopes of all the peoples entrusted to us. Hence, let our concern swiftly focus first of all on those who are especially lowly, poor, and weak. Like Christ, we would have pity on the multitude weighed down with hunger, misery, and lack of knowledge. We want to fix a steady gaze on those who still lack the opportune help to achieve a way of life worthy of human beings. As we undertake our work, therefore, we would emphasize whatever concerns the human dignity, whatever contributes to a genuine community of peoples. "Christ's love impels us," for "he who sees his brother in need and closes his heart against him, how does the love of God abide in him?"

The Supreme Pontiff, John XXIII, in a radio address delivered on September 11, 1962, stressed two points especially. The first dealt with peace between peoples. There is no one who does not hate war, no one who does not strive for peace with burning desire. But the Church desires it most of all, because she is the Mother of all. She strives with all her might to bring peoples together and to develop among them a mutual respect for interests and feelings. The Supreme Pontiff also pleads for social justice. The Church is supremely necessary for the modern world if injustices and unworthy inequalities are to be denounced, and if the true order of affairs and of values is to be restored, so that people's lives can become more human according to the standards of the gospel.

We humbly and ardently call for all people to work along with us in building up a more just and brotherly city in this world. Our prayer is that in the midst of this world there may radiate the light of our great hope in Jesus Christ, our only Savior.

THE CHURCH IN THE WORLD

Gaudium et spes is a lengthy document written in two parts. The first part presents the church's understanding of the human person in relation to the world. The second part, "Problems of Special Urgency," includes discussion of marriage and the family, the development of culture, socioeconomic life, political community, and the promotion of peace. The selection in this chapter is limited to the first section. We see that the council holds a more comprehensive and dynamic view of the person than earlier natural-law descriptions allowed.

The first words of this document powerfully indicate the sense of the bishops: "The joys and the hopes, the griefs and the anxieties of the people of this age, especially those who are poor or in any way afflicted, these are the joys and hopes, the griefs and anxieties of the followers of Christ." There is a dramatic link between the lives of people—all people, but especially the poor and suffering—with the lives of those who confess to be Christian. What is the foundation of this link? The council presents a view of the human person, understood through theological concepts, that forms the unity of persons. When reading the document notice its view of humans, human nature, and human experience. See if you can relate your experiences with the description of persons presented. Note the discussions of conscience, of atheism, and of moral responsibility. Note also the council's views of concern for the neighbor and the social conditions necessary for a life of dignity.

Given the content and the form of the document, it can be called, in the words of theologian David Hollenbach, "the most authoritative and significant document of Catholic social teaching issued in the twentieth century."[6]

Gaudium et Spes (abridged and edited)
Pope Paul VI, December 7, 1965

PREFACE

The joys and the hopes, the griefs and the anxieties of the people of this age, especially those who are poor or in any way afflicted, these are the joys and hopes, the griefs and anxieties of the followers of Christ. Hence this Second Vatican Council now addresses itself to the whole of humanity.

The council brings to all the light kindled from the Gospel, and puts at its disposal those saving resources that the Church herself, under the guidance of the Holy Spirit, receives from her Founder. For the human person deserves to be preserved and human society deserves to be renewed. Hence the focal point of this document will be the person, whole and entire, body and soul, heart and conscience, mind and will.

INTRODUCTION: THE MODERN WORLD

The Church scrutinizes the signs of the times and interprets them in the light of the Gospel. Thus, in language intelligible to each generation, she responds to the questions that persons ask about this present life and the life to come, and about the relationship between the two.

A NEW AND DYNAMIC SENSE OF REALITY

Today, the human race is involved in a new stage of history. Profound and rapid changes are spreading around the whole world. Hence we can speak of a true cultural and social transformation, one that has repercussions on religious life.

Never has the human race enjoyed such an abundance of wealth, resources and economic power, and yet a huge proportion of the world's citizens are still tormented by hunger and poverty. Countless numbers suffer from total illiteracy. Never before have humans had so keen an understanding of freedom, yet at the same time new forms of social and psychological slavery make their appearance. Although the world of today has a very vivid awareness of its unity, political, social, economic, racial and ideological disputes bitterly continue. As humans painstakingly search for a better world, they often neglect the corresponding spiritual advancement.

Today's spiritual agitation and the changing conditions of life are part of a broader and deeper revolution. History itself speeds along on so rapid a course that an individual person can scarcely keep abreast of it. Thus, the human race has passed from a rather static concept of reality to a more dynamic, evolutionary one.

A change in attitudes and in human structures frequently calls accepted values into question; this leads to an upheaval in the norms of behavior. These new conditions have their impact on religion. On the one hand we have developed a more critical ability to distinguish religion from superstition. As a result many people are achieving a more vivid sense of God. On the other hand, growing numbers of people are abandoning religion. Indeed it is not unusual today for the rejection of religion to be presented as a requirement for scientific progress or of a certain new humanism. Today many people are shaken.

EQUALITY AND INEQUALITY IN THE WORLD

Development in the world has been uneven. It has intensified the inequalities and imbalances of the world. Various tensions now exist between races and between various kinds of social orders. Tensions exist between wealthy nations and those that are needy. To this we must add the collective greed existing in nations and other groups. The result is mutual distrust, enmities, conflicts and hardships.

People hounded by hunger call upon those better off. Women claim equality with men before the law and in fact. Laborers and farmers seeking to provide for the necessities of life for all also seek to develop the gifts of their personality by their labors and indeed to take part in regulating economic, social, political and cultural life. Now, for the first time in human history all people are convinced that the benefits of culture ought to be and actually can be extended to everyone.

The modern world is at once powerful and weak. It is capable of the noblest deeds or the foulest. Today before us we have the path to freedom or to slavery, to progress or retreat, to brotherhood or hatred. We must take responsibility to properly guide forces we have unleashed.

CHRIST IS THE KEY TO HUMAN HISTORY

The underlying truth here is that the tensions in the world mirror the more basic tension rooted in the heart of persons. In each person many elements wrestle with one another. Each person suffers from internal divisions and from these flow so many great discords in society. Even in the modern world with all its development, people all over ask the most basic questions: what does it mean to be human? Why do we still suffer despite so much progress? What follows this earthly life?

The Church firmly believes that in Christ we can find the key, the focal point and the goal of the person and human history. The Church maintains that beneath all changes in the modern world there are many realities that do not change and have their ultimate foundation in Christ. The council wishes to speak to all people in order to shed light on the mystery of humanity and to cooperate in finding the solution to the outstanding problems of our time.

1. THE HUMAN PERSON

According to the almost unanimous opinion of believers and unbelievers alike, all things on earth should be related to persons as their center and crown.

THE NATURE OF THE HUMAN PERSON

But what is the human person? There are many divergent and even contradictory opinions. The Church offers answers to this question, so that the truth about persons, their defects, dignity and destiny, can be portrayed. Sacred Scripture teaches that humans were created "in the image of God" (Gen. 1:27), capable of knowing and loving God, and master of all earthly creatures. We are to subdue them and use them to God's glory.

By one's innermost nature a person is a social being, for from the beginning "male and female he created them" (Gen. 1:27). Their companionship produces the primary form of interpersonal communion. Unless they relate to others, persons can neither fully live nor develop their potential.

From the very onset of history humans abused their liberty. They set themselves against God. People today find that they too have inclinations toward evil. When we refuse to acknowledge God we disrupt our proper relationships to God, ourselves, other people and indeed the whole of creation.

People often feel internally split. As a result, all of human life, whether individual or collective, shows itself to be a dramatic struggle between good and evil, between light and darkness. The call to grandeur and the depths of misery, both of which are a part of human experience, find their ultimate and simultaneous explanation in the light of this revelation.

Though made of body and soul, a person is a unity. Our bodies are good, honorable and created by God. Our interior qualities, however, surpass all material things. God probes our hearts. We plunge into the depths of reality whenever we enter into our own hearts. There we find God waiting for us.

Humans know that through intellect they surpass the material universe, and through this intellect share in the light of the divine mind. The intellectual nature of the human person is perfected by wisdom and a love for what is true and good. The contemporary world is in desperate need of people with wisdom. We note that often people poor in economic goods are quite rich in wisdom and ought to be a source of wisdom for others.

Conscience is the most secret core and sanctuary of a person. In conscience one is alone with God. It is where one can hear God. In the depths of conscience, people can perceive a law obliging them to love good and avoid evil. This law is fulfilled by love of God and neighbor. To obey conscience is the very dignity of a person, indeed one will be judged according to how one obeyed one's conscience.

Following an informed conscience pushes us from simple blind choice and toward the objective norms of morality. Conscience, through human limitation, may frequently err but it never loses its primacy.

Only in freedom can one move toward goodness. Hence a person's dignity demands that he or she act with knowledge and freedom, motivated from within. True choice is not made under blind internal impulse nor is it a result of external pressure.

In the face of death the riddle of human existence grows most acute. Although the mystery of death utterly challenges human imagination, the Church firmly teaches that God has created humans for a blissful purpose beyond the reach of earthly misery. For God has called all people to be joined to Him in an endless sharing of divine life.

ATHEISM IN THE CONTEMPORARY WORLD

The fundamental justification for human dignity lies in our call to communion with God. Thus atheism must be accounted among the most serious problems of this age, and is deserving of closer examination.

There are many distinct forms of atheism. Some people simply reject God. Others are skeptical that anyone can really know God. There are people who believe that science can explain all things. Still others reject the notion of any absolute truth. Some people place humankind in a place reserved for God. Some people who argue against God really have a misinformed view of the reality of God. There are many people who never come to ask about God's existence.

Sometimes the evils of the world lead people to atheism. Sometimes people are so engaged in the world they do not think of God.

Those who willfully shut out God from their hearts are not following the dictates of their consciences, and are not free of blame. Yet it has to be acknowledged that believers themselves frequently bear some responsibility for this situation. For, taken as a whole, atheism is not a spontaneous development but stems from a variety of causes, including a critical reaction against religious beliefs, and in some places against the Christian religion in particular. Hence believers can have more than a little to do with the birth of atheism. To the extent that they neglect their own training in the faith, or teach erroneous doctrine, or are deficient in their religious, moral or social life, they must be said to conceal rather than reveal the authentic face of God and religion.

Modern atheism often takes on a systematic expression. Those who profess atheism of this sort maintain that it gives persons freedom to be an end unto themselves. They claim that this freedom cannot be reconciled with the affirmation of a Lord who is author and purpose of all things. Not to be overlooked among the forms of modern atheism is that which anticipates the liberation of persons especially through economic and social emancipation.

In her loyal devotion to God and persons, the Church has already repudiated those poisonous doctrines and actions that contradict reason and the common experience of humanity. At the same time she strives to detect in the atheistic mind the hidden causes for the denial of God. The Church is conscious that the questions atheism raises are serious. The Church holds, however, that the recognition of God is in no way hostile to human dignity.

The remedy for atheism is to be sought in a proper presentation of the Church's teaching as well as in the integral life of the Church and her members. For it is the function of the Church to make God the Father and His Incarnate Son present and in a sense visible. This result is achieved chiefly by the witness of a living and mature faith, namely, one trained to see difficulties clearly and to master them. This faith needs to prove its fruitfulness by penetrating the believer's entire life, including its worldly dimensions, and by activating him toward justice and love, especially regarding the needy. What most reveals God's presence, however, is the communal charity of the faithful who are united in spirit as they work together for the faith of the Gospel.

While rejecting atheism the Church professes that all people must work for the betterment of this world. We know that such an ideal cannot be realized without sincere and prudent dialogue. She courteously invites atheists to examine the Gospel of Christ with an open mind.

THE SPIRITUAL TRUTH OF THE HUMAN CONDITION

The truth is that only in the mystery of the incarnate Word does the mystery of humanity take on light. He who is "the image of the invisible God" (Col. 1:15) is Himself the perfect human. For by His incarnation the Son of God has united

Himself in some fashion with every person. He worked with human hands. He thought with a human mind, acted by human choice and loved with a human heart. Born of the Virgin Mary, He has truly been made one of us, like us in all things except sin. By suffering for us He not only provided us with an example for our imitation, He blazed a trail, and if we follow it, life and death are made holy and take on a new meaning.

Such is the mystery of the human person, and it is a great one, as seen by believers in the light of Christian revelation. Through Christ and in Christ, the riddles of sorrow and death grow meaningful. Apart from His Gospel, they overwhelm us. Christ has risen, destroying death by His death. He has lavished life upon us so that we can cry out, "Abba, Father."

2. THE HUMAN COMMUNITY

A significant feature of the modern world is the growing interdependence of people because of technical advances. Yet more than technological advances are needed to deepen dialogue between persons. True dialogue depends on mutual respect based on the recognition of the spiritual dignity of the person. This document will now call to mind some of the basic truths about Christian doctrine and human society.

ONE HUMAN FAMILY

God, who has loving concern for everyone, has willed that all people constitute one family. For this reason, love for God and neighbor is the first and greatest commandment. For humanity growing daily more dependent on one another, and to a world becoming more unified every day, this truth proves to be of paramount importance.

Indeed, the Lord Jesus, when He prayed to the Father, "that all may be one . . . as we are one" (John 17:21–22) opened up vistas closed to human reason, for He implied a certain likeness between the union of the divine Persons, and the unity of people in truth and charity. This likeness reveals that persons, who are the only creatures on earth that God willed for themselves, cannot fully find themselves except through a sincere gift of self.

The subject and the goal of all social institutions is and must be the human person. The social element of life is not something added on to a person. It is through relationships with others, through reciprocal duties, and through true dialogue that a person develops his or her gifts and is able to rise to his or her destiny.

HUMAN INTERDEPENDENCE

The ties of the family and political community are most intimate to a person's nature. Other ties originate from choice. In our times voluntary associations play a critical role in socialization. When the structure of affairs is flawed by the consequences of sin, a person, already born with a bent toward evil, finds new inducements to sin, which cannot be overcome without strenuous efforts and the assistance of grace.

Every day human interdependence grows more tightly drawn and spreads by degrees over the whole world. As a result the common good (the sum of those conditions of social life which allow social groups and their individual members relatively thorough and ready access to their own fulfillment) today takes on an increasingly universal complexion and consequently involves rights and duties with respect to the whole human race.

With the growth of interdependence, there is a growing awareness of the exalted dignity proper to the human person. Each person stands above things, and has rights and duties that are universal and inviolable. All people must then have the things necessary for leading a life truly human. These include food, clothing, and shelter. They also include the right to choose a state of life freely and to found a family, the right to education, to employment, to a good reputation, to respect, to appropriate information, to act in accord with the upright norm of one's own conscience, to protection of privacy and rightful freedom including religious freedom.

The social order must be founded on truth, built on justice and animated by love; in freedom it should grow every day toward a more humane balance.

ACTIVE CONCERN FOR THE NEIGHBOR

In our times a special obligation binds us to make ourselves the neighbor of every person without exception. We must actively aid the needy neighbor when he or she crosses our path. The neighbor may be an old person, a foreign laborer unjustly looked down upon, a refugee, a child born of an unlawful union, or a hungry person. All of these and others can disturb our conscience. Recall the voice of the Lord, "As long as you did it for one of these the least of my brethren, you did it for me" (Matt. 25:40).

Whatever is opposed to life, for example any type of murder, genocide, abortion, euthanasia or willful self-destruction as well as other shameful and evil actions, poisons human society. Such actions harm more those who practice them than those who suffer from the injury. They are supreme dishonor to the Creator.

Whatever violates the integrity of the human person, such as mutilation, torments inflicted on body or mind, attempts to coerce the will itself as well as other shameful and evil actions, poisons human society. Such actions harm more those who practice them than those who suffer from the injury. They are supreme dishonor to the Creator.

Whatever insults human dignity, such as subhuman living conditions, arbitrary imprisonment, deportation, slavery, prostitution, the selling of women and children, disgraceful working conditions (where people are treated as mere tools for profit rather than as free and responsible persons) as well as other shameful and evil actions, poisons human society. Such actions harm more those who practice them than those who suffer from the injury. They are supreme dishonor to the Creator.

LOVE AND GOODWILL

Respect and love ought to be extended to those who think or act differently than we do in social, political and even religious matters. In fact, the more deeply we come to understand their ways of thinking through courtesy and love, the more easily will we be able to enter into dialogue with them.

This love and good will, however, must not render us indifferent to truth and goodness. Indeed love itself impels the disciples of Christ to speak the saving truth to all people. But it is necessary to distinguish between error, which always merits repudiation, and the person in error, who never loses the dignity of being a person. God alone is the judge and searcher of hearts, for that reason He forbids us to make judgments about the internal guilt of anyone.

The teaching of Christ even requires that we forgive injuries, and extends the law of love to include every enemy, according to the command of the New Law: "You have heard that it was said: You shall love your neighbor and hate your enemy. But I say to you: love your enemies, and pray for those who persecute you" (Matt. 5:43–44).

FUNDAMENTAL HUMAN DIGNITY

A fundamental equality exists among all people. We all possess a rational soul. All people have been created in God's likeness and thus share the same nature and origin. Since Christ has redeemed us, all people share the same divine calling and destiny. Thus every type of discrimination, whether social or cultural, whether based on sex, race, color, social condition, language or religion, is to be overcome and eradicated. Discrimination is contrary to God's will. Yet even today, the basic personal rights of many people are not honored.

Although individuals are unique and differences do exist between people, the equal dignity of persons demands that a more humane and just condition of life be brought about. Excessive economic and social differences between the members of the one human family or within particular communities undermine social justice, equity, and the dignity of the human person, as well as social and international peace.

MORAL RESPONSIBILITY

The profound and rapid changes in the modern world require that we cannot be content with a simple individualistic morality. Justice and love demand that each person make a positive contribution to the common good and promote public and private institutions dedicated to bettering the conditions of human life. Yet many people today do not care about the needs of society. People do not hesitate to resort to deception in avoiding just taxes or other debts due to society. Everyone must consider it a sacred obligation to make an effort for the common good. Our time calls for morally strong people from all walks of life to commit to the service of the human community.

There are many obstacles to developing a moral sense and responsibility in people. Human freedom is crippled, for example, when persons live in extreme poverty. Degrading living conditions hamper a person's sense of dignity. On the other hand when a person is deeply entrenched in life's comforts and luxury he or she can be imprisoned in splendid isolation. If one lives either in degrading poverty or is held captive by comfort, it may be very difficult to rise to the destiny one is called to, that is to say, to give oneself to God for the welfare of others.

God did not create humans to live in isolation. Humans are created to live in social unity. Indeed they have been created to be members of a certain community. This communitarian character of persons is developed and consummated in the work of Jesus Christ. For the very Word made flesh willed to share in the human fellowship. He was present at the wedding of Cana, visited the house of Zacchaeus, and ate with publicans and sinners. He revealed the love of the Father and the sublime vocation of people in the most common social realities and by making use of the speech and the imagery of plain everyday life. He sanctified human ties, especially family ones, which are the source of social structures. He chose to lead the life proper to His time and place.

3. HUMAN ACTIVITY IN THE WORLD

Through our labor and our native endowments we have ceaselessly striven to better human life. Today, however, especially with the help of science and technology, humans have extended mastery over nearly the whole of nature. Thanks to increased opportunities for many kinds of social contact among nations, the human family is gradually recognizing that it comprises a single world community. Hence many benefits people once looked for from heavenly powers, they have now enterprisingly procured for themselves.

The Church guards the heritage of God's word and draws from it moral and religious principles without always having at hand the solution to particular problems. As such she desires to add the light of revealed truth to human experience so that the path which humanity takes will not be a dark one.

THE MANDATE OF FAITH

Throughout the course of the centuries, people have labored to better their lives and their social conditions. Christians believe such activity accords with God's will. Humans, created to God's image, are to subject the earth and all it contains, and to govern the world with justice and holiness. We have a mandate to relate ourselves and all things to God. This mandate refers to all human activity. For while providing the substance of life for themselves and their families, men and women also benefit society. They ought to consider their labor as part of the unfolding of the Creator's work. Christians are convinced that the development of the human race is a sign of God's grace and the flowering of His own mysterious design. Hence it is clear that the Christian message compels people to build up the world and to address the welfare of their fellows.

Human activity takes its significance from relationships. Through work people develop products, society and themselves. Working for justice and right relations between peoples has greater worth than technical advances. Hence, the norm of human activity is this: In accord with the divine plan and will, human action ought to harmonize with the genuine good of the human race, and allow people, as individuals and as members of society, to pursue and fulfill their total vocation.

A FAITH INTEGRATED INTO LIFE

Now many of our contemporaries seem to fear that a closer bond between human activity and religion will work against the independence of people, of societies, and of the sciences.

If methodical investigation is carried out in a genuinely scientific manner and in accord with moral norms, it never truly conflicts with faith, for earthly matters and the concerns of faith derive from the same God. The hand of God, who holds all things in existence and gives them their identity, is nevertheless leading whoever labors to penetrate the secrets of reality with a humble and steady mind.

Sacred Scripture teaches the human family what the experience of the ages confirms: that while human progress is a great advantage to man, it brings with it a strong temptation. Caught in this conflict, people must constantly wrestle to cling to what is good. Persons cannot achieve their own integrity without great efforts and the help of God's grace.

All human activity, constantly imperiled by pride and selfishness, must be purified and perfected by the power of Christ's cross and resurrection. Redeemed by Christ and made a new creature in the Holy Spirit, a person is able to love the things themselves created by God, and ought to do so.

For God's Word, through Whom all things were made, was Himself made flesh and dwelt on the earth. While we are warned that it profits a person nothing to gain the whole world and lose himself or herself, the expectation of a new earth must not weaken but rather stimulate our concern for cultivating this one. For here grows the body of a new human family, a body which even now is able to give some kind of foreshadowing of the new age. The earthly progress must be carefully distinguished from the growth of Christ's kingdom. Yet to the extent that earthly progress can contribute to the better ordering of human society, it is of vital concern to the Kingdom of God.

For after we have obeyed the Lord, and in His Spirit nurtured on earth the values of human dignity, community and freedom, and indeed all the good fruits of our nature and enterprise, we will find them again. But when we find them again they will be freed of stain, burnished and transfigured, when Christ hands over to the Father a kingdom eternal and universal, a kingdom of truth and life, of holiness and grace, of justice, love and peace. On this earth that Kingdom is already present in mystery. When the Lord returns it will be brought into full flower.

4. THE CHURCH AND THE WORLD

Everything we have said about the dignity of the human person, the human community and the meaning of human activity, lays the foundation for the relationship between the Church and the world, and provides the basis for dialogue between the Church and the world. We now consider this Church living and acting in the world.

THE CHURCH PROMOTES HUMAN DIGNITY

Coming forth from the eternal Father's love, founded by Christ the Redeemer and made one in the Holy Spirit, the Church has a saving and an eschatological purpose. This purpose can be fully attained only in the future world. The Church, at once a visible association and a spiritual community, goes forward together with humanity as it experiences the same earthly reality. She serves as a leaven and a soul for human society as it is to be renewed in Christ and transformed into God's family.

Pursuing the saving purpose that is proper to her, the Church communicates divine life to all and casts the reflected light of that life over the entire earth. It does this by healing and elevating the dignity of the person, by strengthening human society and instilling meaning on the everyday activity of people.

Humanity is on the road to a more thorough development of human personality, as well as to the increased awareness of its basic rights. But only God, Who created persons in His own image and ransomed them from sin, provides the most adequate answers to the basic questions. God does this through His revelation in Christ. Whoever follows Christ, the perfect human, becomes more of a human.

Thanks to this belief, the Church can anchor the dignity of human nature against all tides of opinion. No human law can better aptly safeguard the personal dignity and liberty than it is by the Gospel. The Church, by virtue of the Gospel, proclaims the fundamental human rights. She acknowledges and greatly esteems the contemporary movements that advance human rights. She recognizes that these movements must be penetrated by the spirit of the Gospel and protected against any kind of false autonomy.

THE CHURCH IS NOT BOUND TO A PARTICULAR CULTURE

The union of the human family is greatly fortified and fulfilled by the unity, founded on Christ, of the family of God's children. Christ, to be sure, gave His Church no proper mission in the political, economic or social order. The purpose that He set before her is a religious one. But out of this religious mission itself come a function, a light and an energy that can serve to structure and consolidate the human community according to the divine law. When circumstances of time and place produce the need, she can and indeed should initiate activities on behalf of people, especially the needy, such as the works of mercy and similar undertakings.

With great respect, therefore, this council regards all the true, good and just elements inherent in the very wide variety of institutions that the human race has established for itself and constantly continues to establish. The Church has no fiercer desire than that in pursuit of the welfare of all she may be able to develop herself freely under any kind of government which grants recognition to the basic rights of person and family, to the demands of the common good and to the free exercise of her own mission.

THE CHURCH CALLS ALL TO RESPONSIBILITY

This council exhorts Christians to strive to discharge their earthly duties conscientiously and in response to the Gospel spirit. Christians are mistaken if they think they may shirk their earthly responsibilities. Such people forget faith demands that they fulfill these duties, each according to his or her proper vocation. Christians are mistaken if they think that faithfulness consists only in acts of worship. People who immerse themselves in earthly affairs divorced from their religious life are also mistaken. One of the more serious errors of our age is this split between faith and daily life. The Prophets of the Old Testament fought against this scandal, as did Jesus Christ. Therefore, let there be no opposition between professional and social activities on the one part, and religious life on the other. The Christian who neglects temporal duties, who neglects duties toward the neighbor and God, jeopardizes his or her eternal salvation.

Secular duties and activities belong properly although not exclusively to lay people. Through their well-formed conscience they must see to it that the divine law is inscribed in the life of the earthly city. While they look to priests for spiritual light and nourishment, lay people ought not imagine that pastors are always experts in every problem. Lay people, enlightened by Christian wisdom and giving close attention to the teaching of the Church, must take their own distinctive role.

Often the Christian view will indicate a specific solution in a particular circumstance. Yet it often happens that Christians might disagree on a particular issue. Christians in this situation should always try to enlighten each another through honest discussion, preserving mutual charity and caring above all for the common good. Lay people have an active role to play in the life of the Church. They are to penetrate the world with a Christian spirit and are called to be witnesses to Christ in human society.

Bishops, together with their priests, should preach the news of Christ so all the earthly activities of the faithful will be bathed in the light of the Gospel. All pastors should remember that by their daily conduct and concern they are revealing the face of the Church to the world. People will judge the power and truth of the Christian message through their lives. They must do their part to establish dialogue with the world including dialogue with those who have differing opinions.

Although by the power of the Holy Spirit the Church will remain the faithful spouse of her Lord and will never cease to be the sign of salvation on earth, still she is very well aware that among her members, both clerical and lay, some have been unfaithful to the Spirit of God during the course of many centuries. The Church realizes that in working out her relationship with the world she always has great need of the ripening that comes with the experience of the centuries. Led by the Holy Spirit, Mother Church unceasingly exhorts her members to purify and renew themselves so that the sign of Christ can shine more brightly on the face of the Church.

With the help of the Holy Spirit, it is the task of the entire People of God, especially pastors and theologians, to hear, distinguish and interpret the many voices of our age, and to judge them in the light of the divine word, so that revealed truth can always be more deeply penetrated, better understood and set forth to greater advantage.

CONCLUSION

While helping the world and receiving many benefits from it, the Church has a single intention: that God's kingdom may come, and that the salvation of the whole human race may come to pass. For every benefit which the People of God during its earthly pilgrimage can offer to the human family stems from the fact that the Church is the universal sacrament of salvation simultaneously manifesting and actualizing the mystery of God's love.

The Lord is the goal of human history, the focal point of the longings of history and of civilization. He is the center of the human race, the joy of every heart and the answer to all our yearnings. He was raised from the dead by God; lifted on high and stationed at His right hand. He is the judge of the living and the dead. Enlivened and united in His Spirit, we journey toward the consummation of human history, one that fully accords with the counsel of God's love: "To reestablish all things in Christ, both those in the heavens and those on the earth" (Eph. 11:10).

FREEDOM, CONSCIENCE, AND TRUTH

Gaudium et spes is the most important Vatican II document concerning Catholic social thought. There are, however, three other relevant documents with significant roles in the tradition. We read these in two sections. The first section includes excerpts from *Nostra aetate* and *Lumen gentium*. These texts address the complicated question of how a Catholic ought to understand other religions. The second section contains *Dignitatis humanae*, which addresses the fundamental theme of religious freedom.

Christianity in Relation to Other Religions

Most conversations about the topic of religious pluralism suggest there are three ways of looking at this issue: relativism, exclusivism, and inclusivism. Relativism holds that all religions are fundamentally the same. It does not matter to which religion you belong or even if you have no religious faith at all. No religion is more true than any other religion. *Nostra aetate* rejects relativism. Exclusivism holds that one religion is the only true religion and that there is no truth in other religions. One religion has exclusive possession of the truth. *Nostra aetate* also rejects this view. Against these two extreme positions, *Nostra aetate* holds something of a middle ground. While asserting the centrality of Christ and the Catholic religion, it promotes an inclusivist view of other religions, suggesting that there may be truth in them.

This is a very important faith-based position to anchor social activism. It highlights the commonality among religions in moral truth and social aspirations. At the same time it allows Christians to walk side by side with members of other religions in the pursuit of social justice. An inclusivist world view encourages Christians and Catholics to claim and to live their own religious identity while acknowledging the many spiritual expressions and traditions in the contemporary world. This has direct implications for programs for charity and justice. Inclusivism does not ask people to make a faith statement or to convert to Catholicism before being given help. Blessed Mother Teresa states this idea succinctly:

Our purpose is to take God and His love to the poorest of the poor, irrespective of their ethnic origin or the faith that they profess. Our discernment of aid is not the belief but the necessity. We never try to convert those who we receive to Christianity but in our work we bear witness to the love of God's presence and if Catholics, Protestants, Buddhists or agnostics become for this reason better people—simply better—we will be satisfied. Growing up in love they will be nearer to God and will find Him in His goodness.[7]

Likewise, Pope Benedict XVI writes in his encyclical *Deus caritas est*:

Charity, furthermore, cannot be used as a means of engaging in what is nowadays considered proselytism. Love is free; it is not practiced as a way of achieving other ends. But this does not mean that charitable activity must somehow leave God and Christ aside. For it is always concerned with the whole person. Often the deepest cause of suffering is the very absence of God. Those who practice charity in the Church's name will never seek to impose the Church's faith upon others. They realize that a pure and generous love is the best witness to the God in whom we believe and by whom we are driven to love. (#31)

Nostra aetate also makes what is perhaps the strongest and most direct statement against discrimination in official Catholic social thought. Following the text from *Nostra aetate* is a paragraph from another Vatican II document, *Lumen gentium*, which directly addresses the question of whether non-Christians can be saved.

Nostra Aetate (abridged and edited)
Pope Paul VI, October 28, 1965

PLURALISM AND TRUTH

In our time when humanity is being drawn closer together and ties between different peoples are becoming stronger, the Church examines more closely the relationship to non-Christian religions. In her task of promoting unity and love among people and nations, the Church considers what all have in common and what draws humanity together in fellowship.

One reality is the community of all peoples. Humanity is one in its origin, for God made the whole human race to live over the face of the earth. Another reality is humanity's final goal, that is to say, God. God's providence, manifestations of goodness, and saving design extend to all people.

From ancient times down to the present, people of various places and cultures have perceived that hidden power in life and history. At times some have recognized this as the Supreme Being, or even of a Father. This perception penetrates their lives with a profound religious sense.

RELATIONS TO PARTICULAR RELIGIONS

Religions in advanced cultures have struggled to answer the same questions as ancient peoples by means of more refined concepts and a more developed language. Hinduism and Buddhism and indeed other religions found throughout the world try to counter the restlessness of the human heart, each in its own manner, by proposing "ways," comprising teachings, rules of life, and sacred rites. The Catholic Church rejects nothing that is true and holy in these religions. She regards with sincere reverence those ways of conduct and of life, those precepts and teachings which, though differing in many aspects from the ones she holds and sets forth, nonetheless often reflect a ray of that Truth which enlightens all people.

The Church exhorts her sons and daughters to dialogue and collaborate with the followers of other religions. She exhorts them to act with prudence and love and to witness Christian faith and life while at the same time recognizing and promoting the good things, spiritual and moral, as well as the socio-cultural values found among others.

The Church also esteems Muslims. They adore the one God, living and subsisting in Himself; merciful and all-powerful, the Creator of heaven and earth, who has spoken to men. Muslims take pains to submit wholeheartedly to even His inscrutable decrees, just as Abraham, with whom the faith of Islam takes pleasure in linking itself, submitted to God. Though they do not acknowledge Jesus as God, they revere Him as a prophet. They also honor Mary, His virgin Mother; at times they even call on her with devotion. In addition, they await the day of judgment when God will render their deserts to all those who have been raised up from the dead. Finally, they value the moral life and worship God especially through prayer, almsgiving and fasting.

The Church urges all to forget the past and to work sincerely for mutual understanding. She urges all to preserve and promote social justice and moral welfare, peace and freedom.

As the sacred synod searches into the mystery of the Church, it remembers the bond that spiritually ties the people of the New Covenant to Abraham's stock. Thus the Church acknowledges that the beginnings of her faith and her election are found already among the Patriarchs, Moses and the prophets. The Church cannot forget that she received the revelation of the Old Testament through the people with whom God in His inexpressible mercy concluded the Ancient Covenant. Nor can she forget that she draws sustenance from the root of that well-cultivated olive tree onto which have been grafted the wild shoots, the Gentiles. The Church keeps ever in mind that the Apostles, the Church's pillars, as well as most of the early disciples, were Jewish.

As Holy Scripture testifies, most Jews at the time of Jesus did not accept the Gospel. Some even opposed its spreading. Jewish authorities at the time and those who followed them did call for His death. It is important to note, however, that what happened in His passion cannot be charged against all Jews alive then, nor against the Jews today. The Scriptures testify that the Church is the new people of God, yet it does not hold that the Jews are rejected or accursed by God. God holds the Jews most dear for the sake of their Fathers. He does not repent of the gifts He makes nor of the calls He issues. In company with the Prophets and the same Apostle, the Church awaits that day, known to God alone, on which all peoples will address the Lord in a single voice and "serve him shoulder to shoulder" (Soph. 3:9).

Since the spiritual patrimony common to Christians and Jews is so great, the Church recommends biblical and theological studies as well as fraternal dialogues for mutual understanding and respect. Furthermore Church decries hatred, persecutions, and displays of anti-Semitism, directed against Jews at any time and by anyone.

CONDEMNATION OF DISCRIMINATION

Christ underwent His passion and death freely, because of the sins of all and out of infinite love, in order that all may reach salvation. It is, therefore, the burden of the Church's preaching to proclaim the cross of Christ as the sign of God's all-embracing love and as the fountain from which every grace flows.

We cannot truly call on God, the Father of all, if we refuse to treat others as brothers and sisters, created in the image of God. Our relation to God the Father and our relation to others as brothers and sisters are so linked together. Scripture says: "He who does not love does not know God" (1 John 4:8). There is no justification for discrimination between persons or between nations. Human dignity and human rights that flow from that dignity reject a discriminatory theory or practice. The Church rejects, as foreign to the mind of Christ, any discrimination or harassment people based on race, color, condition of life, or religion.

The extract below is paragraph 16 from *Lumen gentium*. In this selection the council considers the question of salvation for people outside Christianity. It begins with words about the Jews.

Lumen Gentium (abridged and edited)
Pope Paul VI, November 21, 1964

Finally, those who have not yet received the Gospel are related in various ways to the people of God. In the first place we must recall the people to whom the testament and the promises were given and from whom Christ was born according to the flesh. On account of their fathers this people remains most dear to God, for God does not repent of the gifts He makes nor of the calls He issues. But the plan of salvation also includes those who acknowledge the Creator. In the first place among these there are the Muslims, who, professing to hold the faith of Abraham, along with us adore the one and merciful God, who on the last day will judge humankind. Nor is God far distant from those who in shadows and images seek the unknown God, for it is He who gives to all people life and breath and all things, and as Savior wills that all people be saved.

Those also can attain to salvation who through no fault of their own do not know the gospel of Christ or His Church, yet sincerely seek God and moved by grace strive by their deeds to do His will as it is known to them through the dictates of conscience. Nor does divine Providence deny the helps necessary for salvation to those who, without blame on their part, have not yet arrived at an explicit knowledge of God and with His grace strive to live a good life. The Church as a preparation for the gospel looks upon whatever good or truth is found among them. She knows that it is given by Him who enlightens all people so that they may finally have life.

But rather often persons, deceived by the Evil One, have become vain in their reasonings and have exchanged the truth of God for a lie, serving the creature rather than the Creator. Or some there are who, living and dying in this world without God, are exposed to final despair. Wherefore, to promote the glory of God and procure the salvation of all of these, and mindful of the command of the Lord, "Preach the gospel to every creature," the Church fosters the missions with care and attention.

Religious Freedom

Dignitatis humanae addresses the fundamental theme of religious freedom. At least two points should be noted. First, the notion of freedom advanced in the text seems very close to the view of religious freedom that developed in the American context. Second, along with the defense of freedom in the Catholic tradition comes the significant call for individual responsibility. Freedom here is not simply freedom from government. It necessarily includes responsibility to act in an appropriate manner. Freedom here is freedom to seek the truth. Fr. John Courtney Murray, whose work we studied in the previous chapter, was a primary author of *Dignitatis humanae*.

Dignitatis Humanae (abridged and edited) Pope Paul VI, December 7, 1965

A sense of the dignity of the human person has impressed itself more and more deeply on the consciousness of contemporary people. Increasingly the demand is made that people should act on their own judgment, making use of a responsible freedom, and motivated by a sense of duty, that is to say, not driven by coercion.

The Vatican Council professes that the one true religion subsists in the Catholic and Apostolic Church, to which the Lord Jesus committed the duty of spreading it abroad among all people. The council also professes that all people are bound to seek the truth, to embrace the truth they come to know, and to hold fast to it. The truth cannot impose itself except by virtue of its own truth, as it makes its entrance into the mind at once quietly and with power.

The Church declares that each human person has a right to religious freedom. This freedom means that all people are to be immune from coercion whether from individuals, social groups or any other any human power. No one ought to be forced to act in a manner contrary to his or her own beliefs, whether privately or publicly, whether alone or in association with others.

The Church further declares that the right to religious freedom has its foundation on the dignity of the human person. Human dignity is known both through the Sacred Scripture and through human reason. This right of the human person to religious freedom must be recognized in the constitutional law of every nation and thus be a civil right in every country.

With the personal right is personal responsibility. All people are impelled by nature and bound by a moral obligation to seek the truth, especially religious truth. They are also bound to adhere to the truth, once it is known, and to order their whole lives accordingly. The right to religious freedom, however, continues to exist even in those who do not live up to their obligation of seeking the truth.

In all activity, a person is bound to follow his or her conscience. Through conscience a person perceives and acknowledges the imperatives of the divine law so that he or she may come to God, the end and purpose of life. No person ought to be forced to act in manner contrary to conscience.

Provided the just demands of public order are observed, religious communities also have religious freedom. They may govern themselves according to their own norms, honor the Supreme Being in public worship, assist their members in the practice of the religious life, strengthen members by instruction, and join together for the purpose of ordering their own lives in accordance with their religious principles.

Families share in this right. Parents have the right to determine, in accordance with their own religious beliefs, the kind of religious education that their children are to receive.

The common good consists in those conditions of social life under which all enjoy the possibility of achieving their perfection in a certain fullness and with some relative ease. The common good chiefly consists in the protection of human rights, and in the performance of the duties. The protection and promotion of human rights is an essential duty of government. Indeed all members of society must promote rights including the right to religious freedom.

Finally, governments must protect the equality of citizens before the law, which itself is an element of the common good. There must be no discrimination, including religious discrimination in its treatment of citizens. The freedom of persons is to be respected as far as possible and is not to be curtailed except when and insofar as necessary.

A major tenet of Catholic doctrine is that a person's response to God in faith must be free. No one is to be forced to embrace the Christian faith against his or her will. It is therefore completely in accord with the nature of faith that in matters religious every manner of coercion should be excluded.

The Christian is bound to understand the truth received from Christ, to proclaim it faithfully, and to defend it vigorously never using means incompatible with the spirit of the Gospel. The love of Christ urges Christians to love and have prudence and patience in dealing with those who are in error or in ignorance with regard to the faith.

May the God and Father of all people grant that the human family, observing the principle of religious freedom, may be brought by the grace of Christ and the power of the Holy Spirit to the sublime and unending and "glorious freedom of the children of God."

INTEGRAL HUMAN DEVELOPMENT

In the 1950s and 1960s a new way to fight global poverty developed. This new model was based on the realization that the best way to help the poor was through economic development programs. Donal Dorr writes:

> Essentially this change was the widespread acceptance of the belief that each individual country, and the world as a whole, can "grow" out of poverty. Prior to this time justice was primarily a matter of ensuring the proper distribution of existing wealth and resources. Now it could be seen in terms of the production of increased resources which would be used to overcome poverty and to ensure that those who had little could catch up with those who had more.[8]

Pope Paul VI responds to this movement and essentially redefines the meaning of the term development. *Populorum progressio* can be read as a Christian directive on the meaning and importance of full human development. So important is this concept, notes Paul, that it is "a new name for peace." That is to say, much like Pope Leo XIII's concern in *Rerum novarum* that the conditions for moral economic order lie in deep respect for and responsibility to workers as persons, Paul holds that the conditions for moral global order lie in deep respect for and responsibility to the marginalized and powerless throughout the world.

Populorum Progressio (abridged and edited)
Pope Paul VI, March 26, 1967

INTRODUCTION: ON THE DEVELOPMENT OF PEOPLES

The development of peoples is an object of deep concern to the Church. We think of those peoples trying to escape the ravages of hunger, poverty, endemic disease and ignorance; of those peoples seeking a larger share in the benefits of civilization and a more active improvement of their human qualities; of those peoples consciously striving for fuller growth. The Church judges it her duty to explore this serious problem in all its dimensions, and to impress upon all people the need for concerted action at this critical time. Today the social question is worldwide. The hungry nations of the world cry out to the peoples blessed with abundance. The Church hears this cry and shudders. She asks each and every person to hear this cry, this cry from their brothers and sisters, and answer it lovingly.

1. TRUE DEVELOPMENT IS INTEGRAL DEVELOPMENT

POVERTY AND PROGRESS

Today we see people trying to secure a sure food supply, cures for diseases, and steady employment. We see people trying to eliminate every ill, to remove every obstacle that offends human dignity. People today strive to exercise greater personal responsibility, to do more, to learn more, and to have more. At the same time, many are condemned to live in conditions that make these legitimate desires an illusion. The imbalance between rich and poor nations grows with each passing day. As some nations produce a food surplus, other nations are in desperate need.

At the same time, social unrest has gradually spread throughout the world. The acute restlessness engulfing the poorer classes in countries that are now being industrialized has spread to other regions where agriculture is the mainstay of the economy. There are the flagrant inequalities in possessions, and even more in the exercise of power. In certain regions a privileged minority enjoys the refinements of life, while the rest of the inhabitants, impoverished and disunited, are deprived of almost all possibility of acting on their own initiative and responsibility, and often subsist in living and working conditions unworthy of the human person.

Moreover, traditional culture comes into conflict with the advanced techniques of modern industrialization; social structures out of tune with today's demands are threatened with extinction. The sad fact is that we often see the older moral, spiritual and religious values give way without finding any place in the new scheme of things.

THE CHRISTIAN UNDERSTANDING OF DEVELOPMENT

The Church has never failed to foster the progress of people to which she brings the faith. As the Church built churches, she also built hospitals, long-term care facilities, schools and universities. While we admit that at times the work of missionaries was not perfect, they did protect and promote indigenous institutions. Many missionaries were pioneers in promoting the country's material and cultural progress in the face of dominant foreign powers. In the present day, however, the Church notes that individual and group effort is not enough. The world situation requires the concerted effort of everyone and a thorough examination of every facet of the problem.

The Church clearly states that the two realms, Church and state, are distinct and supreme in their own sphere of competency. But since the Church lives in the world, she has the duty of scrutinizing the signs of the times and of interpreting them in the light of the Gospel. Sharing the noblest aspirations of people and suffering when she sees these aspirations not satisfied, she wishes to help people attain their full realization. So she offers people her distinctive contribution: a global perspective on the person and human race.

More than Wealth: Authentic human development is not restricted to economic growth. To be authentic, development must be integral; it must foster the development of each person and the whole person. In God's plan, every person is born to seek self-fulfillment, for God calls every human person to some task. Endowed with intellect and free will, each person is responsible to work for self-fulfillment and seek salvation. Our nature, developed through personal effort and responsible activity, is indeed destined for a higher state of perfection. United with Christ, human life is enhanced.

Each person is a member of society and a member of the human community. The reality of human solidarity brings benefits and obligations.

The pursuit of life's necessities is quite legitimate; hence we are duty-bound to do the work that enables us to obtain them. But the acquisition of worldly goods can lead people to be greedy, to the unrelenting desire for more, to the pursuit of greater personal power. Rich and poor alike fall prey to avarice and soul stifling materialism.

No person or nation should regard the possession of more and more goods as its ultimate objective. The development of wealth is ambivalent. It is necessary if a person is to grow as a human being yet wealth can also enslave a person. The exclusive pursuit of material possessions prevents true growth and stands in opposition to a person's true grandeur. Greed, in individuals and in nations, is the most obvious form of moral underdevelopment.

A New Humanism: As authentic human development is not simply equated with wealth it is also not simply a matter of more or greater technology. Authentic human development includes wisdom and the search for a new humanism. A new humanism will encourage and enable all people to embrace the higher values of love and friendship, of prayer and contemplation. Authentic human development demands that people move from living conditions that are "less than human" to living conditions that are "truly human."

What are "less than human" conditions? "Less than human" conditions include material poverty. People must not be denied the bare necessities of life. "Less than human" conditions also include moral poverty. Many people live crushed under the weight of their own self-love. "Less than human" conditions include oppressive political structures as well as the abuse of ownership and power. "Less than human" conditions include the exploitation of workers and unjust systems of economic transactions.

What are "truly human" conditions? "Truly human" conditions include the movement from poverty toward the acquisition of life's necessities. "Truly human" conditions include the elimination of social ills and broadening the horizons of knowledge. "Truly human" conditions include the move toward culture and the growing awareness of other people's dignity. "Truly human" conditions include a rejection of materialism, an active interest in the common good, and a desire for peace. "Truly human" conditions encourage a person to acknowledge God as the author of the highest values. Finally, "truly human" conditions include faith, God's gift to all people of good will, and loving unity in Christ.

The Purpose of Creation: In the very first pages of Scripture we read these words: "Fill the earth and subdue it" (Gen 1:28). The earth was created to provide humanity with the necessities of life and the tools for progress. Thus each person has the right to glean what one needs from the earth. All other rights, whatever they may be, including the rights of property and free trade, are to be subordinated to the principle of the universal purpose of creation.

The Fathers of the Church unambiguously laid down the duty of the rich toward the poor. As St. Ambrose put it: "You are not making a gift of what is yours to the poor person, but you are giving him back what is his. You have been appropriating things that are meant to be for the common use of everyone. The earth belongs to everyone, not to the rich."

The Conditional Right to Private Property: The right to private property is not absolute and unconditional. No one may appropriate surplus goods solely for one's own private use when others lack the bare necessities of life. If large privately owned estates impede the general prosperity because they are extensive, unused or poorly used, or because they bring hardship to peoples or are detrimental to the interests of the country, the common good sometimes demands their expropriation. It is not permissible for citizens who have garnered sizeable income from the resources and activities of their own nation to deposit a large portion of their income in foreign countries for the sake of their own private gain alone, taking no account of their country's interests. Such activity clearly violates the principle of the common good.

Industrialism is necessary for economic growth and human progress yet unfortunately the rise of economic progress often produces hardships, unjust practices, and conflicts. The economy is to serve persons yet the opposite often occurs. This happens when economics become simply equated with profit, when competition becomes unbridled, and when the system of private ownership lacks any sense of social responsibility. These abuses cannot be condemned too strongly.

The Meaning of Work: God gave humans intelligence, sensitivity and the power to produce in conjunction with these attributes. We have the tools to finish and perfect the work He began. Every worker, whatever the work, is, to some extent, a creator. Consider the worker in relation to the product; bent over a material that resists efforts, the worker leaves an imprint on it. Consider also the worker at work developing one's own powers of persistence, inventiveness and concentration. Further, when work is done in common, when hope, hardship, ambition and joy are shared, it brings together and firmly unites the wills, minds and hearts of people.

Work, too, has a certain ambiguity. Since it promises money, pleasure and power, it stirs up selfishness in some and incites other to revolt. On the other hand, it also fosters a professional outlook, a sense of duty and love of neighbor. Even though it is now being organized more scientifically and efficiently, work systems still can threaten human dignity and enslave a person. Work is human only if it results from the worker's use of intellect and free will.

2. CHRISTIAN VIEW OF SOCIAL ACTION

A Crisis Situation: We must not delay. Too many people are suffering. While some people make progress, others stand still or move backwards. The gap between the rich and the poor is widening. The injustice of these situations cries out to God. Because of these oppressive conditions many people are moved to revolt or revolution. Yet revolutionary uprisings are not the answer, except where there is manifest, longstanding tyranny. Violence often does great damage to fundamental personal rights and to the common good of the country. It often induces new injustices, new inequities and new disasters.

At the same time it must be said that the present state of affairs must be confronted boldly. Injustices must be challenged and overcome. Continuing development calls for bold innovations and profound changes. This is a crisis situation that must be corrected without delay.

Programs to Serve Persons: Individual initiative and competition alone will not ensure satisfactory development. Organized programs are necessary for directing, stimulating, coordinating, supplying and integrating the work of individuals and intermediary organizations. Public authorities must establish goals, plans and methods.

Organized programs designed to increase productivity should have but one aim: to serve human persons. They should reduce inequities, eliminate discrimination, free people from the bonds of servitude, and thus give them the capacity, in the sphere of temporal realities, to improve their lot, to further their moral growth and to develop their spiritual endowments.

Basic education is the first objective for any nation seeking to develop itself. Lack of education is as serious as lack of food; the illiterate person is a starved spirit. When a person learns how to read and write, he or she is equipped to do a job and to shoulder a profession.

Family as Foundation: A person finds true identity within social relations and here the family plays the basic and most important role. The natural family, stable and monogamous—as fashioned by God and sanctified by Christianity, is the basis of society.

There is no denying that the accelerated rate of population growth brings many added difficulties to the problems of development. A context may reach an impasse when the size of the population grows more rapidly than the quantity of available resources. In such circumstances people are inclined to apply drastic remedies to reduce the birth rate. Public authorities, within limits, can intervene in this situation. They can instruct citizens on this subject and adopt appropriate measures, so long as these are in conformity with the dictates of the moral law and the rightful freedom of married couples is preserved. When the inalienable right of marriage and of procreation is taken away, so is human dignity.

It is up to parents to decide upon the number of their children. This is an obligation they take upon themselves, following the dictates of their own consciences informed by God's law authentically interpreted, and bolstered by their trust in Him. The fundamental responsibility of development belongs to the family.

True Humanism: The ultimate goal here is a complete and integral humanism, that is to say, the fulfillment of the whole person and of every person. A narrow humanism, closed in on itself and not open to the values of the spirit and to God, could achieve only apparent success. A humanism set apart from God will end up being directed against persons. A humanism closed off from spiritual realities becomes inhuman. True humanism points the way toward God and acknowledges the task to which we are called, the task that offers us the real meaning of human life. A person becomes truly a person when he or she passes beyond himself or herself.

3. HUMAN SOLIDARITY AND DEVELOPMENT

The Moral Obligations of the Rich: Development of the individual necessarily entails an effort in solidarity for the development of the human race as a whole. This duty concerns first and foremost the wealthier nations. They have a threefold obligation. The first obligation is solidarity. Richer nations must give aid to developing nations. The second obligation is social justice. Inequitable trade relations between strong and weak nations must be rectified. The third obligation is universal charity. Rich countries must work to build a more humane world community, where all can give and receive, and where the progress of some is not bought at the expense of others. The matter before us is urgent, on it depends the future of world civilization.

Today no one can be unaware of the fact that on some continents countless men and women are ravished by hunger and countless children are undernourished. Many children die at an early age; many more of them find their physical and mental growth retarded. Thus whole populations are immersed in pitiable circumstances and lose heart. It is not just a question of eliminating hunger and reducing poverty. It is not just a question of fighting wretched conditions, though this is an urgent and necessary task. Our task is to build a human community where people can live truly human lives, free from discrimination based on race, religion or nationality. We must build a human community free from slavery, one that protects persons from natural elements. We must build a human community where liberty is not an idle word, where the needy Lazarus can sit down with the rich man at the same banquet table.

All people must examine their conscience. They must be prepared to support, at their own expense, projects and undertakings designed to help the needy. They must be prepared to pay higher taxes so public authorities may expand development projects. People must be prepared to pay more for imported goods, so that foreign producers may make a fairer profit.

Worldwide Effort: World leaders ought to set aside part of their military expenditures for a world fund to relieve the needs of impoverished peoples. Only a concerted effort on the part of all nations through an organized world fund will stop senseless rivalries and promote fruitful, friendly dialogue between nations. Such a fund would reduce the need for those other expenditures that are motivated by fear and pride. Countless millions are starving, countless families are destitute, countless people are steeped in ignorance; countless people need schools, hospitals, and homes worthy of the name. In such circumstances, we cannot tolerate public and private expenditures of a wasteful nature; we cannot but condemn lavish displays of wealth by nations or individuals; we cannot approve a debilitating arms race. It is Our solemn duty to speak out against them. If only world leaders would listen to Us, before it is too late!

Nations Must Dialogue: The contributing nations and receiving nations must be in dialogue. Rates of interest and time for repayment of the loan could be so arranged as not to be too great a burden on either party, taking into account free gifts, interest-free or low-interest loans, and the time needed for liquidating the debts. Donor nations could certainly ask for assurances on how the money will be used. On the other hand, the recipients would certainly have the right to demand that no one interfere in the internal affairs of their government or disrupt their social order. As sovereign nations, they are entitled to manage their own affairs, to fashion their own policies, and to choose their own form of government.

This task undoubtedly calls for concerted, continuing and courageous effort. But let there be no doubt about it, it is an urgent task. The very life of needy nations, civil peace in the developing countries, and world peace itself are at stake.

Trade Relations as an Obstacle to Development: Efforts are being made to help the developing nations, yet the unstable trade relations between rich and poor nations nullify such efforts. Highly industrialized nations export their own manufactured products. Less developed nations, on the other hand, have nothing to sell but raw materials and agricultural crops. As a result of technical progress, the price of manufactured products is rising rapidly and they find a ready market. But the basic crops and raw materials produced by the less developed countries are subject to sudden and wide-ranging shifts in market price; they do not share in the growing market value of industrial products.

This poses serious difficulties to the developing nations. They depend on exports for a balanced economy and for further steps toward development. Thus the needy nations grow more destitute, while the rich nations become even richer. It is apparent that the principle of free trade, by itself, is no longer adequate for regulating international agreements. It certainly can work when both parties are economically equal. In these cases free trade stimulates progress and rewards effort. That is why industrially developed nations see an element of justice in this principle.

But the case is quite different when the nations involved are dramatically unequal. Market prices that are freely agreed upon can be most unfair. The teaching set forth by Leo XIII in *Rerum novarum* is still valid today. When two parties are in very unequal positions, their mutual consent alone does not guarantee a fair contract. The rule of free consent remains subservient to the demands of the natural law. In *Rerum novarum* this principle was set down with regard to a just wage for the individual worker; here we apply it to contracts made between nations. Trade relations based solely on the principle of free competition often create economic dictatorship. Free trade can be called just only when it conforms to the demands of social justice.

Nationalism and Racism Are Obstacles to Development: Nationalism and racism are also obstacles to the creation of a more just social order and to the development of world solidarity. While it is natural for nations with longstanding traditions to be proud of their traditional heritage, haughty pride in one's own nation divides nations and isolates people. Commendable respect for national identity must be infused with a love for the human family.

Racism is an obstacle to justice and solidarity throughout the world. In developing nations racism hides beneath the rivalries of clans and warring political parties. It is an obstruction to collaboration among disadvantaged nations and a cause of division and hatred within all, particularly when people are unjustly subjected to a regime of discrimination because of their race or their color.

Obligations of the Poor: This state of affairs causes the Church great distress and anguish. But We cherish this hope: that distrust and selfishness among nations will eventually be overcome by a stronger desire for mutual collaboration and a heightened sense of solidarity. We hope that the developing nations will themselves organize within geographical regions. We hope that they will draw up joint programs, coordinate investment funds wisely, divide production quotas fairly, and exercise management over the marketing of these products. We also hope that multilateral and broad international associations will undertake the necessary work of organization to find ways of helping needy nations, so that these nations may escape from the fetters now binding them; so that they themselves may discover the road to cultural and social progress, while remaining faithful to the native genius of their land.

That is the goal toward which we must work. An ever more effective world solidarity should allow all peoples to become the artisans of their destiny. May the day come when international relationships will be characterized by respect and friendship. May the day come when mutual cooperation will be the hallmark of collaborative efforts, and when concerted effort for the betterment of all nations will be regarded as a duty by every nation.

The Meaning of Solidarity: The world is ill. The cause is not only the depletion of natural resources, nor the monopolistic control of these resources by a privileged few. The sickness is caused by the weakening of the ties of human solidarity between individuals and nations.

We cannot insist too much on the duty of giving foreigners a hospitable reception. Young people, in particular, must be given a warm reception. They must be shielded from feelings of loneliness, distress and despair that would sap their strength. These young people should be guarded against the corrupting influence of their new surroundings, where the contrast between the dire poverty of their homeland and the lavish luxury of their present surroundings is, as it were, forced upon them. And finally, it must be done so that they may be protected from subversive notions and temptations to violence. In short, they should be welcomed in the spirit of love, so that the concrete example of wholesome living may give them a high opinion of authentic Christian charity and of spiritual values.

Immigrant workers should also be given a warm welcome. Their living conditions are often inhuman, and they must scrimp on their earnings in order to send help to their families who have remained behind in their native land in poverty.

We would also say a word to those who travel to newly industrialized nations for business purposes: industrialists, merchants, managers and representatives of large business concerns. It often happens that in their own land they do not lack a social sense. Why is it, then, that they give in to baser motives of self-interest when they set out to do business in the developing countries? Their more favored position should rather spur them on to be initiators of social progress and human betterment in these lands. Their organizational experience should help them to figure out ways to make intelligent use of the labor of the indigenous population, to develop skilled workers, to train engineers and other people in management, to foster these people's initiative and prepare them for offices of ever-greater responsibility. In this way they will prepare these people to take over the burden of management in the near future.

Sincere dialogue between cultures, as between individuals, paves the way for ties of solidarity. This dialogue will be fruitful if it shows the participants how to make economic progress and how to achieve spiritual growth as well; if the technicians take the role of teachers and educators; if the training provided is characterized by a concern for spiritual and moral values, so that it ensures human betterment as well as economic growth. Then the bonds of solidarity will endure, even when the aid programs are past and gone. Is it not plain to all that closer ties of this sort will contribute immeasurably to the preservation of world peace?

Forms of Service: We are delighted to learn that in some nations their requirement of military duty can be fulfilled, in part at least, by social service or, simply, service. We commend such undertakings and those of good will who take part in them. Would that all those who profess to be followers of Christ might heed His plea: "I was hungry and you gave me to eat; I was thirsty and you gave me to drink; I was a stranger and you took me in; naked and you covered me; sick and you visited me; I was in prison and you came to me" (Mt. 25:35–36). No one is permitted to disregard the plight of brothers and sisters living in dire poverty, enmeshed in ignorance and tormented by insecurity. The Christian, moved by this sad state of affairs, should echo the words of Christ: "I have compassion on the crowd" (Mk. 8:2).

4. DEVELOPMENT IS THE NEW NAME FOR PEACE

Peace Is Not Merely the Absence of War: Extreme economic, social and educational disparity between nations provokes jealousy and discord, putting peace in jeopardy. Know that when people fight poverty and oppose unfair conditions they promote the physical as well as the spiritual and moral development of people. Peace is not simply the absence of warfare. Peace can never truly be based on a precarious balance of power. Peace is fashioned by efforts directed day after day toward the establishment of the ordered universe willed by God. Nations are the architects of their own development, and they must bear the burden of this work; but they cannot accomplish peace if they live in isolation from others.

Such international collaboration among the nations of the world certainly calls for institutions that will promote, coordinate and direct it, until a new juridical order is firmly established and fully ratified.

We must travel this road together, united in minds and hearts. Hence We feel it necessary to remind everyone of the seriousness of this issue in all its dimensions, and to impress upon all persons the need for action. The moment for action has reached a critical juncture. Can countless innocent children be saved? Can countless destitute families obtain more human living conditions? Can world peace and human civilization be preserved? Every individual and every nation must face up to this issue, for it is the problem of all.

The Appeal to Catholics: We appeal, first of all, to you. Lay people, throughout the world, must consider it their task to improve the temporal order. The hierarchy has the role of teaching and interpreting the moral laws that apply in this matter; the laity have the duty of using their own initiative and taking action in this area. They must not wait passively for directives and precepts from others. They must work to infuse a Christian spirit into their outlook and daily behavior, as well as into the laws and structures of their civil communities. The needed social transformations must be permeated with the spirit of the Gospel.

The Appeal to Other Christians: We are sure that Christians will want to cooperate and expand their collaborative efforts to reduce human immoderate self-love and haughty pride, to eliminate quarrels and rivalries, and to repress demagoguery and injustice—so that a more human way of living is opened to all, with each person helping others out of love. We ask our brothers and sisters to do all in their power to promote living conditions truly worthy of the children of God.

The Appeal to Other People of Good Will: Civil progress and economic development is the only road to peace. Delegates to international organizations, public officials, persons in the media, teachers and educators—all of you must realize that you have your part to play in the construction of a new world order. We ask God to enlighten and strengthen you all, so that you may persuade all to turn their attention to these grave questions and prompt nations to work toward their solution.

Educators must inspire young people with a love for the needy. Members of the media must place before our eyes the initiatives that are being taken to promote mutual aid, and the tragic spectacle of misery and poverty that people tend to ignore in order to salve their consciences. Through your means the wealthy will know that the poor stand outside their doors waiting to receive some leftovers from their banquets.

Government leaders must draw your communities into closer ties of solidarity. Delegates to international organizations must see to it that the senseless arms race and the dangerous power plays give way to mutual collaboration between nations, a collaboration that is friendly, peace oriented, and divested of self-interest, a collaboration that contributes greatly to the common development of humanity and allows the individual to find fulfillment.

CONCLUSION: SEEK AND YOU SHALL FIND

We call upon people of deep thought and wisdom—Catholics and Christians, believers in God and devotees of truth and justice, and all people of good will—to take as their own Christ's injunction, "Seek and you shall find" (Lk. 11:9). Blaze the trails to mutual cooperation among people, to deeper knowledge and more widespread charity, to a way of life marked by true solidarity, to a human society based on mutual harmony.

We bless you with all Our heart, and We call upon all persons of good will to join forces with you as a band of brothers and sisters. Knowing that in our day development means peace, who among us would not want to work for authentic development with every ounce of his or her strength? In the name of the Lord, We beseech all of you to respond wholeheartedly to Our urgent plea.

***

SOME QUESTIONS FOR CONSIDERATION

1. Highlight and discuss three ideas or themes from *Dignitatis humanae* and *Nostra aetate* that you find to be important for Catholic social thought.
2. Discuss *Gaudium et spes* from the perspective of the "vocation" of the Catholic social tradition.
3. Using the "look, judge, and act" model, discuss what the Vatican Council sees in the world, what it judges, and what actions it determines to be appropriate.
4. Discuss *Populorum progressio* and *Rerum novarum*. Compare the ways Pope Leo XIII and Pope Paul VI present their positions. Do they use different methods of persuasion? Does Paul simply update Leo's concerns, or does Paul have something new or innovative to contribute to the tradition of Catholic social thought?
5. Present a Christian view of personal and human development.
6. Analyze the description of human nature—what it means to be a person—in *Gaudium et spes*.
7. Analyze the view of the human condition in the world presented by *Gaudium et spes*.
8. Summarize and comment on the presentation of religious pluralism in this chapter.
9. Review the principles of Catholic social thought from the first chapter—the dignity of the human person, the common good, subsidiarity, and solidarity—and describe how they are expressed in this chapter.
10. How do the authors of the selections in this chapter defend and support their positions? Review the discussion of moral arguments from the first chapter. Do the authors argue from authority or do they use theological, biblical, philosophical, common sense, or pragmatic arguments?
11. Review the three spheres of Catholic social action: works of mercy and justice, public expression and personal commitment, and social analysis for social change. How do the readings in this chapter express these spheres?
12. Discuss the four forms of moral discourse—narrative, prophetic, ethical, and policy—and how they are expressed in this chapter.

The Beatitudes

"Blessed are the poor in spirit, for theirs is the kingdom of heaven.

"Blessed are they who mourn, for they will be comforted.

"Blessed are the meek, for they will inherit the earth.

"Blessed are those who hunger and thirst for righteousness, for they will be filled.

"Blessed are the merciful, for they will receive mercy.

"Blessed are the pure in heart, for they will see God.

"Blessed are the peacemakers, for they will be called children of God.

"Blessed are those who are persecuted for righteousness' sake, for theirs is the kingdom of heaven.

"Blessed are you when people revile you and persecute you and utter all kinds of evil against you falsely on my account. Rejoice and be glad, for your reward is great in heaven, for in the same way they persecuted the prophets who were before you.

"You are the salt of the earth; but if salt has lost its taste, how can its saltiness be restored? It is no longer good for anything, but is thrown out and trampled under foot.

"You are the light of the world."

—MATTHEW 5:3–14

Chapter Six

Liberation

We Plant Seeds

It helps, now and then, to step back and take a long view. The kingdom is not only beyond our efforts, it is even beyond our vision. We accomplish in our lifetime only a tiny fraction of the magnificent enterprise that is God's work. Nothing we do is complete, which is a way of saying that the kingdom always lies beyond us. No statement says all that could be said. No prayer fully expresses our faith. No confession brings perfection. No pastoral visit brings wholeness. No program accomplishes the church's mission. No set of goals and objectives includes everything.

This is what we are about. We plant the seeds that one day will grow. We water seeds already planted, knowing that they hold future promise. We lay foundations that will need further development. We provide yeast that produces far beyond our capabilities.

We cannot do everything, and there is a sense of liberation in realizing that. This enables us to do something, and to do it very well. It may be incomplete, but it is a beginning, a step along the way, an opportunity for the Lord's grace to enter and do the rest.

We may never see the end results, but that is the difference between the master builder and the worker. We are workers, not master builders; ministers, not messiahs. We are prophets of a future not our own. Amen.[1]

—BISHOP KENNETH UNTENER

From 1961 to 1975 nine major documents in official Catholic social thought were released. In 1961 Pope John issued *Mater et magistra. Pacem in terris* came two years later. In 1965 the Second Vatican Council produced *Gaudium et spes, Dignitatis humanae,* and *Nostra aetate.* Sixteen months later Pope Paul VI issued *Populorum progressio (On the Development of Peoples),* in 1971 *Octogesima adveniens (A Call to Action),* and in 1975 *Evangelii nuntiandi (Evangelization in the Modern World).* In 1971 the world Synod of Bishops issued *Justice in the World.* These years mark the most significant time of growth in the history of the tradition. Yet the official documents from Rome tell only part of the story. The most dramatic contribution in the last part of the twentieth century to the Catholic social tradition came from a most surprising location—Latin America. Highly Catholic and, for the most part, very poor, Latin American countries had been victims of unfair international relations and brutal military and political leaders for decades. By the mid 1980s Latin America, that place of great suffering, had become a beacon of moral strength to the global Catholic community.

This chapter includes two writings by Pope Paul VI—*Octogesima adveniens* and *Evangelii nuntiandi*—as well as *Justice in the World* by the Synod of Bishops. It also considers several critical events in Catholic life and practice in Central America and South America. These events had a dramatic impact on public practice of Catholic social thought.

A CALL TO ACTION

Eighty years after the publication of *Rerum novarum*, Pope Paul VI issued *Octogesima adveniens (A Call to Action)*. The document, officially an apostolic letter, not an encyclical, includes one of the most often quoted sections in the tradition of official Catholic social thought:

> In the face of such widely varying situations it is difficult for us to utter a unified message and to put forward a solution that has universal validity. Such is not our ambition, nor is it our mission. It is up to the Christian communities to analyze with objectivity the situation that is proper to their own country, to shed on it the light of the Gospel's unalterable words and to draw principles of reflection, norms of judgment and directives for action from the social teaching of the Church. (#4)

This quotation serves to empower people to understand Catholic social teaching within their own political context and thus promotes pluralistic understanding of the tradition.

A Call to Action captures Paul VI's urgency. For him, "Christians must become involved in social reforms as part of their mission as Christians."[2] He was influenced by theological movements and developments in Latin America (see the sections that follow in this chapter). He also addresses the option for the poor as well as science and true human progress.

Octogesima Adveniens (abridged and edited)
Pope Paul VI, May 14, 1971

INTRODUCTION

The eightieth anniversary of the publication of *Rerum novarum*, the message of which continues to inspire action for social justice, prompts us to take up again and to extend the teaching of our predecessors, in response to the new needs of a changing world.

There are grave problems in our days. Flagrant inequalities exist in the economic, cultural and political development of nations. Some regions are heavily industrialized; others are still at the agricultural stage. Some countries enjoy prosperity; others are struggling against starvation. Some peoples have a high standard of culture; others are still engaged in eliminating illiteracy. From all sides there rises a yearning for more justice and a desire for guaranteed peace and mutual respect.

There is a wide diversity in the situations that Christians find themselves in. In some places they are reduced to silence. In other places they are a weak minority. In some nations Christians are tempted by radical and violent solutions to oppression. On the other hand, many Christians seem unaware of present injustices and work to prolong the existing situations.

In the face of such widely varying situations it is difficult for us to utter a unified message and to put forward a solution that has universal validity. Such is not our ambition, nor is it our mission. It is up to the Christian communities to analyze with objectivity the situation that is proper to their own country, to shed on it the light of the Gospel's unalterable words and to draw principles of reflection, norms of judgment and directives for action from the social teaching of the Church.

EQUALITY AND PARTICIPATION

With ever advancing scientific and technological progress and the continual changes in patterns of knowledge, work, consumption and relationships, two aspirations persistently grow stronger in persons. These are aspirations for equality and participation. They are expressions of human dignity and freedom.

While progress has been made inscribing these two aspirations in deeds and structures, various forms of discrimination continually reappear. Legislation is necessary, but not sufficient, to set up true relationships of justice and equity. The Gospel instructs us in the preferential respect due to the poor and the special situation they have in society. The more fortunate should renounce some of their rights so as to place their goods more generously at the service of others. If there is no deeper sense of respect for others beyond the law, discrimination, exploitation and indeed contempt will continue to exist.

The aspirations for equality and participation promote a democratic type of society. The Christian has the duty to take part in the organization and life of political society.

SCIENCE, TECHNOLOGY, AND PROGRESS

The "human sciences" enjoy significant growth. On the one hand they offer a critical and radical examination of accepted knowledge about human nature. On the other hand, they often give a privileged position to a specific aspect of human nature. This scientific reductionism can mutilate human nature and make it impossible to understand the fullness of being human.

Each individual scientific discipline, given in its own particular emphasis, is able to grasp only a partial truth about human nature. Nevertheless the sciences promise a positive function that the Church willingly recognizes. They can widen the horizons of human liberty to a greater extent than the current circumstances allow us to. They could assist Christian social morality, which no doubt will see its field restricted when it comes to suggesting certain models of society. The use of the sciences will assist Christian social morality make critical judgments by its showing the relative character of the behavior and values presented by a particular society as definitive and inherent to human nature. Science does not provide the complete and definitive answer to the desire that springs from the innermost being of persons.

This better knowledge of human actions makes it possible to pass a critical judgment upon the motive, measure, and goal of modern societies, that is to say, on progress. Since the nineteenth century, Western societies (and, as a result, many other societies) have put their hopes in indefinite progress. They saw this progress as the human effort for freedom in face of the demands of nature and of social constraints. Progress was the condition for and the yardstick of human freedom. Yet a doubt arises about the value and the result of this ideology of progress. There has been condemnation of the limits of merely quantitative economic growth. The quality and the truth of human relations, the degree of participation and of responsibility, are no less significant and important for the future of society than the quantity and variety of the goods produced and consumed.

Genuine progress is to be found in the development of moral consciousness. This will lead people to exercise wider solidarity so they open themselves freely to others and to God. For a Christian, progress necessarily comes up against the eschatological mystery of death. The death of Christ and his resurrection and the outpouring of the Spirit of the Lord help one to place his or her freedom, in creativity and gratitude, within the context of the truth of all progress and the only hope which does not deceive.

JUSTICE IN THE TIME OF GLOBALIZATION

BEYOND VIOLENCE

There is a need to establish a greater justice in the sharing of goods, both within national communities and on the international level. In international exchanges there is a need to go beyond relationships based on force, in order to arrive at agreements reached with the good of all in mind. Relationships based on force have never in fact established justice in a true and lasting manner, even if at certain times the alteration of positions can often make it possible to find easier conditions for dialogue. The use of force moreover leads to the setting in motion of opposing forces, and from this springs a climate of struggle that opens the way to situations of extreme violence and to abuses.

AUTONOMY AND SOLIDARITY

The most important duty of justice is to allow each country to promote its own development, within the framework of cooperation free from economic or political domination. Thus it is necessary to have the courage to undertake a revision of the relationships between nations. This includes the question of the international division of production, the structure of exchanges, the control of profits, the monetary system—without forgetting the actions of human solidarity—to question the models of growth of the rich nations and change people's outlooks, so that they may realize the prior call of international duty, and to renew international organizations so that they may increase in effectiveness.

NEW FORMS OF GLOBAL POWER

Under the driving force of new systems of production, national frontiers are breaking down. We can see new economic powers emerging. Multinational enterprises can conduct autonomous strategies largely independent of the national political powers. They are therefore not subject to control from the point of view of the common good. By extending their activities, these private organizations can lead to a new and abusive form of economic domination. The excessive concentration of means and powers that Pope Pius XI already condemned on the fortieth anniversary of *Rerum novarum* is taking on a new and very real image.

INTERIOR LIBERATION

Today people yearn to free themselves from need and dependence. This liberation starts with the interior freedom that all must find in relation to their goods and their powers. They will never reach this without a transcendent love for persons, and, in consequence, through a genuine readiness to serve. Revolutionary ideologies lead only to a change of masters; once installed in power, these new masters surround themselves with privileges, limit freedom and allow other forms of injustice to become established.

Today many people are reaching the point of questioning the very model of society. The ambition of many nations is to attain technological, economic and military power so as to compete and oppose other nations. The ambition to powers accentuates inequalities and creates a climate of distrust and struggle that can compromise peace.

THE NEED FOR POLITICAL ACTIVITY

Economic activity is necessary. If it is at the service of persons it can be a source of unity and a sign of Providence. It is the occasion of concrete exchanges between persons, of rights recognized, of services rendered and of dignity affirmed in work. Though it is often a field of confrontation and domination, it can give rise to dialogue and foster cooperation. Yet it runs the risk of taking up too much strength and freedom. This is why the need is felt to pass from economics to politics. It is true that the term "politics" is ambiguous. Yet everyone knows that in the social and economic field, both national and international, the ultimate decision rests with political power.

Political power, which is the natural and necessary link for ensuring the cohesion of the social body, must have as its aim the achievement of the common good. While respecting the legitimate liberties of individuals, families and subsidiary groups, it acts in such a way as to create, effectively and for the well-being of all, the conditions required for attaining a person's true and complete good, including a person's spiritual end. It acts within the limits of its competence, which can vary from people to people and from country to country. It always intervenes with care for justice and with devotion to the common good, for which it holds final responsibility. It does not, for all that, deprive individuals and intermediary bodies of the field of activity and responsibility which are proper to them and which lead them to collaborate in the attainment of this common good. In fact the true aim of all social activity should be to help individual members of the social body, but never to destroy or absorb them. According to the vocation proper to it, the political power must know how to stand aside from particular interests in order to view its responsibility with regard to the good of all, even going beyond national limits.

To take politics seriously at its different levels is to affirm the duty of people, of every person, to recognize the concrete reality and the value of the freedom of choice that is offered to him or her to seek to bring about both the good of the city and of the nation and of humankind. While recognizing the autonomy of the reality of politics, Christians who are invited to take up political activity should try to make their choices consistent with the Gospel and, in the framework of a legitimate plurality, to give both personal collective witness to the seriousness of their faith by effective and disinterested service of all.

SOCIAL RESPONSIBILITY

The passing to the political dimension expresses a demand made by people today, namely, a greater sharing in responsibility and in decision-making. This legitimate aspiration becomes more evident as the cultural level rises, as the sense of freedom develops and as people become more aware of how the choices of today condition the life of tomorrow. Pope John XXIII stressed how much the admittance to responsibility is a basic demand of human nature, a concrete exercise of freedom and a path to development. Today the field is wider, and extends to the social and political sphere in which a reasonable sharing in responsibility and in decisions must be established and strengthened. In order to counterbalance increasing technocracy, modern forms of democracy must be devised, not only making it possible for each person to become informed and to express himself or herself, but also by involving him or her in a shared responsibility.

FREEDOM

Thus human groups will gradually begin to share and to live as communities. Thus freedom, which too often asserts itself as a claim for autonomy by opposing the freedom of others, will develop in its deepest human reality. Such freedom will involve itself and spend itself building up active and lived solidarity. For the Christian, it is by losing oneself in God who sets one free that one finds true freedom, renewed in the death and resurrection of the Lord.

A CALL TO ACTION

In the social sphere, the Church has always wished to assume a double function. The Church seeks to enlighten minds and to take part in action and to spread, with a real care for service and effectiveness, the energies of the Gospel.

It is to all Christians that we address a fresh and insistent call to action. Every person must be self-reflective and honestly examine himself or herself, to see what he or she has done up to now, and what he or she ought to do. It is not enough to recall principles, state intentions, point to crying injustice and utter prophetic denunciations; these words will lack real weight unless they are accompanied for each individual by a livelier awareness of personal responsibility and by effective action.

In concrete situations, and taking account of solidarity in each person's life, one must recognize a legitimate variety of possible options. The one Christian faith leads to a variety of types of social commitments. The Church invites all Christians to take up a double task of inspiring and innovating, in order to make structures evolve, so as to adapt them to the real needs of today. Today more than ever the Word of God will be unable to be proclaimed and heard unless it is accompanied by the witness of the power of the Holy Spirit, working within the actions of Christians in the service of their brothers and sisters.

THE MORAL VOICE FROM LATIN AMERICA

In 1968 Pope Paul VI traveled to Latin America and attended the opening of the Medellín Conference of Latin American bishops. The conference, influenced by the Second Vatican Council and Paul's encyclical *Populorum progressio*, addressed in an honest and very direct way the conditions of extreme poverty and oppression in Latin America. The immediate result was the publication of the *Medellín Documents on Justice, Peace, Family and Demography, and Poverty of the Church*. The conference had a far-reaching impact. The bishops, following the path set out in *Rerum novarum*, "reoriented the Latin American church to social justice."[3] They described and condemned the injustice and oppression of the poor and explicitly sided with the poor in their struggle. Note the passion with which the bishops confronted social problems. The bishops wanted to awaken a sense of justice in people. They invited Christians to create small, faith-based communities in the face of the dominant and powerful groups in society. They also shifted the traditional conversation in Catholic thought from wealth and the right to own property to the scandal of poverty. The bishops also directly addressed violence and offered insight into understanding the levels and types of violence. This part of the chapter includes selections from the Medellín documents. Following the bishops' documents are selections from two prominent books from Latin American priests published in 1971.

For readers from countries with strong economies that have legal protection of individual rights and some forms of safety nets to protect the poor, it is vital to set the context in which Catholic liberation movements started. As a student once asked, "What do they want to be liberated from?" Before reading the literature from Latin America, here are three "snapshots" of the context, all from Guatemala.

Narratives for Liberation

The first narrative: Journalist Penny Lernoux opens her 1989 book *People of God* with the following true story:

In the misty highlands of northwestern Guatemala there thrives a strange and wondrous church. Most of its members are illiterate Indian peasants who earn a subsistence living from farming the grudging hillsides and by weaving palm hats. Once a week they gather to celebrate the Word of God, sometimes in hidden forest glades, depending on the extent of military persecution. In these simple ceremonies the Indians share their feelings about a reading from the Bible, reflecting on what it means to be a Christian in the midst of extreme poverty and repression. They also remember their martyrs, the children who were burned alive, the pregnant women who were bayoneted, whole families that were tortured to death by the army because a Bible was found, buried beneath the dirt floor of a hut.

Every village in this region of El Quiche has a bloody story to tell. During an eight-year reign of terror that did not begin to subside until a civilian president took office in 1986, thousands of Indians were killed or relocated to concentration camps. By the army's own count, it destroyed 440 Indian villages, some dating to pre-Columbian times. Persecution against the Catholic Church was so ferocious that not a single priest or nun remained in the Quiche diocese. All the chapels were closed, and convents were occupied by troops. In order to celebrate Communion, undercover catechists traveled hours on foot, carrying consecrated Hosts hidden among ears of corn or in baskets of beans or tortillas. Anyone caught with such "subversive material" could expect a slow death by torture. Yet the people kept faith.[4]

In 1982 the Guatemalan army took over the town of Santa Cruz. It gathered the villagers and told them that the religion teachers were "subversives" and that they had to be killed. The army's threat to the people was clear: Either kill them tonight or we return tomorrow and burn down all the villages in the area. Could you imagine being in such a situation? If you were a citizen, how would you respond? Lernoux continues,

> The villagers had refused to do the deed, but the five catechists insisted that they must: "It is better for us to die than for thousands to die." At 4:00 A.M. a weeping procession, led by the catechists, arrived at the cemetery. Graves were dug, the people formed a circle around the kneeling men, and relatives of the five drew their machetes. Many could not watch the scene; some fainted as the blades fell, and the executioners' tears mingled with the blood of the catechists. The bodies were wrapped in plastic and buried. The villagers returned home in silence.[5]

The second narrative: As the above account suggests, the 1980s were a time of great violence in Guatemala. Indeed, from 1960 to 1996 there was great turmoil in that country. In 1998, Bishop Juan Gerardi of Guatemala issued an official report from the archdiocese titled, *The Recovery of Historical Memory Project* (REMHI), published in English as *Guatemala: Never Again*. The report was the result of many interviews conducted by diocesan officials with people who had experienced the violence committed by the Guatemalan army during those years. The result was a very moving and gut-wrenching document. Gerardi reported that from 1960 to 1996 the army committed 25,123 murders and additionally attacked 5,537 people. The army illegally detained 5,079 people; threatened 4,620 people; and tortured 4,219 people; 3,893 people "disappeared." Of all the people who were abducted, 715 people were released. Finally, 152 women told church officials that members of the army had raped them.[6]

Half of the massacres recorded include the collective murder of children. In keeping with the indiscriminate violence of massacres, descriptions of children's deaths often contain atrocities (incineration, machete wounds, and drawing and quartering, and most frequently, severe head trauma). Many young girls were raped during massacres or while detained. Cases of children killed by indiscriminate fire or machine-gun strafing of communities are reported less frequently. This suggests direct, deliberate aggression consistent with the overall treatment suffered by communities in these situations.

During the massacres, the violence against pregnant women sometimes included extreme cruelty toward the children they carried in their wombs. Many infant victims of the horror never appeared in the statistics on violence because they never had a name: they were murdered before they were born.

In many massacres, however, violence against children was not only part of the violence against the community in general but also had a deliberate purpose. In the testimonies gathered by REMHI, soldiers or patrollers frequently refer to the killing of children as a way of eliminating the possibility of rebuilding the community and of circumventing the victims' efforts to attain justice.

Information on the deaths of children and survivors' accounts of atrocities also are consistent with testimonies about military training methods and the instruction that was given at that time to soldiers in order to implement the scorched earth policy. During those years (1980–82), regarding the entire civilian population of many villages as members of guerrilla groups and physically eliminating them, including the children, was part of a carefully designed strategy.

Threatening and torturing children was also a means of torturing their families. The torture of children was a means of forcing people to collaborate, inducing people to denounce others, and destroying community. [In the words of one of the persons interviewed] "First they killed the children. It was a way of torturing the people, the parents. And I thought about all of that, but thank God it didn't happen. And so someone was still able to escape. They took the baby out of the woman. She was alive and they took out the child she was expecting, in front of her husband and her children. And the woman died and her children died too. They killed the others; the only one who remained was the one who escaped."

The murder of children has had an enormous impact on the survivors. It is accompanied by an even deeper feeling of injustice and symbolizes utter destruction. Such violence against children is an assault on community identity, which encompasses the ancestors and descendants.[7]

Two days after the release of the report, Bishop Gerardi was beaten to death with a concrete block in his garage.

The third narrative: The same year that Bishop Gerardi's report came out, Sr. Dianna Ortiz, an American Ursuline nun working in Guatemala, was abducted and brutally tortured. Her memoir, *The Blindfold's Eyes: My Journey from Torture to Truth,*[8] not only details the vicious cruelty inflicted on her while she was held captive but it also describes her courageous attempts to seek justice through the Guatemalan and U.S. (which funded the Guatemalan military) legal systems. Her story raised serious questions about the role of the U.S. military's relationship with the Guatemalan army. Reading the book takes one away from naive and abstract academic debates about the morality of torture to the reality of this evil practice.

The Medellín Conference of Latin American Bishops (abridged and edited) 1968

FUNDAMENTAL THEMES

The Church as Moral Voice: People must form a social conscience and a realistic perception of the problems of the community and the social structures. We bishops must awaken the social conscience of all and promote dialogue in community life.

Base Communities: It is necessary that small basic communities be developed in order to establish a balance with the groups in power.

The Church Is on the Side of the Poor: The Church, the People of God, will lend its support to the downtrodden of every social class so that they might come to know their rights and how to make use of them.

Peace in the Context of Violence: Given the tensions today that conspire against peace tempting violence and given the demands of the Christian understanding of peace, the Latin American Bishops must assume concrete responsibilities. For to create a just social order, without which peace is illusory, is an eminently Christian task. As Pastors of the Church, we have the duty to educate the Christian conscience. We must inspire, stimulate and help orient initiatives that contribute to the formation of persons. We must also denounce everything that, opposing justice, destroys peace.

POVERTY

The Latin American bishops cannot remain indifferent in the face of the tremendous social injustices that currently exist in Latin America. These conditions keep the majority of our people in dismal poverty and inhuman wretchedness.

Within the context of the poverty and wretchedness in which the great majority of the Latin American people live, we, bishops, priests and religious, have the necessities of life and a certain security. The poor, on the other hand, lack basic necessities and struggle between anguish and uncertainty. Some of them feel that their bishops, pastors and religious, do not really identify with them or with their problems and afflictions. They too often feel that Church officials do not always support people who work with them or plead their cause.

The Types of Poverty. Given this situation we reflect on the nature of poverty. We begin by distinguishing three types of poverty.

The first form of poverty is the lack of material goods needed to live a life worthy of human dignity. This form of poverty is in itself evil. The prophets denounce it as contrary to the will of the Lord. Usually this form of poverty is the consequence of injustice and sin.

The second form of poverty is spiritual poverty, the poor of God (See Lk 1:46–55). Spiritual poverty is when one opens oneself up to God. It is the ready disposition of one who hopes for everything from the Lord (Mt 5:3). In this sense of poverty a person values material goods but he or she does not become attached to them. The person recognizes the higher value of the riches of the Kingdom (Am 2:6–7; 4:1; Jer 5:28; Mi 6:12–13; Is 10:2).

The third form of poverty is voluntary or evangelical poverty. This is a loving commitment to share the conditions of the poor. Through this form of poverty people bear witness to the evil of material poverty. They follow the example of Christ who took to himself all the consequences of sinful condition of people (Phil 2:5–8) and who "being rich became poor" (2 Cor 8:9) in order to redeem us. Evangelical poverty bears witness to spiritual liberty in the face of material goods.

The Theology of Poverty. The Church then,

1. Denounces the sinful and unjust lack of material goods for the poor;

2. Preaches and lives in spiritual poverty, as an attitude of spiritual childhood and openness to the Lord;

3. Is committed to material poverty. All members of the church are called to live in evangelical poverty, but not all in the same way. There are diverse vocations to this poverty that tolerate diverse styles of life and various modes of acting.

Christ, our Savior, not only loved the poor, but rather "being rich he became poor." He lived in poverty. His mission centered on advising the poor of their liberation. He founded his Church as the sign of that poverty among men.

The Latin American Church, given the continent's conditions of poverty and underdevelopment, experiences the urgency of translating that spirit of poverty into actions, attitudes and norms that make it a more lucid and authentic sign of its Lord. The poverty of so many of our brothers and sisters cries out for justice, solidarity, open witness, commitment, strength, and exertion directed to the fulfillment of the redeeming mission to which it is committed by Christ.

The poverty of the Church and of its members in Latin America ought to be a sign and a commitment—a sign of the inestimable value of the poor in the eyes of God, an obligation of solidarity with those who suffer.

PASTORAL DIRECTIONS

We wish the Latin American Church to be the evangelizer of the poor and one with them, a witness to the value of the riches of the Kingdom, and the humble servant of all our people. Its pastors and the other members of the People of God have to correlate their life and words, their attitudes and actions, to the demands of the Gospel and the necessities of the people of Latin America.

The Lord's distinct commandment to "evangelize the poor" ought to bring us to a distribution of resources and apostolic personnel that effectively gives preference to the poorest and most needy. We, the bishops, wish to come closer to the poor in sincerity and brotherhood, making ourselves accessible to them. We ought to sharpen the awareness of our duty of solidarity with the poor. We must make their problems and their struggles ours. We must be critics of injustice and oppression.

We must live lives that give testimony to poverty and detachment from material goods. Authentic examples of detachment and freedom of spirit will encourage other members of the People of God to give a similar witness to poverty. A sincere conversion of all is needed to change our individualistic mentality into a mentality of social awareness and concern for the common good.

CONCLUSION

We want our Latin American church to be free from worldly possessions so that her mission of service will be stronger and clearer. We want her to be present in life and in secular works, reflecting the light of Christ, present in the construction of the world.

We recognize the value and legitimate autonomy of temporal works. We desire to respect all people and listen to them in order to serve them in their problems and afflictions. Thus the Church, carrying on the work of Christ ("For you know the gracious act of our Lord Jesus Christ, that for your sake he became poor although he was rich, so that by his poverty you might become rich" [2 Cor 8:9]), presents before the world a clear and unmistakable sign of the poverty of her Lord.

Liberation Theology

The most influential book in Catholic theology written between Vatican II
and the beginning of this century is Gustavo Gutiérrez's *A Theology of
Liberation* (1971). Fr. Gutiérrez was born in Peru in 1928 and educated in
Europe. He was, however, "trained" in the slums of Lima. The following
paragraph introduces the book and clearly captures its objectives:

> This book is an attempt at reflection, based on the gospel and the expe-
> riences of men and women committed to the process of liberation in the
> oppressed and exploited land of Latin America. It is a theological reflec-
> tion born of the experience of shared efforts to abolish the current unjust
> situation and to build a different society, freer and more human.[9]

In the introduction to the fifteenth anniversary edition of *A Theology of
Liberation*, Gutiérrez explains some of the basic tenets of the movement.

> Liberation theology is closely bound up with this new presence of those
> who in the past were always absent from our history. They have gradu-
> ally been turning into active agents of their own destiny and beginning a
> resolute process that is changing the condition of the poor and oppressed
> of this world. Liberation theology (which is an expression of the right of
> the poor to think out their own faith) has not been an automatic result of
> this situation and the changes it has undergone. It represents rather an
> attempt to accept the invitation of Pope John XXIII and the Second
> Vatican Council and interpret this sign of the times by reflecting on it
> critically in the light of God's word. (xxi)

> This is the context of a theme that is central in liberation theology and
> has now been widely accepted in the universal church: the preferential
> option for the poor . . . The very word "preference" denies all exclusive-
> ness and seeks rather to call attention to those who are the first, though
> not the only ones, with whom we should be in solidarity . . . The great
> challenge was to maintain both the universality of God's love and God's
> predilection for those on the lowest rung of the ladder of history. To
> focus exclusively on the one or the other is to mutilate the Christian
> message. (xxv–xxvi)

> God's love for the poor is manifested in Christ . . . In other words, the
> poor deserve preference not because they are morally or religiously bet-
> ter than others, but because God is God, in whose eyes "the last are
> first." This statement clashes with our narrow understanding of justice;
> this very preference reminds us, therefore, that God's ways are not ours.
> (xxviii)

The combination of these two factors, the message that is at the heart of biblical revelation, and the profound longing of the Latin American peoples, led us to speak of liberation in Christ and to make this the essential content of evangelization. (xxxviii)

The Controversy Surrounding Liberation Theology

The publication of *A Theology of Liberation* spurred a host of other Latin American theologians to work, study, and write in this area. The book became the focal point for an influential movement. Liberation theology spread to a variety of other geographical and cultural contexts: Asian liberation theology, black liberation theology, and liberation theology for women, among others. The movement was not without controversy. The primary criticism of liberation theology was its relation to or dependence on Marxist (communist) sources. The links to Marxism in the literature are clear. Liberation theologians often used Karl Marx's critique of capitalism in their analysis of current economic systems. Some Catholics in Latin American countries, perhaps inspired by liberation theology, joined communist-backed revolutionary movements.

There are, then, two issues here regarding liberation theology and Marxism. The first is that liberation theology undoubtedly used forms of Marxian social analysis. The second is that concurrently, communist sources did play an important role in Latin America, often advocating the overthrow of or violence against oppressive governments. A key point for critics of liberation theology was its ambiguity on the question of violence and revolution.

As we have seen, there are elements of Marxism that conflict with Catholic thought. The primary concern is the atheism Marx advocated. Marx held that religion was an ideology, that is, a system developed and controlled by the rich to justify their economic system and their privileged place in that system. Religion was part of the social structure that kept rich people rich and poor people poor. Thus Marx rejected religion. Communist societies that followed were officially atheistic; they denied the right of religious freedom. As we have seen in this book, the popes present a public ethic, that is, they hold that faith has a crucial place in society.

A second concern that social Catholicism has had with Marxism is Marx's view of society. The popes have traditionally held an organic view of society. Put simply, society naturally comprises different sorts of people in different social positions. Everybody has a social function. If all persons perform their respective social responsibilities, there will be cooperation among the social classes. Marx, on the other hand, held that social classes were fundamentally in conflict. The rich were rich because the poor were poor. The only option for the poor to gain any social goods was violent revolution against the rich. Marx ends his *Communist Manifesto* with the famous words:

"The Communists disdain to conceal their views and aims. They openly declare that their ends can be attained only by the forcible overthrow of all existing social conditions. Let the ruling classes tremble at a Communistic revolution. The proletarians have nothing to lose but their chains. They have a world to win. WORKING MEN OF ALL COUNTRIES, UNITE!"[10]

A most interesting response to the question of violence in Latin America and in liberation theology was offered by Dom Hélder Câmara (1909–99). Câmara was for twenty years a bishop in the archdiocese of Recife and Olinda, a very poor area of Brazil. He was known for his deep faith and his active life of service. Although he lived under a brutal military dictatorship, he was a staunch defender of the poor and a promoter of human rights and democracy. He was also a tireless advocate for nonviolent action in the work of justice. In short, he lived and preached Catholic social thought. Given his context and his faith, his life was constantly threatened. He lived for a good deal of time under constant monitoring by his government.

The following selections are taken from his influential book *Spiral of Violence*.[11] First, note how Câmara defines *violence*. People usually think of violence as some direct physical action used to harm persons (or things). Câmara describes violence in a much broader sense. He calls poverty violence, a violence caused by injustice. This wider use of the term *violence* is characteristic of liberation theology and Catholic social thought. Second, note Câmara's theory that violence causes violence. The violence of poverty invites revolt; revolt invites repression; and the social situation spirals downward.

> There exists what could be called a heritage of poverty. It is common knowledge that poverty kills just as surely as the most bloody war. But poverty does more than kill; it leads to physical deformity, to psychological deformity, and to moral deformity. (25–26)

> Look closely at the injustices in the underdeveloped countries, in the relations between the developed world and the underdeveloped world. You will find that everywhere the injustices are a form of violence. One can and must say that they are everywhere the basic violence, violence No. 1.
>
> A human being condemned to a sub-human situation is like an animal, an ox or a donkey, wallowing in the mud. Now the egoism of some privileged groups drives countless human beings into this sub-human condition, where they suffer restrictions, humiliations, and injustices; without prospects, without hope; their condition is that of slaves. This established violence, this violence No. 1, attracts violence No. 2, revolt, either of the oppressed themselves or of youth, firmly resolved to battle for a more just and human world. (29–30)

The young no longer have the patience to wait for the privileged to discard their privileges. The young very often see governments too tied to the privileged classes. The young are losing confidence in the churches, which affirm beautiful principles, great texts, remarkable conclusions, but without ever deciding, at least so far, to translate them into real life. (33)

If there is some corner of the world which has remained peaceful, but with a peace based on injustices, the peace of a swamp with rotten matter fermenting in its depths, we may be sure that that peace is false. Violence attracts violence. Let us repeat fearlessly and ceaselessly: injustices bring revolt.

And then comes repression: When conflict comes out into the streets, when violence No. 2 tries to resist violence No. 1, the authorities consider themselves obliged to preserve or reestablish public order, even if this means using force; this is violence No. 3. Sometimes they go even further, and this is becoming increasingly common: in order to obtain information, which may indeed be important to public security, the logic of violence leads them to use moral and physical torture. (33–34)

Let us have the honesty to admit . . . in the light of some typical reactions, that violence No. 3, governmental repression, under the pretext of safeguarding public order, national security, the free world, is not a monopoly of the underdeveloped countries. (36)

If violence is met by violence, the world will fall into a spiral of violence; the only true answer to violence is to have the courage to face the injustices that constitute violence No 1. (55)

A third area of conflict between Marxism and the Catholic tradition (the first was atheism *vs.* the necessary affirmation in God; the second was the conflictual understanding of society and social relations *vs.* the organic understanding) is the moral legitimacy of private property. Marx strongly argued against the notion of private property, a concept that has become central to Catholic social thought.

The Congregation for the Doctrine of the Faith at the Vatican offered a critique of liberation theology in 1984 with the publication of the document "Instruction on Some Aspects of Liberation Theology" (it published a related document in 1986). There it warned of the dangers of theologians using Marxism in an "insufficiently critical" fashion.

Liberation theology is not atheistic. It is, however, very critical of the distribution of the world's goods and the unjust patterns of land ownership in Latin America. Its view on violence, particularly violence against oppressive

regimes, is ambiguous. The movement has had strong defenders of the right
to self-defense and of the responsibility to nonviolence. The fundamental
question for many was whether a theology could use part of a problematic
philosophy and not be influenced by its other ideas. For people sympathetic
to liberation theology, the answer is yes; for critics, it remains no. The label
of communism was often applied to liberation theology. Perhaps the most
quoted words on this topic were by Dom Hélder Câmara. His simple words
touch the heart of liberation theology: "When I gave food to the poor they
called me a saint. When I asked why the poor were hungry they called me a
communist."

THE BLOOD OF THE MARTYRS

In the year 197 C.E., Tertullian, a leader in early Christianity, wrote a
treatise entitled "Apology," in which he responded to various charges made
against the Christians from members of the Roman community. (For example, he writes, "We are accused of observing a holy rite in which we kill
little children and eat them.")[12] At the end of the book he speaks about the
persecution of Christians and boldly proclaims, "The oftener we are mown
down by you, the more in number we grow; the blood of Christians is
seed."[13] In these powerful words Tertullian addressed the power of martyrdom. *Martyr* means "witness." As stated in the *Catechism of the Catholic
Church*, "Martyrdom is the supreme witness given to the truth of the faith:
it means bearing witness even unto death" (#2473).

From the earliest times Christians were killed because they were thought
to pose a threat to the political status quo. The Roman emperor Decius, for
example, in 250 C.E. ordered the universal persecution of Christians.[14] Dana
Gioia describes the complex interrelationship among faith, politics, and
martyrdom.

> Virtually all martyrdoms contain a political element. The paradigm of
> Christian martyrdom is the individual who refuses to bend his or her
> faith to the demands of the political authority. The martyr represents the
> heroic integrity of the conscientious individual resisting the expedient
> moral compromises of the collective society. Although the martyr's resis-
> tance is fundamentally spiritual, the state will inevitably view it in politi-
> cal terms . . . The martyr's task is not armed resistance; nor is it even
> passive suffering. Persecution and death are only the by-products of the
> martyr's true role, to witness the truth uncompromised . . . A tyrant can
> kill bodies but not ideas; especially not ideas the just consider worth
> dying for. The moral example of martyrs not only outlives the empires
> that persecute them; it gradually transforms them.[15]

The Tertullian quotation highlights the dramatic irony of martyrdom. When a political power kills people in an attempt to wipe out a movement, the opposite often occurs. The movement is strengthened. People who before may have been lukewarm in their support become inspired by the deaths of the martyrs. As theologian William Cavanaugh writes, "A martyr is a public witness who makes the truth visible in her or his own body . . . The historical lesson of the Colosseum is widely known: the more the Roman Empire treated its citizens to the public spectacle of Christians going peacefully and prayerfully to their deaths at the hand of gladiators and beasts, the more the church grew, eventually overtaking the empire itself." The significance of martyrdom is not, however, the glorification of an individual. The significance of martyrdom is that it builds the church. Cavanaugh continues, "The very process of naming a martyr is part of the act of memory that gives the community its identity. Not everyone who is killed is a martyr; some are merely victims. To be a martyr one must be recognized as such by the discernment of the community; a martyr must be named as such by those who remain alive."[16]

While the Medellín documents and the writing of Gutiérrez had far-reaching consequences, it was the martyrdom of so many Catholic leaders, teachers, missionaries, and people that captured the attention of Catholics around the globe. Their blood was seed for the faith of others. The Latin American church has given us many, many martyrs, some of whose words follow.

First, we look at the life and words of Archbishop Romero. Oscar Romero was born in El Salvador in 1917; he was ordained a priest in 1942. In preparation for ordination he studied in Rome. His reputation as a student and young priest was that he was serious and scholarly, with no real interest in political matters. When Romero became a bishop in 1967, observers thought he would support the political status quo in his country. According to biographers,[17] the most significant event in Romero's life came on March 12, 1977, when his friend Fr. Rutilio Grande was murdered. Grande worked in a very poor Salvadoran village. A strong advocate for social justice, a month before his death he preached a passionate sermon denouncing social conditions and the arrest and torture of priests. The following words from that sermon capture the spirit of faith-based calls for justice:

I'm quite aware that very soon the Bible and the Gospel won't be allowed to cross our borders. We'll get only the bindings, because all the pages are subversive. And I think that if Jesus himself came across the border at Chalatenango, they wouldn't let him in . . . It is dangerous to be a Christian in our world. It is almost illegal to be a Catholic in our world, where the very preaching of the Gospel is subversive and where priests are exiled for preaching it![18]

Fr. Grande was driving an old man and some children to town the day of his death. Members of the police force ambushed the car. The man and one of the boys were murdered along with the priest. Robert Ellsberg writes:

> Romero was deeply shaken by this event, which marked a new level in the frenzy of violence overtaking the country. In the weeks and months following Grande's death Romero underwent a profound transformation. Some would speak of it as a conversion, as astonishing to his new friends as it was to his foes. From a once timid and conventional cleric, there emerged a fearless and outspoken champion of justice. His weekly sermons, broadcast by radio throughout the country, featured an inventory of the week's violations of human rights, casting the glaring light of the gospel on the realities of the day.[19]

The following quotations are collected from Romero's sermons, published in James Brockman's *The Violence of Love*.[20] In these texts it is easy to see Romero's option for the poor. Note also his response to accusations that he encourages violence and that he is a communist:

> We have never preached violence, except the violence of love, which left Christ nailed to a cross, the violence that we must each do to ourselves, to overcome our selfishness and such cruel inequalities among us. The violence we preach is not the violence of the sword, the violence of hatred. It is the violence of love, of brotherhood, the violence that wills to beat weapons into sickles for work. (12)

> The church . . . believes that in each person is the Creator's image and that everyone who tramples it offends God. As holy defender of God's rights and of his images, the church must cry out. It takes as spittle in its face, as lashes on its back, as the cross in its passion, all that human beings suffer, even though they be unbelievers. They suffer as God's images. There is no dichotomy between persons and God's image. Whoever tortures a human being, whoever abuses a human being, whoever outrages a human being, abuses God's image, and the church takes as its own that cross, that martyrdom. (26)

> I repeat . . . addressing by radio those who perhaps caused so many injustices and acts of violence, those who have brought tears to so many homes, those who have stained themselves with the blood of so many murders, those who have hands soiled with tortures, those who have calloused their consciences, who are unmoved to see under their boots a person abased, suffering, perhaps ready to die. To all of them I say: no matter your crimes. They are ugly and horrible, and you have abased the

highest dignity of a human person, but God calls you and forgives you. And here perhaps arises the aversion of those who feel they are laborers from the first hour. How can I be in heaven with those criminals? Brothers and sisters, in heaven there are no criminals. The greatest criminal, once he has repented of his sins, is now a child of God. (91)

Those who do not understand transcendence cannot understand us. When we speak of injustice here below and denounce it, they think we are playing politics. It is in the name of God's just reign that we denounce the injustices of the earth. (162–63)

By what right have we cataloged persons as first-class persons or second-class persons? In the theology of human nature there is only one class: children of God. (199)

In August 1979 Romero published his fourth pastoral letter to the people of El Salvador: "The Church's Mission amid the National Crisis." The text below contains excerpts from the letter. Here Romero distinguishes several types of violence and considers the moral evaluation of each.

—Violence—
Given the escalation of the violence that casts a shadow over so many families in our homeland I want to address violence. Would that this reflection might persuade Salvadorans to lay unjust attitudes aside, and to get them, with sincere change of heart, to wash clean so many hands and consciences stained by social injustice and human blood! Inspired by the gospel, the church feels itself driven to seek peace before all else. But the peace that the church urges is the work of justice *(opus justitiae pax)*.

—Structural Violence—
The church condemns "structural" or "institutionalized" violence, the unjust situation in which the majority of men, women, and children in our country find themselves deprived of the necessities of life. The church condemns this violence not only because it is unjust in itself. It is an objective expression of personal and collective sin. The church condemns this as it is the cause of other innumerable cruelties and more obvious acts of violence.

—Arbitrary Violence of the State—
The church likewise condemns the arbitrary and repressive violence of the state. We in El Salvador well know how any dissent against the present form of capitalism and against the political institutions that support it is repressed with ever increasing violence and ever greater injustice,

inspired by the theory of national security. We also know how the majority of the campesinos, the laborers, slum dwellers, and others who
have organized themselves to defend their rights and to promote legitimate structural changes are simply declared to be "terrorists" or
"subversives." They are therefore arrested, tortured, murdered, or they
simply disappear and all without reference to the law or to any judicial
institution that might protect them or give them the chance to defend
themselves and prove their innocence. Faced with this prejudicial and
unjust situation, many have decided that they had no alternative but to
defend themselves with violence. And recently they have encountered, in
response, the arbitrary violence of the state.

Public authority certainly has the right to punish social disorder. But
in order to do so there must be the intervention of a court of justice that
gives the accused the chance to defend themselves. Any other kind of
sanction, arbitrary and repressive, is an abuse of authority.

—Violence of the Extreme Right—

The church equally condemns the violence favored by right-wing gangs
of terrorists. They go absolutely unpunished, which makes one suspect
official connivance. Their intention is to try to uphold the unjust social
order. Therefore they, more than anyone else, are involved in the injustice of the system.

—Terrorist Violence—

The church also condemns the violence perpetrated by politico-mili-
tary groups or individuals when they intentionally victimize innocent
persons, or when the damage they do is disproportionate to the positive
effect they wish to achieve.

—Insurrectional Violence—

According to Pope Paul VI in *Populorum progressio*, insurrection is
legitimate "in the very exceptional circumstances of an evident, prolonged
tyranny that seriously works against fundamental human rights and seriously damages the common good of the country, whether it proceeds
from one person or from clearly unjust structures."

—Violence of Legitimate Defense—

For the violence of insurrection or of defense to be legitimate, the
following is required:

1. The violence of legitimate defense must not be greater than the
unjust aggression.

2. All other possible peaceful means have been tried.

3. The violence used in defense must not bring in retaliation an even greater evil than that being resisted.

In practice it is very difficult to take account these theoretical measures. History has taught us how cruel and painful is the price of blood, and how difficult it is to repair social and economic damage caused by war. This is an opportune moment to recall that celebrated phrase of Pope Pius XII on war: "Nothing is lost by peace, everything may be lost in war."

The most reasonable and effective thing for a government to do is to use its moral and coercive force not to defend the structural violence of an unjust order, but to guarantee a truly democratic state, one that defends the fundamental rights of all its citizens, based on a just economic order.

—The Christian Is Peaceful, But Not Passive—

In this atmosphere of violence and of change in the country, how much to the point, and how valuable, have those guidelines become that Medellín expressed: "The Christian is peaceful and not ashamed of it. He is not simply a pacifist for he can fight, but he prefers peace to war. He knows that violent changes in structures would be fallacious, ineffectual in themselves, and not conforming to the dignity of man."[21]

Archbishop Romero was killed on March 24, 1980. He was shot while saying Mass for nuns in a hospital chapel. The previous day he had preached a passionate sermon which had been broadcast on the radio. Consider the words with which he challenges members of the military to disobey unjust orders from their superiors: "We are your people. The peasants you kill are your own brothers and sisters. When you hear the voice of the man commanding you to kill, remember instead the voice of God. Thou Shalt Not Kill . . . In the name of God, in the name of our tormented people whose cries rise up to heaven, I beseech you, I beg you, I command you, stop the repression."[22] As Catholic historian Thomas Bokenkotter notes, "These words sealed his death warrant."[23]

Nine months after the murder of Archbishop Romero, and after the deaths and disappearances of untold peasants, the Salvadoran military killed four American women working as missionaries in El Salvador. They are remembered today for their sacrifice and their commitment to Christian love and justice for the people of that war-torn country. Two of the martyrs were members of the Maryknoll order of nuns, Maura Clark and Ita Ford. Dorothy Kazel was a member of the Ursuline order, and Jean Donovan was a lay missionary. Two of the women were raped before being shot.

A few words from these women are appropriate here. Ita Ford, in a letter to her teenage niece, wrote:

This is a terrible time in El Salvador for youth . . . The reasons why so many people are being killed are quite complicated, yet there are some clear, simple strands. One is that people have found a meaning to live, to sacrifice, struggle, and even die . . . Some things hold true wherever one is, and at whatever age. What I'm saying is that I hope you can come to find that which gives life a deep meaning for you, something that energizes you, enthuses you, enables you to keep moving ahead.[24]

Jean Donovan, also in a letter, shows the same commitment to others, the same grounding in Christian vocation:

There's one think I know, I'm supposed to be down here, right now . . . You can contribute a lot and make a big difference in the world if you realize that the world you're talking about might be very small, maybe one person, or two people. And . . . if you can find a place to serve, you can be happy.[25]

Nine years later, early on the morning of November 16, 1989, an almost unthinkable event occurred. A battalion of the army, under the direction of the top military commanders of El Salvador, stormed the priests' residence at the University of Central America in San Salvador. They executed six Jesuit priests—Ignacio Ellacuría, Ignacio Martin Baro, Segundo Montes, Amano Lopez, Joaquin Lopez y Lopez, and Juan Ramon Moreno—and the housekeeper, Elba Ramos, and her teenage daughter Celina.[26]

Why were these priests, these college professors, targeted by the government? If we read Ron Hansen's reflections on Ignacio Ellacuría we get a sense of their threat to the oppressive status quo. Hansen, describing Ellacuría's vision for the University of Central America, wrote: "Ellacuría felt the institution ought to fully engage the harsh realities of the third world and through teaching, research, and persuasion, to be a voice for those who have no voice, to change or annihilate the world's inhuman and unjust structures, and to help assuage the agony of the poor."[27] This vision should be part of the mission statement of every college or university that calls itself Catholic.

The Controversy Surrounding U.S. Involvement in Latin America

A month before his death Archbishop Romero wrote a letter to the president of the United States, Jimmy Carter. He told the president that vast amounts of U.S. military aid to El Salvador had "violently repressed the people." He wrote:

For this reason, given that as a Salvadoran and archbishop of the archdiocese of San Salvador, I have an obligation to see that faith and justice reign in my country, I ask you, if you truly want to defend human rights: to forbid that military aid be given to the Salvadoran government; to guarantee that your government will not intervene directly or indirectly, with military, economic, diplomatic, or other pressures, in determining the destiny of the Salvadoran people.[28]

For many American Catholics, the United States appeared to be on the wrong side of this struggle. This concern increased when it became public that American-trained soldiers were involved in the deaths of Romero, the four missionary women, and the martyrs at the University of Central America. In each case either the commanders or the killers themselves were trained at the School of the Americas in Fort Benning, Georgia (in 2001 the school was renamed the Western Hemisphere Institute for Security Cooperation). Catholics and others have been for many years actively involved in attempts to close the school.

The civil war in El Salvador ended in 1992. It had lasted twelve years and claimed over seventy thousand lives. The peace was brokered by the United Nations.

JUSTICE IN THE WORLD

With the Second Vatican Council we see the reemergence of groups of bishops working together to respond to particular issues in their region. The Medellín Conference is one example of this. In 1971 Pope Paul VI asked the international bishops to meet to articulate and promote "the Church's engagement in the cause of social justice."[29] An interesting feature of this synod (the term here refers to the convening of the bishops to serve in an advisory role for the pope) is that more than half of the bishops came from third-world countries. Theologian Kenneth Himes comments, "It was the first time leaders of churches in poor nations had a formal opportunity to dialogue about justice with members of the curia and bishops from the wealthy nations."[30]

Justice in the World contains what is probably the most quoted text in the whole of official Catholic social thought: "Action on behalf of justice and participation in the transformation of the world fully appear to us as a constitutive dimension of the preaching of the Gospel, or, in other words, of the Church's mission for the redemption of the human race and its liberation from every oppressive situation." Much has been written about the meaning and intent of the word *constitutive*. Is action on behalf of justice "integral" to preaching the gospel? Or is action on behalf of justice "essential" to preaching the gospel? Himes, after reviewing the debate, notes, "It is fair to conclude, therefore, that the synod was making a powerful claim that the ministry of justice is of the very essence of the Church's mission."[31]

In this document the church for the first time applies its standards of justice to itself. Reading the documents one cannot but note the self-understanding of the church as a transformative actor in the world.

Justice in the World (abridged and edited)
World Synod of Catholic Bishops, 1971

INTRODUCTION

We, the Catholic Bishops of the world, gathered in this Synod to consider the mission of the People of God to further justice in the world. Scrutinizing the "signs of the times," we listened to the Word of God so we might fulfill the divine plan for the salvation of the world.

We have listened to the cry of those who suffer violence and are oppressed by unjust systems and structures. We see a world that contradicts the plan of its Creator and we share the Church's vocation to proclaim the Good News to the poor, freedom to the oppressed, and joy to the afflicted.

Action on behalf of justice and participation in the transformation of the world fully appear to us as a constitutive dimension of the preaching of the Gospel, or, in other words, of the Church's mission for the redemption of the human race and its liberation from every oppressive situation.

1. READING THE SIGNS OF THE TIMES

OUR CURRENT CONDITION

The world in which the Church lives and acts is held captive by a tremendous paradox. Never before have the forces working for bringing about a unified world society appeared so powerful and dynamic. Moreover, people are beginning to grasp a new and more radical dimension of unity; for they perceive that their resources are not infinite, but on the contrary must be saved and preserved as belonging to all human beings.

The paradox lies in the fact that within this unity the forces of division and antagonism seem today to be increasing in strength. At the same time new divisions are being born to separate people from their neighbors. Unless combated and overcome by social and political action, the new order favors the concentration of wealth and power in the hands of a controlling group. Economic injustice and lack of social participation keep people from attaining their basic human and civil rights.

During the last twenty-five years a hope has spread through the human race that economic growth would bring about such a quantity of goods that it would be possible to feed the hungry. This has proved a vain hope. The stifling oppressions of the rapid growth of population, rural stagnation, lack of agrarian reform, as well as the massive migratory flow to the cities have left many workers unemployed. These conditions give rise to great numbers of "marginal" persons, ill-fed, inhumanly housed, illiterate, deprived of political power and unable to attain the suitable means of acquiring responsibility and moral dignity.

If all people in this world used the natural resources as the rich nations currently do, and if all people of the world polluted the air and water as the rich nations currently do, there would be irreparable damage done to the essential elements of life on earth.

These current conditions, namely, the drive towards global unity; the unequal distribution of income, investment and trade; the insufficiency of measuring progress in merely economic terms; and the recognition of the limits of the biosphere, makes us aware of the fact that in today's world new modes of understanding human dignity are demanded.

HUMAN DIGNITY AND HUMAN DEVELOPMENT

In the face of international systems of domination, justice depends on the determined will of people to work for human development. In the poorer nations the will to promote human dignity asserts itself in a struggle of claiming individual rights. This aspiration to justice begins a consciousness of enhancement of personal worth. This is expressed in an awareness of the right to development. We understand the "right to development" is the culmination of all fundamental human rights.

Social structures can place obstacles in the way of conversion of hearts and the realization of charity. There must be an end to the systematic barriers and discrimination that exclude so many people. By taking their future into their own hands through a determined will for progress, the poorer peoples and nations will manifest their own personalization and attain liberation through development so as not to be the victims of international economic forces.

It is impossible to conceive true progress without the recognition of the necessity of human development that overcomes the imbalances in economic growth, participation, wealth and social progress. Participation is a right in both economics and politics.

DEFENDING THE RIGHT TO LIFE

A particular set of injustices is at the heart of today's problems. Justice demands that we be prepared to take new responsibilities in every aspect of human life. Above all, our action must be directed to the victims of injustice, those people who because of oppression are silent and voiceless. We think, for example of many types of workers, and farm workers, particularly migrant workers who are forced to leave their own country to find work and often treated in an inhuman manner. We also remember the millions of refugees and people suffering racial, ethnic, or religious persecution. Justice is violated when people are oppressed, when prisoners are tortured and denied due process or when they are subject to arbitrary legal procedures. Justice is violated when prisoners of war are treat in an inhuman manner.

People defend the right to life by working to bring an end to war, by working to bring an end to legalized abortion and by working to bring an end to forced contraception.

The world needs to create a lasting atmosphere of dialogue. The progressive realization of this atmosphere of dialogue can be made when people are not hampered by geopolitical, ideological or socioeconomic conditions.

2. THE GOSPEL AND THE MISSION OF THE CHURCH

In the face of the present-day situation of injustice in the world, we recognize both our responsibility and our inability to overcome it by our own strength. We must listen with a humble and open heart to the word of God, as he shows us new paths towards action in the cause of justice in the world.

THE BIBLICAL TESTIMONY

In the Old Testament God reveals himself to us as the liberator of the oppressed and the defender of the poor, demanding from people faith in him and justice towards one's neighbor.

By his action and teaching Christ united people to God and people to each other. Christ lived his life in the world as a total giving of himself to God for the salvation and liberation of people. In his preaching he proclaimed the fatherhood of God towards all people and the intervention of God's justice on behalf of the needy and the oppressed (Lk 6: 21–23). In this way he identified himself with his "least ones," as he stated: "As you did it to one of the least of these who are members of my family, you did it to me" (Mt 25:40).

Faith in Christ, the Son of God and the Redeemer, and love of neighbor constitute a fundamental theme of the writers of the New Testament. According to St. Paul, the whole of the Christian life is summed up in faith effecting love and service of neighbor which includes fulfilling the demands of justice.

Our relationship to our neighbor is bound up with our relationship to God; our response to the love of God is shown to be effective in Christ's love and service of people. Christian love of neighbor and justice cannot be separated. For love implies a recognition of the dignity and rights of one's neighbor. Justice attains its inner fullness only in love. Because every person is truly a visible image of the invisible God and a sibling of Christ, the Christian finds in every person God himself and God's absolute demand for justice and love.

THE CHURCH IN THE WORLD

The present situation of the world, seen in the light of faith, calls us back to the very essence of the Christian message. The Gospel dictates that we should dedicate ourselves to the liberation of people.

The Church has received from Christ the mission of preaching the Gospel message. This message contains a call to people to turn away from sin to the love of the Father, universal kinship and a consequent demand for justice in the world. This is the reason why the Church has the duty to proclaim justice and to denounce instances of injustice on the social, national and international levels. The Church has the responsibility to give witness before the world of the need for love and justice. This witness must be carried out both in Church institutions and in the lives of Christians. The mission of the Church includes defending and promoting the dignity and fundamental rights of the human person.

Christians ought to fulfill their temporal obligations with fidelity and competence. They should act as a leaven in the world, in their family, professional, social, cultural and political life. They must accept their responsibilities in the world and respond informed by the Gospel and the teaching of the Church.

3. THE PRACTICE OF JUSTICE

Christians give witness to justice by various modes of action inspired by love in accordance with the grace they have received from God. The priority of love draws Christians to prefer the way of non-violent action and work in the area of public opinion. Anyone who ventures to speak about justice must first be just.

JUSTICE IN THE CHURCH

Within the Church rights must be preserved. No member should be deprived of his or her ordinary rights within the Church. Those who serve the Church should receive a sufficient livelihood and enjoy that social security which is customary in their region. Lay people should be given fair wages and a system for promotion. They should also exercise important roles regarding the administration of Church property. Women should share responsibility and participation in the Church and in the community.

The Church recognizes everyone's right to suitable freedom of expression and thought. This includes the right of everyone to be heard in a spirit of dialogue that preserves a legitimate diversity within the Church.

In its judicial procedures, the Church should allow people accused the right to know accusers, a right to a proper defense and a timely process, particularly in marriage cases. All members of the Church should have some share in the decision-making process.

The Church must never give mixed messages regarding its material possessions. While it is difficult to draw a line between appropriate possession and prophetic

witness, we must keep firm the principle that our faith demands we use possessions sparingly. The Church must live and use goods so that the Gospel is proclaimed to the poor. If the Church appears to be among the rich and the powerful it loses its credibility. Our examination of conscience now turns to the lifestyle
of it members: bishops, priests, religious and lay people. We must ask ourselves if
we practice what we preach. Millions of hungry people throughout the world
need to be fed. Do our life styles contribute to their hunger or their satisfaction?

JUSTICE AND EDUCATION

On a day-to-day basis a Christian's specific contribution to justice is to be the
leaven of the Gospel in family, school, work and social and civic life.

True education demands a renewal of heart as it recognizes both individual
sin and its social manifestations. True education instills justice, love and simplicity.
It awakens a critical sense, enabling people to reflect on their society and its
values. Such education enables people to renounce social values that do not
promote justice for all people. In the poorer countries, this education awakens
consciences to knowledge of the situation and calls people to work for social
improvement. Education makes people decidedly more human and helps as they
take control of their own destinies. This education is practical. It comes through
action, participation and vital contact with the reality of injustice. The first school
for justice is the family.

The content of this education is respect for the person and for his or her
dignity. All humans, according to God's plan, are born into the human family and
are destined to become in Christ sharers in the divine nature.

Like the apostle Paul, we insist that the Word of God should be present in the
center of human situations. Our mission demands that we should courageously
denounce injustice with charity, prudence and firmness. Our mission demands
sincere dialogue with all parties concerned.

The liturgy, which is the heart of the Church's life, can greatly serve education
for justice. For it is a thanksgiving to the Father in Christ, which through its
communitarian form places before our eyes the bonds of our brotherhood and
again and again reminds us of the Church's mission. The liturgy of the word,
catechesis and the celebration of the sacraments have the power to help us to
discover the teaching of the prophets, the Lord and the Apostles on the subject
of justice. The preparation for baptism is the beginning of the formation of the
Christian conscience. The practice of penance should emphasize the social dimension of sin and of the sacrament. Finally, the Eucharist forms the community
and places it at the service of people.

For the Church to be the sign of that solidarity it must in its own life show
greater cooperation and communion between the Churches of rich and poor
regions. The Churches, through social solidarity, ought to coordinate the administration of God's gifts. This solidarity encourages autonomy and responsibility on

the part of the beneficiaries particularly in the determination and implementation of programs. Such programs should include activities aimed at developing that human and spiritual formation serving as the leaven for integral human development.

COLLABORATION AND THE WORK OF JUSTICE

We highly commend cooperation with our separated Christian brethren for the promotion of justice in the world, development of peoples and establishing peace. This cooperation concerns first and foremost activities for securing human dignity and people's fundamental rights, especially the right to religious liberty. This is the source of our common efforts against discrimination on the grounds of differences of religion, race and color, culture and the like. Collaboration extends also to the study of the teaching of the Gospel insofar as it is the source of inspiration for all Christian activity.

In the same spirit we commend collaboration with all believers in God in the fostering of social justice, peace and freedom; indeed we commend collaboration also with those who, even though they do not recognize the Author of the world, nevertheless, in their esteem for human values, seek justice sincerely and by honorable means.

AN EXAMINATION OF CONSCIENCE

We urge Catholics to consider the following propositions:

1. The international order is rooted in the inalienable rights and dignity of the human being. The United Nations Declaration of Human Rights should be ratified and fully observed by all Governments.

2. It is absolutely necessary that international conflicts should not be settled by war, but that other methods better befitting human nature should be found. Strategies of non-violence should be fostered and each nation ought to recognize the validity of conscientious objection. The United Nations and other international organizations ought to be supported particularly as they are able to restrain the arms race, discourage the trade of weapons, secure disarmament and settle conflicts by peaceful methods including legal action, arbitration and international police action.

3. The aims of the Second Development Decade should be fostered. These aims include the transfer of a percentage of the annual income of the richer countries to the developing nations, fairer prices for raw materials, the opening of the markets of the richer nations and, in some fields, preferential treatment for exports of manufactured goods from the developing nations.

4. The concentration of power (which consists in almost total domination of economics, research, investment, freight charges, sea transport and securities) should be progressively balanced. Developing nations ought to have full participation in international organizations concerned with development.

5. There is a critical need for international attention to provide sufficient food and protein for the mental and physical development of children. We support the specialized agencies of the United Nations concerned with the acute questions of world poverty particularly agrarian reform and agricultural development, health, education, employment, housing, and rapidly increasing urbanization.

6. Governments must continue their individual contributions to a development fund, but they must also work multilaterally. Development efforts must include the responsibility of the developing nations in decision-making processes.

7. Richer nations must accept a less material way of life, with less waste, in order to avoid the destruction of the heritage which they are obliged by absolute justice to share with all other members of the human race. It is impossible to see what right the richer nations have to keep up their claim to increase their own material demands, if the consequence is either that others remain in misery or that the danger of destroying the very physical foundations of life on earth is precipitated.

8. In order that the right to development may be fulfilled by action: people should not be hindered from attaining development in accordance with their own culture; all peoples, through mutual cooperation, should be able to become the principal architects of their own economic and social development; every person, as an active and responsible member of human society, should be able to cooperate for the attainment of the common good on an equal footing with other persons.

4. A WORD OF HOPE

The power of the Spirit, who raised Christ from the dead, is continuously at work in the world. Through the generous sons and daughters of the Church, the People of God is present in the midst of the poor and in those who suffer oppression and persecution.

Let Christians therefore be convinced that they will yet find the fruits of their own nature and effort in the new earth that God is now preparing for them, and in which there will be the kingdom of justice and love, a kingdom that will be fully perfected when the Lord will come himself.

At the same time as it proclaims the Gospel of the Lord, its Redeemer and Savior, the Church calls on all, especially the poor, the oppressed and the afflicted, to cooperate with God to bring about liberation from every sin and to build a world which will reach the fullness of creation.

EVANGELIZATION AND JUSTICE

The final section of this chapter covers an excerpt from a short document from Pope Paul VI. It reflects on the relation between culture and the gospel. Theologian Donal Dorr suggests that in this document the pope makes a distinctive contribution to Catholic social thought. To put Dorr's analysis in context, consider a debate in matters of social change. Advocates of change to end racism or poverty or violence often take one of two positions. Ought we work to change systems, structures, and laws? Or ought we work to change people's hearts and minds? Dorr's point is that Paul challenges this dichotomy. It is not an either/or proposition:

The pope is here taking the word culture in a broad and rich sense. It refers to the shared understanding and attitudes of any group of people who together live in their own particular "world" . . . These shared attitudes and values might be called structures or patterns of thinking and feeling. They become embodied in traditions and in this way they are passed on from one generation to the next . . .

The most helpful aspect of this whole account is the way in which it bridges the gap that is usually presumed to exist between attitudinal change and structural change. It is commonly assumed that changing one's attitudes is a matter of personal morality; and this is generally what people have in mind when they speak of "conversion." Structural changes, on the other hand, are thought of as belonging to the political order, extrinsic to the person as such, and not a matter of personal morality in the usual sense . . . [The pope's statements] suggest that perhaps the most important structures in our world are our patterns of thinking and feeling and valuing. These are deeply personal; yet in many respects they transcend the individual. They are social realities which are often our unexamined presuppositions. They are "within" the person without being private . . .

To change the collective conscience of a people is to change their value system; and this is linked to changes in the social, political, and economic structures of their society.

People can be oppressed by structures of the mind, by distorted value-systems and patterns of action, by misguided expectations, and by inherited prejudices and insensitivities . . .

Liberation calls not only for the transformation of society structures in the sphere of economics and polities but also for radical changes in the patterns and structures that mould the way groups of people think and feel and evaluate.[32]

The following section is from Pope Paul VI's *Evangelii nuntiandi (Evangelization in the Modern World)*. It was written in response to a request from the World Synod of Bishops in 1974.

Evangelii Nuntiandi (abridged and edited)
Pope Paul VI, December 8, 1975

EVANGELIZATION AND LIBERATION

Christ proclaims salvation as the kernel and center of His Good News. This great gift of God which is liberation from everything that oppresses persons but which is above all liberation from sin and the Evil One, in the joy of knowing God and being known by Him, of seeing Him, and of being given over to Him.

"Evangelization" means bringing the Good News into all the levels of human experience so as to transform humanity from within and making it new. But there is no new humanity if there are not first of all new persons renewed by Baptism and by lives lived according to the Gospel. The purpose of evangelization is interior change. To put it simply and directly the Church evangelizes when she seeks to convert, through the divine power of the message she proclaims, both the personal and collective consciences of people, the activities in which they engage, and the lives and concrete milieu that are theirs. Evangelization means bringing the Good News into all the levels of human experience so as to transform humanity from within and making it new.

EVANGELIZATION AND PERSONS

Christians are to evangelize human culture always taking the person as the starting-point and always coming back to the relationships of people among themselves and with God. The Gospel and evangelization are not to be identified with any particular culture; they are independent of all cultures. Nevertheless, the kingdom proclaimed in the Gospel is lived by people profoundly linked to a particular culture. Building up of the kingdom cannot avoid borrowing the elements of human culture or cultures.

Complete evangelization always takes into account the interplay of the Gospel and of human life, personal and social. The explicit message of evangelization, adapted to the different situations, is about the rights and duties of every human being. It is about personal growth and development possible in and through family life. It is about life in society, about international life, peace, justice, development and liberation.

Many people are deeply engaged in the struggle to overcome all that condemns them to live on the margin of life: famine, chronic disease, illiteracy, poverty, injustices in international relations and in commercial exchanges, and situations of economic and cultural neo-colonialism. The Church has many duties in this work. She proclaims the liberation of millions of people, including many Christians. She assists in the birth of this liberation, gives witness to this liberation and ensures its completion. This work is not foreign to evangelization.

CONVERSION AND LIBERATION

There are profound links between evangelization and human advancement, development and liberation. People after all are not abstract beings. They are persons living within social and economic situations. There are also theological links between evangelization and human development. The plan of creation cannot be separated from the plan of Redemption. Redemption touches the very concrete situations of injustice to be combated and of justice to be restored. How can one proclaim Jesus' new commandment without promoting justice, peace and authentic human development?

The Church considers it to be undoubtedly important to build up structures that are more human, more just, more respectful of the rights of the person and less oppressive and less enslaving. She also is conscious that the best structures and the most idealized systems soon become inhuman if those who live in these structures or who rule them do not undergo a conversion of heart and of outlook.

THE REJECTION OF VIOLENCE

The Church cannot accept violence, especially the force of arms and indiscriminate death, as the path to liberation. She knows that violence always provokes violence. She knows that violence irresistibly engenders new forms of oppression and enslavement that are often harder to bear than those from which they claimed to bring freedom. We exhort people not to place their trust in violence and revolution. They are contrary to the Christian spirit. Violence and revolution, moreover often delay lawful social development. Violence is not in accord with the Gospel. It is not Christian.

CONCLUSION

The Church encourages Christians to devote themselves to the liberation of people. She provides the inspiration of faith, the motivation of fraternal love, and her social teaching as a foundation of wisdom. From these sources and through experience Christians can develop plans for action, participation and commitment.

SOME QUESTIONS FOR CONSIDERATION

1. Compare liberation theology and the writings of Archbishop Romero to *Rerum novarum*. In what ways are these two aspects of the tradition similar? In what ways do they differ?

2. Respond to ideas in this chapter that have influenced your thinking. Be specific. Give examples from the readings.

3. Review the sources from Latin America (Medellín, liberation theology, and the writings of Archbishop Romero) and compare them with the writings of Pope Paul VI. In what ways have these sources influenced the pope's writings?

4. Critique the discussion of violence and the types of violence discussed in this chapter.

5. Using the "look, judge, and act" model, discuss what Pope Paul sees in the world, what his judgment is, and what actions he determines to be appropriate.

6. Review the principles of Catholic social thought from the first chapter—the dignity of the human person, the common good, subsidiarity, and solidarity—and describe how they are expressed in this chapter.

7. Discuss the main themes of liberation theology in relation to the cultural context of current U.S. middle-class Catholicism. Are there any links or ways liberation theology might inform or challenge the American Catholic church?

8. How do the authors of the selections in this chapter defend and support their positions? Review the discussion of moral arguments from the first chapter. Do the authors argue from authority, or do they use theological, biblical, philosophical, common sense, or pragmatic arguments?

9. Review the three spheres of Catholic social action: works of mercy and justice, public expression and personal commitment, and social analysis for social change. How do the readings in this chapter express these spheres?

10. Discuss the four forms of moral discourse—narrative, prophetic, ethical, and policy—and how they are expressed in this chapter.

God's Voice Today

It is not difficult to hear God's call today in the world about us. It is difficult to do more than offer an emotional response, sorrow and regret. It is even more difficult to give up our comfort, break with old habits, let ourselves be moved by grace and change our life, be converted.

Come Lord. Do not smile and say you are already with us. Millions do not know you and to us who do, what is the difference? What is the point of your presence if our lives do not alter? Change our lives, shatter our complacency. Make your word flesh of our flesh, blood of our blood and our life's purpose. Take away the quietness of a clear conscience. Press us uncomfortably. For only thus that other peace is made, your peace.[33]

—Dom Hélder Câmara

Chapter Seven

Human Work on God's Earth

You Have Crowned Us with Honor
O LORD, our Sovereign,
   how majestic is your name in all the earth!
You have set your glory above the heavens . . .

When I look at your heavens, the work of your fingers,
   the moon and the stars that you have established;
what are human beings that you are mindful of them,
   mortals that you care for them?

Yet you have made them a little lower than God,
   and crowned them with glory and honor.
You have given them dominion over the works of your hands;
   you have put all things under their feet,
all sheep and oxen,
   and also the beasts of the field,
the birds of the air, and the fish of the sea,
   whatever passes along the paths of the seas.

O LORD, our Sovereign,
   how majestic is your name in all the earth!

—PSALM 8:1, 3–9

No pope has influenced Catholic social thought as much as John Paul II. The reasons for this are many. First, he was pope for nearly twenty-seven years. His was one of the longest pontificates in the history of the church. Second, his time as pope was characterized by extensive travel. He was the first pope of the "globalization" period and witnessed firsthand some of the social problems he addressed. Third, John Paul was an enthusiastic contributor to social Catholicism. He authored three social encyclicals, and his concern for the social order, justice, and peace was communicated through

184

speeches, sermons, messages, and prayers. In his writings there are innumerable references to the person, personalism, and the moral requirements inherent in the dignity of being human.

This chapter, the first of three that center on the work of Pope John Paul II, considers two of his writings. The focus of the chapter is the pope's first social encyclical, *Laborem exercens (On Human Work)*, published in 1981. The second text is his 1990 "World Day of Peace Message" on the environment. In both texts personalism is the fundamental theme. The third section of the chapter builds on a theme highlighted in *Laborem exercens*, namely, the plight of migrants in the contemporary world. This section includes an excerpt from a letter co-written by U.S. and Mexican bishops addressing common concerns of migration and immigration.

ON HUMAN WORK

There is a strange paradox in most of our lives. Few of us would say that our work is the most important thing in our life. If asked, we might give priority to our family, our friends, or our faith. It is those things, we would say, that we value the most. Yet, we spend most of our time when we are awake working. We go to work or we go to school; we come home and prepare meals and clean kitchens and bathrooms. With the aid of the Internet and cell phones, we often work at our paid jobs during our home time (in between loads of laundry). We spend a great deal of time working, paid or otherwise, but we rarely consider ourselves workers.

When we reflect on work, we usually think about the things we do at work. This, according to Pope John Paul II, is not sufficient. Work must be considered in its complex wholeness. Like Pope Leo XIII, John Paul offers a moral examination of the conditions of labor, the rights of workers, unions, and the moral economic order. One might say Leo starts with the worker and looks outward at external conditions. John Paul, on the other hand, explores the subjective nature of work. He calls us to examine who we are and who we become through work. Commenting on the encyclical, theologian Patricia Lamoureux notes that for John Paul, work and all human action have an "inner effect that morally shapes a person."[1] This encyclical, then, is very different from the previous ones we have read. In the words of theologian Donal Dorr: "*Laborem exercens* represents a new style of social teaching. What John Paul offers us here is a painstaking and profound reflection on the nature of human work and the organization of economic life."[2]

The encyclical is divided into four sections. The first considers the worker as a person. The second mediates the classic tension between workers and owners (labor and capital). The third section is a strong affirmation of the rights of workers in the contemporary world. In the final section the pope offers ideas for a spirituality of work.

Laborem Exercens (abridged and edited)
Pope John Paul II, September 14, 1981

INTRODUCTION

Genesis tells us that humans are made in the image and likeness of God (Gen 1:27). From the very beginning humans were called to work, "to subdue the earth" (Gen 1:28). Work is indeed one of the characteristics that distinguish humans from other creatures. Only humans are capable of work, and only humans work.

On this ninetieth anniversary of *Rerum novarum,* we return to the question of work to highlight the fact that human work is the essential key to the whole social question. The solution to the social question is to be found in making "life more human" and work is a primary feature of human life.

WORK AND THE PERSON

CREATION

The Church is convinced that work is a fundamental dimension of human existence. This conviction is confirmed both by reason and faith. The Church finds in the very first pages of the Book of Genesis the source of this conviction. These texts express the fundamental truths about human nature in the context of the mystery of creation. Humans are the image of God partly through the mandate received from the Creator to subdue, to dominate, the earth (Gen 1:28). In carrying out this mandate human beings reflect the action of the Creator.

The expression "subdue the earth" has an immense range. It includes the resources that the earth contains and which, through the conscious activity of humans, can be discovered and used for our ends. And so these words, placed at the beginning of the Bible, never cease to be relevant.

THE OBJECTIVE SENSE OF WORK—SUBDUE THE EARTH

Human dominion over the earth is achieved in and through work. Thus we must consider the "objective" sense of work. Humans have dominated the earth by domesticating animals, rearing them and obtaining from them the food and clothing needed. Humans have further dominated the earth by extracting various natural resources from the land and the seas. "Subduing the earth" is evident through the cultivation and the transformation of the earth's products into human use. Thus agricultural work is a primary field of economic activity and an indispensable factor of production.

The development of industry and technology, especially in the fields of communications and telecommunications, shows how vast the role of technology has become. Technology is a product of human thought, a product of the interaction between the subject and object of work.

If the biblical words "subdue the earth" addressed to humans from the very beginning are understood in the context of the modern age, then they undoubtedly include a relationship with technology, with the world of machinery that is the fruit of the work of the human intellect and a historical confirmation of human dominion over nature.

The recent stage of human history brings an affirmation of technology as a basic coefficient of economic progress; but, at the same time, this affirmation has been accompanied by essential questions concerning human work in relationship to the person. These questions have a particularly ethical and social character. They constitute a challenge for institutions, for states and governments, for systems and international organizations; they also constitute a challenge for the Church.

THE SUBJECTIVE SENSE OF WORK—THE PERSON

In order to continue our analysis of work, we must concentrate on work in the "subjective" sense. Humans are persons, that is to say, subjective beings. Persons are capable of acting in planned and rational ways. They are capable of choice and have a tendency to self-realization. A person therefore is the subject of work. When a person works, he or she performs actions. These actions must serve the realization of the person's humanity. The objective work activity must fulfill the subjective nature of work, that is to say, work must aid the worker in his or her calling to be a person.

The biblical understanding of "dominion" refers both to the objective and subjective dimensions of work. That is to say, it refers to the process whereby people subdue the earth as free and conscious subjects. The moral value of work must consider both dimensions, yet the fundamental moral value of work lies in the subjective dimension. The worker is a person, a subject who decides about himself or herself. This truth constitutes the fundamental and perennial heart of Christian teaching on human work.

All of this is underscored by the fact that Jesus, while being God, became like us in all things. Jesus devoted most of the years of his life on earth to manual work at the carpenter's bench. This circumstance constitutes in itself the most eloquent "Gospel of work"; showing that the basis for determining the value of human work is not primarily the kind of work being done but the fact that the one who is doing it is a person. The source of the dignity of work is to be sought primarily in the subjective dimension, not in the objective dimension.

The primary basis of the value of work is the person, the subject of work. Ethical reflection on the nature of work then begins with the concept that work is "for persons," persons are not "for work." That is to say, the subjective meaning of work has pre-eminence over the objective meaning of work. In the final analysis it is always a person who is the purpose of the work, no matter what kind of work is being done, even if society thinks such work is the most menial, most monotonous, or the most alienating work.

MATERIALISM IS A THREAT TO MORALITY

It is dangerous to understand work as a kind of "merchandise" or as an impersonal "force" needed for production (the expression "workforce" is in fact in common use). A materialistic civilization does just that as it gives primary importance to the objective dimension of work over the subjective dimension. When persons are treated as instruments of production, there is a reversal of the divine ordering. A person must be considered independently of the particular work he or she does.

WORKER SOLIDARITY

There must be continued study of the subject of work and of the subject's living conditions. In order to achieve social justice there is a need for new movements of solidarity of workers and solidarity with workers. This solidarity must be present in situations of social degradation and exploitation of workers and in areas of poverty and hunger. The Church is firmly committed to the cause of social justice and solidarity. This cause is her mission, her service, and a proof of her fidelity to Christ. She aims to be truly the "Church of the poor." Today the "poor" appear under various forms; they appear in various places and at various times; in many cases they appear as a result of the violation of the dignity of human work: either because the opportunities for human work are limited, or because a low value is put on work and the rights that flow from it, especially the right to a just wage and to the personal security of the worker and his or her family.

WORK, TOIL, AND HUMAN DIGNITY

God's fundamental and original intention with regard to humans was not cancelled when Adam, having broken the original covenant with God, heard the words: "In the sweat of your face you shall eat bread." These words refer to the heavy toil that accompanies work. They do not alter the fact that work is the means whereby a person achieves "dominion" over the world, by "subjecting" the earth. Toil is something that is universally known and experienced. It is familiar to those doing physical work under laborious conditions. It is familiar to agricultural workers, who spend long days working the land and to those who work in mines and quarries, to steel-workers at their blast-furnaces, to those who work in builders' yards and in construction work. It is likewise familiar to those at an intellectual workbench; to scientists; to those who bear the burden of grave responsibility for decisions that will have a vast impact on society. It is familiar to doctors and nurses, who spend days and nights at their patients' bedside. It is familiar to women, who, sometimes without proper recognition on the part of society and even of their own families, bear the daily burden and responsibility for their homes and the upbringing of their children. It is familiar to all workers since work is a universal calling. The toil of work is familiar to everyone.

And yet, in spite of all this toil, work is a good thing for a person. It is not only good in the sense that it is useful; work corresponds to human dignity. If one wishes to define more clearly the ethical meaning of work, this truth must be kept in mind. Work is good for humans because through work a person transforms nature and adapts it to his or her own needs. Through work a person achieves fulfillment. Industriousness is a virtue, a moral habit.

It is noted, however, that workers are often exploited and that it is possible to oppress people or punish people through forced labor.

THE THREE SPHERES OF WORK

Having confirmed the personal dimension of human work, we must go on to the second sphere of values linked to work. Work constitutes a foundation for the formation of family life. In a way, work is a condition for making it possible to found a family. Families require the means of subsistence normally gained through work. It must be remembered that the family constitutes one of the most important terms of reference for shaping the social and ethical order of human work.

Another sphere of values that emerges with the view that the worker is the subject of work concerns the society to which the worker belongs. Membership in a nation brings about deep human identity in a person. Through work a person increases the common good and indeed, serves the heritage of the human family.

These three spheres, personal, family, and social, are always important for human work in its subjective dimension. Again, the concrete reality of the worker, takes precedence over the objective dimension of work. Today, the process of "subduing the earth," work, is marked by an immense development of technology. This is a positive phenomenon so long as the objective dimension of work does not gain the upper hand over the subjective dimension and thus deprive the worker of human dignity and human rights.

LABOR AND CAPITAL

THE HISTORICAL TENSION

Even before *Rerum novarum*, work has been described as existing within the great conflict between "capital" and "labor." That is to say, work has been described as part of the conflict between the small but highly influential group of owners or holders of the means of production, and the broader multitude of people who lacked these means and who shared in the process of production through their labor. The conflict originated in the fact that the workers put their powers at the disposal of the owners, and the owners, following the principle of maximum profit, tried to establish the lowest possible wages for the work done by the employees. In addition there were other elements of exploitation, lack of safety in the work place and unhealthy conditions for workers and their families.

Our present day is marked by many conflicts. Technology plays a primary role in many of these, including the threat of nuclear war. In view of this situation we recall a principle that has always been taught by the Church: the principle of the priority of labor over capital. Labor is always the efficient cause of the process of production, while capital, and the means of production, remains an instrumental cause.

THE MORALLY LEGITIMATE SYSTEM OF LABOR

In the light of this truth we see that capital cannot be separated from labor. Labor cannot be opposed to capital or capital be opposed to labor. A morally legitimate labor system overcomes the opposition between labor and capital. That is to say, a just labor system is shaped in accordance with (1) the principle of the priority of labor, (2) the principle of the subjectivity of human labor, and (3) the principle of effective participation of the worker in the whole production process, independent of the nature of the services provided by the worker.

Working at any workbench, whether a relatively primitive or an ultramodern one, a person can see that through work one enters into two inheritances. The first inheritance is what is given to the whole of humanity in the resources of nature. The second is what others have already developed on the basis of those resources, that is to say, instruments for work. In working, a person enters into the labor of others.

The idea that capital cannot be separated from labor, in which the principle of the primacy of person over things is strictly preserved, was broken in human history. The break occurred when labor was separated from capital and set in opposition to it, and capital was set in opposition to labor. Labor and capital were described as though they were two impersonal forces, two production factors juxtaposed in the same economic order. This fundamental error of thought can be called an error of "materialism," in that it includes a conviction that raised material reality to a place of primacy while subordinating the spiritual and the personal. The only chance to overcome this error is through changes in theory and practice. Such changes would include the conviction of the primacy of the person over things, and of human labor over capital.

PARTICIPATION OF THE WORKER

The principle of the priority of labor, that is to say, the subjectivity of human labor, is radically different from the program of Marxist collectivism. It is also different from liberal capitalism. In the latter case, the difference consists in the way the right to ownership or property is understood. Christian tradition has never upheld the right to private property as absolute and untouchable. On the contrary, it has always understood this right within the broader context of the right common to all to use the goods of the whole of creation. The right to private property is subordinated to the right to common use, to the fact that goods are meant for everyone.

From this point of view, one cannot exclude the socialization of certain means of production. Since *Rerum novarum* the Church has always recalled all these principles, going back to the arguments formulated in a much older tradition and the well-known arguments of Saint Thomas Aquinas.

"Rigid" capitalism, the position that defends the exclusive right to private ownership of the means of production as an untouchable "dogma" of economic life, is unacceptable. The principle of respect for work demands that this right should undergo a constructive revision, both in theory and in practice. If it is true that capital, as the whole of the means of production, is at the same time the product of the work of generations, it is equally true that capital is being unceasingly created through the work done with the help of all these means of production, and these means can be seen as a great workbench at which the present generation of workers is working day after day. Obviously we are dealing here with different kinds of work, manual labor and the many forms of intellectual work, including white-collar work and management.

In the light of the above, the many proposals put forward by experts in Catholic social teaching and by the highest Magisterium of the Church take on special significance. These include proposals for joint ownership of the means of work, sharing by the workers in the management and/or profits of businesses, so-called shareholding by labor, etc. Whether these various proposals can or cannot be applied concretely, it is clear that recognition of the proper position of labor and the worker in the production process demands various adaptations in the sphere of the right to ownership of the means of production. This is so not only in view of older situations but also in view of the whole of the situation and the problems in the second half of the present century particularly in poorer and developing countries.

"Rigid" capitalism must undergo continual revision in order to be reformed by human rights. It must be noted that these reforms cannot be achieved by the elimination of private ownership of the means of production. Merely taking these means of production (capital) out of the hands of their private owners is not enough to ensure their satisfactory socialization.

When we speak of "socializing" property we mean only when the subjective character of society is ensured. That is to say, when on the basis of work each person is fully entitled to be considered a part owner, with every one else, of the great workbench at which he or she is working. A way towards this goal could be found by associating labor with the ownership of capital, as far as possible, and by producing a wide range of intermediate organizations with economic, social and cultural purposes.

PERSONALISM AND WORK

The principle of the priority of labor over capital is a fundamental principle in the order of social morality. When a person works he or she wishes to use the fruit of this work. When a person works he or she wishes to take part in the work process as a sharer in responsibility and creativity at the workbench.

Workers desire just remuneration for their work. They also want to know that they are, in a sense, working for themselves. The Church's teaching has always expressed the strong and deep conviction that human work concerns not only the economy but also, and especially, personal values. Every effort must be made to ensure that persons can preserve their awareness of working "for themselves." If this is not fulfilled, incalculable damage is inevitably done throughout the economic process, not only economic damage but first and foremost damage to the person.

THE RIGHTS OF WORKERS

HUMAN RIGHTS

Work is an obligation as well as a source of rights. The human rights that flow from work are part of the broader context of those fundamental rights of the person.

Persons must work, both because the Creator has commanded it and because one must work to maintain and develop one's own humanity. The obligation to work includes responsibility for others, especially for one's own family, but also for one's community. Indeed there are other levels of obligation. The worker is heir to the work of preceding generations and a sharer in building the future for following generations. All this constitutes the moral obligation of work. When we consider the rights of workers, corresponding to these obligations, we must always remember the vast range of points of reference in which the labor of every worker is manifested.

TWO TYPES OF EMPLOYERS

When we speak of the obligation of work and of the rights of the worker we think of the relationship between the employer and the worker. Here we note that we can speak of the employer in one of two ways, as either a direct or indirect employer.

The "direct" employer is the person or institution with whom the worker enters directly into a work contract. The "indirect" employer includes all the other factors that exercise an influence on the shape of the work contract.

The concept of indirect employer includes persons, institutions, and collective labor contracts as well as the principles of conduct laid down by persons and institutions. The responsibility of the indirect employer is not the same as the responsibility of the direct employer but it remains a true responsibility. The indirect employer substantially determines one or more facets of the labor relationship. This dictates the conduct of the direct employer in determining in concrete terms the work contract and labor relations. A policy is morally legitimate when the objective rights of the workers are fully respected.

The concept of indirect employer primarily applies to the government and its system of laws. However, the present system of economic relations is one of dependence between governments. This can easily become an occasion for exploitation. It is easy to see that in these forms of dependence the concept of the indirect employer is extensive. The United Nations and other international organizations must take responsibility here. All of this indicates the importance of the indirect employer in achieving full respect for the worker's rights, since the rights of the human person are the key element in the whole of the social moral order.

When we consider the rights of workers in relation to the "indirect employer" we must first direct our attention to the question of finding work, the issue of suitable employment for all who are capable. Indirect employers have the obligation to provide unemployment benefits, that is to say, grants for the subsistence of unemployed workers and their families. This duty arises from the fundamental principle of the moral order in this sphere, namely, the principle of the common use of goods or, to put it in another and still simpler way, the right to life and subsistence.

JUST WAGES

As we view the human family, we are struck by a disconcerting fact of immense proportion. While conspicuous natural resources remain unused, there are huge numbers of people who are unemployed or under-employed and countless multitudes of people suffering from hunger. This fact demonstrates that something is wrong with the organization of work and employment both within and among political communities.

The key problem of social ethics in this case is that of just remuneration for work. There is no more important way for securing a just relationship between the worker and the employer than remuneration for work. The relationship between the employer (first and foremost the direct employer) and the worker is resolved on the basis of the wage, namely, just remuneration for work done. Here we return once more to the first principle of the whole ethical and social order, namely, the principle of the common use of goods. A just wage is the concrete means of verifying the justice of the whole socioeconomic system.

Just remuneration for the work of an adult who is responsible for a family means remuneration that will suffice for establishing and properly maintaining a family and for providing security for its future. Such remuneration can be given either through a family wage or family allowances. A family wage means that a salary given to a parent is sufficient to meet the needs of the family so the other spouse does not have to seek work outside the home. Family allowance is an example of social programs giving mothers grants to devote themselves exclusively to their families. These grants should correspond to the actual needs, that is, to the number of dependents.

THE ROLE OF WOMEN

Experience confirms that there must be a social re-evaluation of the mother's role, of the toil connected with it, and of the need that children have for care, love and affection in order that they may develop into responsible, morally and religiously mature and psychologically stable persons. It will redound to the credit of society to make it possible for a mother, without inhibiting her freedom, without psychological or practical discrimination, and without penalizing her as compared with other women, to devote herself to taking care of her children and educating them in accordance with their needs, which vary with age. Having to abandon these tasks in order to take up paid work outside the home is wrong from the point of view of the good of society and of the family when it contradicts or hinders these primary goals of the mission of a mother.

The whole labor process must be organized in such a way as to respect the requirements of the person and his or her forms of life. The true advancement of women requires that labor should be structured in such a way that women do not have to pay for their advancement by abandoning what is specific to them and at the expense of the family, in which women as mothers have an irreplaceable role.

OTHER RIGHTS

Besides wages, various social benefits intended to ensure the life and health of workers and their families play a part here. The expenses involved in health care, especially in the case of accidents at work, demand that medical assistance should be easily available for workers, and that as far as possible it should be cheap or even free of charge. Another benefit is the right to rest. In the first place this involves a regular weekly rest comprising at least Sunday, and also a longer period of rest, namely, the holiday or vacation taken once a year or possibly in several shorter periods during the year. A third is the right to a pension and to insurance for old age and in case of accidents at work. A fourth is the right to a working environment and to manufacturing processes that are not harmful to the workers' physical health or to their moral integrity.

THE RIGHT TO FORM UNIONS

Workers have the right of association, that is, the right to form associations for the purpose of defending their vital interests. These associations are called labor or trade unions. Unions are the mouthpieces in the struggle for social justice and rights of working people in accordance with their individual professions. Just efforts to secure the rights of workers should always take into account the limitations imposed by the general economic situation of the country.

One method used by unions in pursuing the rights of their members is the strike or work stoppage. Catholic social teaching recognizes this method as legitimate when carried out in the proper conditions and limits. Workers should be assured the right to strike, without being subjected to personal penal sanctions. While admitting that it is a legitimate means, we must at the same time emphasize that a strike remains, in a sense, an extreme means. It must not be abused. Abuse of the strike weapon can lead to the paralysis of the whole of socioeconomic life, and this is contrary to the requirements of the common good of society.

AGRICULTURAL WORK

The world of agriculture, which provides society with the goods it needs for its daily sustenance, is of fundamental importance. Agricultural work involves considerable difficulties, including unremitting and sometimes exhausting physical effort and a lack of appreciation on the part of society. Added to this are the lack of adequate professional training and of proper equipment, and objectively unjust situations. In certain developing countries, millions of people are forced to cultivate the land belonging to others and are exploited by the big landowners, without any hope of ever being able to gain possession of even a small piece of land of their own.

DISABLED PERSONS AND WORK

Since disabled persons have the same rights as abled persons, they should be helped to participate in the life of society in all its aspects and levels. The disabled person participates fully in humanity. It would be radically unworthy of persons as well as a denial of our common humanity to allow into communal life and work only those who are fully functional. This would be a serious form of discrimination, the strong and healthy against the weak and sick. Here we repeat the principle, work in the objective sense should always be subordinated to human dignity, to the subject of work, and not to economic advantage.

The various bodies involved in the world of labor, both the direct and the indirect employer, should foster the right of disabled people to professional training and work, so that they can be given a productive activity suited to them. Without hiding the fact that this is a complex and difficult task, it is to be hoped that a correct concept of labor in the subjective sense will produce a situation which will make it possible for disabled people to feel that they are not cut off from the working world or dependent upon society, but that they are full-scale subjects of work, useful, respected for their human dignity and called to contribute to the progress and welfare of their families and of the community according to their particular capacities.

EMIGRATION

Finally, we must say at least a few words on the subject of emigration in search of work. This is an age-old phenomenon that is widespread today. A person has the right to leave his or her native land for various motives, and also the right to return, in order to seek better conditions of life in another country. This fact is certainly not without difficulties.

The person working away from his or her native land, whether as a permanent emigrant or as a seasonal worker, should not be placed at a disadvantage in comparison with the other workers in that society in the matter of working rights. Emigration in search of work must in no way become an opportunity for financial or social exploitation. As regards the work relationship, the same criteria should be applied to immigrant workers as to all other workers in the society. The value of work should be measured by the same standard and not according to the difference in nationality, religion or race. The situation of constraint of the emigrant should not be exploited. Once more the fundamental principle must be repeated. The hierarchy of values and the profound meaning of work require that capital should be at the service of labor and not labor at the service of capital.

ELEMENTS FOR A SPIRITUALITY OF WORK

WORK AS SHARING IN THE ACTIVITY OF THE CREATOR

It is right to devote the last part of these reflections to the spirituality of work. Since work in its subjective aspect is always a personal action, it follows that the whole person, body and spirit, participates in it, whether it is manual or intellectual work.

The word of God's revelation is profoundly marked by the fundamental truth that humans, created in the image of God, share in the activity of the Creator. Humans continue the creative activity through the discovery of the resources and values contained in creation. Humans imitate God, their Creator, in working and in resting. Awareness that one's work is a participation in God's activity ought to permeate the most ordinary everyday activities. For, while providing the substance of life for themselves and their families, men and women are performing their activities in a way that appropriately benefits society. They can justly consider that by their labor they are unfolding the Creator's work, aiding their brothers and sisters, and contributing by their personal industry to the realization in history of the divine plan. The knowledge that through working a person shares in the work of creation constitutes the most profound motive for work.

CHRIST—A WORKER

The books of the Old Testament contain many references to human work and to individual professions: for example, the doctor (cf. Sir 38:1—3); the pharmacist (cf. Sir 38:4–8); the craftsman or artist (cf. Ex 31:1–5; Sir 38:27); the blacksmith (cf. Gen 4:22; Is 44:12), we could apply these words to today's foundry workers; the potter (cf. Jer 18:3–4; Sir 38:29–30); the farmer (cf. Gen 9:20; Is 5:1–2); the scholar (cf. Eccles 12:9–12; Sir 39:1–8); the sailor (cf. Ps 107: 23–30; Wis 14: 2–3 a); the builder (cf. Gen 11:3; 2 Kings 12:12–13; 22:5–6); the musician (cf. Gen 4:21); the shepherd (cf. Gen 4:2; 37:3; Ex 3:1; 1 Sam 16:11; et passim); and the fisherman (cf. Ezk 47:10). The words of praise for the work of women are well known (cf. Prov 31:15–27). In his parables on the Kingdom of God Jesus Christ constantly refers to human work: that of the shepherd (e.g. Jn 10:1–16), the farmer (cf. Mk 12:1–12), the doctor (cf. Lk 4:23), the sower (cf. Mk 4:1–9), the householder (cf. Mt 13:52), the servant (cf. Mt 24:45; Lk 12:42–48), the steward (cf. Lk 16:1–8), the fisherman (cf. Mt 13:47–50), the merchant (cf. Mt 13:45–46), the laborer (cf. Mt 20:1–16). He also speaks of the various forms of women's work (cf. Mt 13:33; Lk 15:8–9). He compares the apostolate to the manual work of harvesters (cf. Mt 9:37; Jn 4:35–38) or fishermen (cf. Mt 4:19). He refers to the work of scholars too (cf. Mt 13:52).

This teaching of Christ on work, based on the example of his life during his years in Nazareth, finds a particularly lively echo in the teaching of the Apostle Paul. Paul boasts of working at his trade (he was probably a tent-maker, cf. Acts 18:3).

WORK IN THE LIGHT OF CHRIST

There is yet another aspect of human work, an essential dimension of it, that is profoundly imbued with the spirituality based on the Gospel. All work, whether manual or intellectual, is inevitably linked with toil. The Book of Genesis expresses it in a truly penetrating manner. It says that the original blessing of work connected with human beings created in the image of God is contrasted with the consequences of sin. "Cursed is the ground because of you; in toil you shall eat of it all the days of your life" (Gen 3:17). There is no one on earth who could not apply these words to himself or herself.

In a sense, the final word of the Gospel on this matter as on others is found in the Paschal Mystery of Jesus Christ. It is here that we must seek an answer to these problems so important for the spirituality of human work. The Paschal Mystery contains the Cross of Christ and his obedience unto death, which the Apostle contrasts with the disobedience that from the beginning has burdened human history on earth (cf. Rom 5:19). It also contains the elevation of Christ, who by means of death on a Cross, returns to his disciples in the Resurrection with the power of the Holy Spirit.

Sweat and toil, which work necessarily involves, given the present condition of the human race, present the Christian and everyone who is called to follow Christ with the possibility of sharing lovingly in the work that Christ came to do (cf. Jn 17:4). This work of salvation came about through suffering and death on a Cross. By enduring the toil of work in union with Christ crucified for us, we in a way collaborate with the Son of God for the redemption of humanity. We show ourselves true disciples of Christ by carrying the cross in our turn every day (cf. Lk 9:23) in the activity that we are called upon to perform.

The Christian finds in human work a small part of the Cross of Christ and accepts it in the same spirit of redemption in which Christ accepted his Cross for us. In work, thanks to the light that penetrates us from the Resurrection of Christ, we always find a glimmer of new life, of the new good, as if it were an announcement of "the new heavens and the new earth" (cf. 2 Pt 3:13; Rev 21:1) in which humankind and the world participate precisely through the toil that goes with work. On the one hand this confirms the indispensability of the Cross in the spirituality of human work; on the other hand the Cross that this toil constitutes reveals a new good springing from work itself, from work understood in depth and in all its aspects and never apart from work.

The expectation of a new earth must not weaken but rather stimulate our concern for cultivating this one. For here grows the body of a new human family, a body which even now is able to give some kind of foreshadowing of the new age. Earthly progress must be carefully distinguished from the growth of Christ's kingdom. Nevertheless, to the extent that the former can contribute to the better ordering of human society, it is of vital concern to the Kingdom of God.

A CATHOLIC ENVIRONMENTAL ETHIC

In some ways environmental ethics is new in the Catholic social tradition, yet this new element is grounded in a classic element of Catholic theology. As an area of moral thought and reflection, concern for the environment, both in secular arenas and the Catholic Church, came to the front in the mid to late 1960s with the growing awareness of the impact human choices have on the environment. In 1971 both Pope Paul VI, in *Octogesima adveniens*, and the Synod of Bishops, in *Justice in the World,* recognized the unfolding environmental crisis as a moral problem. Paul wrote that humans are "suddenly becoming aware that by an ill-considered exploitation of nature" they risk destroying nature and in turn risk "becoming the victim of this degradation." The Synod of Bishops noted the potential for "irreparable damage" to the "precious treasures of air and water—without which there cannot be life." These are the first two comments on the environment in official Catholic social thought and they have fostered serious reflection. This section briefly considers the spirituality of nature in Catholic thought as well as the basic moral insights of the tradition. The center of the section is Pope John Paul's 1990 "World Day of Peace Message," which remains the longest reflection on the moral problem of the environmental crisis.

Creation Proclaims the Glory of God

The Catholic moral tradition was well equipped to make a positive contribution to this conversation. The tradition has always had a deep sense of the divine imprint on creation. On the first page of the Bible, for example, we read God's multiple declarations that creation is good (Gen. 1:4, 10, 12, 18, 21, 25). Later books in the Bible proclaim God's ordering and care for creation (see Ps. 104 and Wis. 11:25–26). The Catholic tradition has long held that creation is a form of God's self-disclosure, a form of God's revelation. That is to say, we can know something of God when we reflect on God's creation. Like an artist who communicates an idea or a feeling through art, God communicates to us through nature.

The Canadian Conference of Catholic Bishops captured this idea when it wrote in *You Love All That Exists* (2003), "Standing in awe of creation can assist us to perceive the natural world as a bearer of divine grace" (#15). We can see this illustrated in the Bible. There are many occasions when people immerse themselves in the natural world as they pray. The Gospels tell of Jesus sitting by the sea or going into the wilderness or mountains to pray (Matt. 4:1; Mark 1:12; Luke 4:1; Matt. 14:23; Mark 6:26; Luke 6:12, 9:28; Matt. 13:1). Saints and commentators throughout the ages have written of the place of nature in their prayer and spiritual quest. St. Augustine (354–430), for example, captures this idea in one of his sermons: "Others, in order to find God, will read a book. Well, as a matter of fact there is a certain great big book, the book of created nature. Look carefully at it top and bottom, observe it, read it. God did not make letters of ink for you to recognize him in; he set before your eyes all these things he had made. Why look for a louder voice? Heaven and earth cries out to you, 'God made me.' Observe heaven and earth in a religious spirit."[3]

Perhaps the most famous environmental prayer in the Catholic tradition is the "Canticle of the Sun," credited to (but probably not written by) St. Francis of Assisi (1182–1226). In this prayer Francis calls the sun our brother and the moon our sister. Water, wind, and fire are our siblings, and the earth is our mother. The prayer holds that we see God's ways in their existence:

> O most High, almighty, good Lord God, to you
>   belong praise, glory, honor, and all blessing!
> Praised be my Lord God with all creatures; and
>   especially our brother the sun, which brings us
>   the day and the light; fair is he, and shining
>   with a very great splendor:
> O Lord, he signifies you to us!
> Praised be my Lord for our sister the moon, and for
>   the stars, which God has set clear and lovely
>   in heaven.

> Praised be my Lord for our brother the wind, and
>   for air and cloud, calms and all weather, by
>   which you uphold in life all creatures.
> Praised be my Lord for our sister water, which is
>   very serviceable to us, and humble, and
>   precious, and clean.
> Praised be my Lord for brother fire, through which
>   you give us light in the darkness; and he is
>   bright, and pleasant, and very mighty, and
>   strong.
> Praised be my Lord for our mother the Earth,
>   which sustains us and keeps us, and yields
>   diverse fruits, and flowers of many colors, and
>   grass.
> Praised be my Lord for all those who pardon one
>   another for God's love's sake, and who
>   endure weakness and tribulation; blessed are
>   they who peaceably shall endure, for you, O
>   most High, shall give them a crown!
> Praised be my Lord for our sister, the death of the
>   body, from which no one escapes, Woe to him
>   who died in mortal sin!
> Blessed are they who are found walking by your
>   most holy will, for the second death shall have
>   no power to do them harm.
> Praise you, and bless you the Lord and give thanks
>   to God, and serve God with great humility.[4]

In contemporary times we can look to Pope John Paul II, a great lover of the outdoors, to hear this theme. The following is an excerpt from a prayer he offered while in the Apennines Mountains in Italy.

Here the silence of the mountain and the whiteness of the snow speak to us of God, and they show us the way of contemplation, not only as a way to experience the Mystery, but also as a condition for humanizing life and mutual relations. Today there is a greatly felt need to slow down the sometimes-hectic pace of our days. Contact with nature, with its beauty and its peace, gives us new strength and restores us. Yet, while the eyes take in the wonder of the cosmos, it is necessary to look into ourselves, into the depths of our heart, into the center of our being where we are face to face with our conscience. There God speaks to us and the dialogue with Him gives meaning to our lives. So, dear friends . . . you are, as it were, molded by the mountain, by its beauty and its severity, by its mysteries and its attractions . . . It is a reality, which strongly suggests the journey of the spirit, called to lift itself up from the earth to heaven, to meet God.[5]

Christians believe they can find God in creation. Yet they do not confuse the natural world with God. God may be experienced in and through nature, but nature is not God. Creation is from God and belongs to God. It is good in itself, and it is good for us. Humans are dependent on nature for existence and flourishing, and accountable to God for how we treat nature.

The Moral Response

The environmental disasters of the 1970s and 1980s (Love Canal in 1978; Three Mile Island in 1979; Union Carbide, Bhopal in 1984; Chernobyl in 1986; and the *Exxon Valdez* in 1989) and public recognition of the persistent threats to the environment posed by human action (for example, the extinction and endangerment of plant and animal species; the depletion of natural resources, fisheries, and the ozone layer; water, air, and soil pollution; deforestation; and waste disposal) have made concern for the environment a priority in secular as well as Catholic moral thought.

There are four ways people typically think about human relationship to the natural world.[6] The first and perhaps most popular position holds that the fundamental purpose of nature is to fulfill human needs. If we hold this belief, then we believe that we are allowed and indeed expected to use nature as we see fit. The religious justification for this position is that nature has been given to us by God to fulfill our basic needs and desires. Creation is useful to humans. Its goodness lies in the fact that it is good for us.

The second typical position, one preached by many religions for generations, is that we are stewards of the earth. We are responsible to God, our children, their children, and perhaps our ancestors. We are to use creation wisely to fulfill our needs and desires. We are God's representatives on earth. There are appropriate and inappropriate uses of creation. We should not exhaust it or despoil it.

The third position, unlike the first and second views, rejects the idea that humans are superior to or better than the rest of creation. It holds that there is a fundamental equality or parity within nature. This response is perhaps the most radical one (although from a Christian perspective, the first seems radical as well). People who hold the third position argue that animals have as much right to their existence as humans do to theirs. Animals can make moral claims on people. If the first two positions separate humans from nature, the third rejects humanity's claim of moral dominance. We are but one species among many. Thus to speak of "managing" nature is to put humans in an unwarranted controlling position.

The fourth position mediates between the second and third responses. Like the second view, it holds that humans have a unique position of power

within nature and must use it responsibly. At the same time, influenced by
the third position, it notes that humans are part of the interdependent web
of creation. We are participants in nature with all of creation. Humans are
connected to the patterns and processes of nature.

Briefly put, the four positions are these: One, creation is for humans.
Two, humans are to be stewards of creation. Three, humans, part of creation, hold a moral equivalence with creation. Four, humans are to be responsible for creation while at the same time recognizing that they are interdependent within creation.

The environmental prayer quoted above seems to express the fourth view
as it calls the earth our mother and water, wind, and fire our brothers and
sisters. The position of official Catholic social thought, however, is the second position. It rejects outright the first and third positions. Official Catholic thought emphasizes the person both as responsible for creation and at
the same time as at the center of creation. Thus, the following text has a
human-centered view of the environment. That is to say, we have the responsibility to care for the earth because we need the earth to care for us.
We need clean air and water. We have a responsibility to our children and
future generations to provide a habitable world for them.

The following quotations from John Paul II capture the essence of the
Catholic environmental ethic:

> In front of the majesty of the mountains we are pushed to establish a
> more respectful relationship with nature . . . At the same time . . . we are
> stimulated to meditate upon the gravity of so many desecrations of na-
> ture, often carried out with inadmissible nonchalance.[7]

> It is well known how urgent it is to spread awareness that the resources
> of our planet must be respected . . . For the Christian there is a moral
> commitment to care for the earth so that it may produce fruit and be-
> come a dwelling of the universal human family.[8]

The text that follows is a more detailed expression of the pope's ethic on
the environment.

—"World Day of Peace Message" (abridged and edited)—
Pope John Paul II, January 1, 1990

Introduction

Peace with God the Creator, Peace with all of creation.

In our day, there is a growing awareness that world peace is threatened not only by the arms race, regional conflicts and continued injustices among peoples and nations, but also by a lack of due respect for
nature, by the plundering of natural resources and by a progressive de-
cline in the quality of life. The sense of precariousness and insecurity that

such a situation engenders is a seedbed for collective selfishness, disregard for others and dishonesty.

Faced with the widespread destruction of the environment, people everywhere are coming to understand that we cannot continue to use the goods of the earth as we have in the past. The public in general as well as political leaders are concerned about this problem, and experts from a wide range of disciplines are studying its causes. Moreover, a new ecological awareness is beginning to emerge which, rather than being downplayed, ought to be encouraged to develop into concrete programs and initiatives.

The Ecological Crisis Is a Moral Issue

Certain elements of today's ecological crisis reveal its moral character. First among these is the indiscriminate application of advances in science and technology. Many recent discoveries have brought undeniable benefits to humanity. Indeed, they demonstrate the nobility of the human vocation to participate responsibly in God's creative action in the world. Unfortunately, it is now clear that the application of these discoveries in the fields of industry and agriculture have produced harmful long-term effects. This has led to the painful realization that we cannot interfere in one area of the ecosystem without paying due attention both to the consequences of such interference in other areas and to the well-being of future generations.

The gradual depletion of the ozone layer and the related "greenhouse effect" has now reached crisis proportions as a consequence of industrial growth, massive urban concentrations and vastly increased energy needs. Industrial waste, the burning of fossil fuels, unrestricted deforestation, the use of certain types of herbicides, coolants and propellants: all of these are known to harm the atmosphere and environment. The resulting meteorological and atmospheric changes range from damage to health to the possible future submersion of low-lying lands.

The most profound and serious indication of the moral implications underlying the ecological problem is the lack of respect for life evident in many of the patterns of environmental pollution. Often, the interests of production prevail over concern for the dignity of workers, while economic interests take priority over the good of individuals and even entire peoples. In these cases, pollution or environmental destruction is the result of an unnatural and reductionist vision that at times leads to a genuine contempt for humanity.

On another level, delicate ecological balances are upset by the uncontrolled destruction of animal and plant life or by a reckless exploitation of natural resources. It should be pointed out that all of this, even if carried out in the name of progress and well-being, is ultimately to humankind's disadvantage. Respect for life, and above all for the dignity of the human person, is the ultimate guiding norm for any sound economic, industrial or scientific progress.

The Relation between This Crisis and Other Moral Issues

It is manifestly unjust that a privileged few should continue to accumulate excess goods, squandering available resources, while masses of people are living in conditions of misery at the very lowest level of subsistence. Today, the dramatic threat of ecological breakdown is teaching us the extent to which greed and selfishness—both individual and collective—are contrary to the order of creation, an order that is characterized by mutual interdependence.

The ecological crisis reveals the urgent moral need for a new solidarity, especially in relations between the developing nations and those that are highly industrialized. States must increasingly share responsibility, in complementary ways, for the promotion of a natural and social environment that is both peaceful and healthy.

It must also be said that the proper ecological balance will not be found without directly addressing the structural forms of poverty that exist throughout the world. Rural poverty and unjust land distribution in many countries, for example, have led to subsistence farming and to the exhaustion of the soil. Once their land yields no more, many farmers move on to clear new land, thus accelerating uncontrolled deforestation, or they settle in urban centers which lack the infrastructure to receive them. Likewise, some heavily indebted countries are destroying their natural heritage, at the price of irreparable ecological imbalances, in order to develop new products for export. In the face of such situations it would be wrong to assign responsibility to the poor alone for the negative environmental consequences of their actions. Rather, the poor, to whom the earth is entrusted no less than to others, must be enabled to find a way out of their poverty. This will require a courageous reform of structures, as well as new ways of relating among peoples and States.

But there is another dangerous menace that threatens us, namely, war. Unfortunately, modern science already has the capacity to change the environment for hostile purposes. Alterations of this kind over the long term could have unforeseeable and still more serious consequences. Despite the international agreements that prohibit chemical, bacteriological and biological warfare, the fact is that laboratory research continues to develop new offensive weapons capable of altering the balance of nature.

Today, any form of war on a global scale would lead to incalculable ecological damage. But even local or regional wars, however limited, not only destroy human life and social structures, but also damage the land, ruining crops and vegetation as well as poisoning the soil and water. The survivors of war are forced to begin a new life in very difficult environmental conditions, which in turn create situations of extreme social unrest, with further negative consequences for the environment.

Moral Responsibility

Modern society will find no solution to the ecological problem unless it takes a serious look at its life style. In many parts of the world society is given to instant gratification and consumerism while remaining indifferent to the damage that these cause. As I have already stated, the seriousness of the ecological issue lays bare the depth of the human moral crisis. If an appreciation of the value of the human person and of human life is lacking, we will also lose interest in others and in the earth itself. Simplicity, moderation and discipline, as well as a spirit of sacrifice, must become a part of everyday life, lest all suffer the negative consequences of the careless habits of a few.

An education in ecological responsibility is urgent: responsibility for oneself, for others, and for the earth. This education cannot be rooted in mere sentiment or empty wishes. Its purpose cannot be ideological or political. It must not be based on a rejection of the modern world or a vague desire to return to some "paradise lost." Instead, a true education in responsibility entails a genuine conversion in ways of thought and behavior. Churches and religious bodies, non-governmental and governmental organizations, indeed all members of society, have a precise role to play in such education. The first educator, however, is the family, where the child learns to respect his or her neighbor and to love nature.

When the ecological crisis is set within the broader context of the search for peace within society, we can understand better the importance of giving attention to what the earth and its atmosphere are telling us: namely, that there is an order in the universe which must be respected, and that the human person, endowed with the capability of choosing freely, has a grave responsibility to preserve this order for the well-being of future generations. I wish to repeat that the ecological crisis is a moral issue.

At the conclusion of this Message, I should like to address directly my brothers and sisters in the Catholic Church, in order to remind them of their serious obligation to care for all of creation. The commitment of believers to a healthy environment for everyone stems directly from their belief in God the Creator, from their recognition of the effects of original and personal sin, and from the certainty of having been redeemed by Christ. Respect for life and for the dignity of the human person extends also to the rest of creation, which is called to join us in praising God.

The Canadian bishops in *You Love All That Exists* offer a helpful conclusion for thinking about a Catholic environmental ethic: "Our Christian tradition provides us with at least three interrelated forms of active response:

the Contemplative, the Ascetic and the Prophetic" (#14). The following is
their explanation of these three forms of active response. Before reading
their remarks, however, we will read about a specific environmental concern. When the Canadian bishops discuss the prophetic response, they mention the importance of water. In doing so they follow the lead of the Pontifical Council for Justice and Peace. The following is the church's contribution
to the 2003 international forum on water:

> Water is an essential element for life. Many people must confront daily
> the situation of an inadequate supply of safe water and the very serious
> resulting consequences . . . The management of water and sanitation must
> address the needs of all, and particularly of persons living in poverty.
> Inadequate access to safe drinking water affects the well being of over
> one billion persons and more than twice that number have no adequate
> sanitation. This all too often is the cause of disease, unnecessary suffer-
> ing, conflicts, poverty and even death. This situation is characterized by
> countless unacceptable injustices.
>
> The inadequacy in the supply and access to water has only recently
> taken center stage in global reflection as a serious and threatening phe-
> nomenon. Communities and individuals can exist even for substantial
> periods without many essential goods. The human being, however, can
> survive only a few days without clean, safe drinking water.
>
> Many people living in poverty, particularly in the developing coun-
> tries, daily face enormous hardship because water supplies are neither
> sufficient nor safe. Women bear a disproportionate hardship. For water
> users living in poverty this is rapidly becoming an issue crucial for life
> and, in the broad sense of the concept, *a right to life issue.*
>
> Water is a major factor in each of the three pillars of sustainable de-
> velopment—economic, social and environmental. In this framework, it
> is understood that water must meet the needs of the present population
> and those of future generations of all societies. This is not solely in the
> economic realm but in the sphere of integral human development. Water
> policy, to be sustainable, must promote the good of every person and of
> the whole person.[9]

We conclude with the words of the Canadian bishops:

> The Contemplative Response: Each one of us is called to deepen our
> capacity to appreciate the wonders of nature as an act of faith and love.
> In the silence of contemplation, nature speaks of the beauty of the Cre-
> ator. "If you look at the world with a pure heart, you too will see the
> face of God" (cf. Matthew 5:8). Standing in awe of creation can assist us
> to perceive the natural world as a bearer of divine grace . . . (#15)

The Ascetic Response: Canadians are blessed with an abundance of natural resources, but we also are among the planet's most excessively wasteful inhabitants. Thankfully, there is in our tradition an ascetic response through which we can confidently adjust our lifestyle choices and daily actions to respect ecological limits, attune us to solidarity with vulnerable peoples, as well as encourage the movement of grace in our lives . . . We can challenge the hold of the marketplace over our lives by conscious efforts to avoid over-consumption and by using our purchasing power to promote earth-friendly enterprises. (#16)

The Prophetic Response: All social justice issues have ecological implications: the case of water is a perfect example of this. We can make the links between social and ecological justice more evident in our preaching and community action. The cry of the earth and the cry of the poor are one. Ecological harmony cannot exist in a world of unjust social structures; nor can the extreme social inequalities of our current world order result in ecological sustainability. But the growing movements for eco-justice can contribute substantially to the necessary solutions for both crises. Christian communities, inspired by St. Francis of Assisi—the friend of the poor who was loved by God's creatures—should provide positive recognition and support to those environmentalists, farmers, educators and solidarity activists who have begun to show us the way forward. (#17)

MIGRATION/IMMIGRATION IN CATHOLIC THOUGHT

The final section of this chapter addresses another crucial and controversial issue facing individuals and societies, namely, migration, immigration, and refugees. *Migrants* are people who move, either voluntarily or involuntarily, from one region to another. An *immigrant* moves from his or her original country to another country with the intent to settle there. Defining *refugee* is more difficult. According to the United Nations' Convention Relating to the Status of Refugees, a refugee is

a person who owing to a well-founded fear of being persecuted for reasons of race, religion, nationality, membership of a particular social group, or political opinion, is outside the country of his nationality and is unable or, owing to such fear, is unwilling to avail himself of the protection of that country; or who, not having nationality and being outside the country of his former habitual residence . . . is unable or, owing to such fear, is unwilling to return to it. (Art. 1)

Finally, an *asylum seeker* is a person who asks to be recognized as a refugee by the government of the country he or she wants to enter.

The following section is taken from a pastoral letter written jointly by the Catholic bishops of Mexico and the United States on these issues.

Strangers No Longer, Together on the Journey of Hope (abridged and edited)
The Catholic Bishops of Mexico and the United States, January 22, 2003

THE CATHOLIC CHURCH AND THE RIGHT TO MIGRATE

Catholic teaching has a long and rich tradition in defending the right to migrate. Based on the life and teachings of Jesus, the Church's teaching has provided the basis for the development of basic principles regarding the right to migrate for those attempting to exercise their God-given human rights. Catholic teaching also states that the root causes of migration—poverty, injustice, religious intolerance, armed conflicts—must be addressed so that migrants can remain in their homeland and support their families.

In modern times, this teaching has developed extensively in response to the worldwide phenomenon of migration. Pope Pius XII reaffirms the Church's commitment to caring for pilgrims, aliens, exiles, and migrants of every kind in his 1952 apostolic constitution *Exsul familia (On the Spiritual Care of Migrants)*, affirming that all peoples have the right to conditions worthy of human life and, if these conditions are not present, the right to migrate.

While recognizing the right of the sovereign state to control its borders, *Exsul familia* also establishes that this right is not absolute, stating that the needs of immigrants must be measured against the needs of the receiving countries. According to Pius: "Since land everywhere offers the possibility of supporting a large number of people, the sovereignty of the State, although it must be respected, cannot be exaggerated to the point that access to this land is, for inadequate or unjustified reasons, denied to needy and decent people from other nations, provided of course, that the public wealth, considered very carefully, does not forbid this."

In his landmark encyclical *Pacem in terris*, Blessed Pope John XXIII expands the right to migrate as well as the right to not have to migrate: "Every human being has the right to freedom of movement and of residence within the confines of his own country; and, when there are just reasons for it, the right to emigrate to other countries and take up residence there." Pope John XXIII placed limits on immigration, however, when there are "just reasons for it." Nevertheless, he stressed the obligation of sovereign states to promote the universal good where possible, including an obligation to accommodate migration flows. For more powerful nations, a stronger obligation exists.

The Church also has recognized the plight of refugees and asylum seekers who flee persecution. In his encyclical letter *Sollicitudo rei socialis*, Pope John Paul II refers to the world's refugee crisis as "the festering of a wound." In his 1990 Lenten message, Pope John Paul II lists the rights of refugees, including the right to be reunited with their families and the right to a dignified occupation and just wage. The right to asylum must never be denied when people's lives are truly threatened in their homeland.

Pope John Paul II also addresses the more controversial topic of undocumented migration and the undocumented migrant. In his 1995 message for World Migration Day, he notes that such migrants are used by developed nations as a source of labor. Ultimately, the pope says, elimination of global underdevelopment is the antidote to illegal immigration. His letter *Ecclesia in America*, which focuses on the Church in North and South America, reiterates the rights of migrants and their families and the respect for human dignity "even in cases of non-legal immigration."

MORAL PRINCIPLES ON MIGRATION

Both of our episcopal conferences have echoed the rich tradition of church teachings with regard to migration. Five principles emerge from such teachings, which guide the Church's view on migration issues.

I. Persons have the right to find opportunities in their homeland.

All persons have the right to find in their own countries the economic, political, and social opportunities to live in dignity and achieve a full life through the use of their God-given gifts. In this context, work that provides a just, living wage is a basic human need.

II. Persons have the right to migrate to support themselves and their families.

The Church recognizes that all the goods of the earth belong to all people. When persons cannot find employment in their country of origin to support themselves and their families, they have a right to find work elsewhere in order to survive. Sovereign nations should provide ways to accommodate this right.

III. Sovereign nations have the right to control their borders.

The Church recognizes the right of sovereign nations to control their territories but rejects such control when it is exerted merely for the purpose of acquiring additional wealth. More powerful economic nations, which have the ability to protect and feed their residents, have a stronger obligation to accommodate migration flows.

IV. Refugees and asylum seekers should be afforded protection.

Those who flee wars and persecution should be protected by the global community. This requires, at a minimum, that migrants have a right to claim refugee status without incarceration and to have their claims fully considered by a competent authority.

V. The human dignity and human rights of undocumented migrants should be respected.

Regardless of their legal status, migrants, like all persons, possess inherent human dignity that should be respected. Often they are subject to punitive laws and harsh treatment from enforcement officers from both receiving and transit countries. Government policies that respect the basic human rights of the undocumented are necessary. (#33–38)

The U.S. and Mexican bishops offer several policy recommendations for their respective countries. First, they call both countries to address the root causes of migration. Their particular concern is the economic condition in Mexico. Steps taken to reduce poverty in Mexico would help ease migration pressures. Their second recommendation is to change migration law. Here they have three proposals: (1) They advocate family-based immigration laws. The bishops note that many families are separated through migration. Current policy calls for long waits, up to eight years, for spouses to join legal permanent residents. (2) The bishops also support a policy that would lead to the legalization of undocumented persons. (3) They call for the development of work-visa (permanent and temporary) programs. Their third general recommendation is for humane enforcement of policy. They demand that human rights of migrants, including due-process rights, be protected.

SOME QUESTIONS FOR CONSIDERATION

1. Explain Pope John Paul II's view of work in its subjective and objective dimensions. Give examples of the different types of objective work that a person might do in a week and how those activities might affect the subject of work, the worker.
2. Using Pope John Paul II's ideas on personalism and capitalism (including rights and participation), discuss what a moral work place might look like.
3. Comment on the various theological themes John Paul relates to work in the section entitled "Elements for a Spirituality of Work" in *Laborem exercens.*
4. Using the "look, judge, and act" model, discuss what John Paul sees in the world, what his judgment is, and what actions he determines to be appropriate.
5. A theme that appears in both *Laborem exercens* and the "World Day of Peace Message" is that persons participate in God's creative activity in

the world. Examine this theme and explain its theological and/or moral ramifications.

6. Summarize John Paul's environmental ethic and respond to its various elements.

7. Compare the discussion of "subduing the earth" in *Laborem exercens* with the pope's call for an environmental ethic in his "World Day of Peace Message."

8. Consider the three spheres of Catholic social action: works of mercy and justice, public expression and personal commitment, and social analysis for social change. Discuss these spheres in relation to environmental ethics. How do the readings in this chapter express those spheres?

9. Review the principles of Catholic social thought from the first chapter—the dignity of the human person, the common good, subsidiarity, and solidarity—and describe how they are expressed in the chapter.

10. How do the authors of the selections in this chapter defend and support their positions? Review the discussion of moral arguments from the first chapter. Do the authors argue from authority or do they use theological, biblical, philosophical, common sense, or pragmatic arguments?

11. Discuss the four forms of moral discourse—narrative, prophetic, ethical, and policy—and how they are expressed in this chapter.

Christ Has No Body But Yours

Christ has no body here but yours. He has no eyes but yours, no hands but yours and no feet but yours. Your eyes are the eyes though which Christ's compassion must look onto the world. Your feet are the feet through which Christ is to go and do good. Your hands are the hands through which Christ is to bless us.

—ATTRIBUTED TO ST. TERESA OF AVILA, 1515–82

Chapter Eight

Solidarity and Justice

The Rich Man and Lazarus
"There was a rich man who was dressed in purple and fine linen and who feasted sumptuously every day. And at his gate lay a poor man named Lazarus, covered with sores, who longed to satisfy his hunger with what fell from the rich man's table; even the dogs would come and lick his sores. The poor man died and was carried away by the angels to be with Abraham. The rich man also died and was buried. In Hades, where he was being tormented, he looked up and saw Abraham far away with Lazarus by his side. He called out, 'Father Abraham, have mercy on me, and send Lazarus to dip the tip of his finger in water and cool my tongue; for I am in agony in these flames.' But Abraham said, 'Child, remember that during your lifetime you received your good things, and Lazarus in like manner evil things; but now he is comforted here, and you are in agony. Besides all this, between you and us a great chasm has been fixed, so that those who might want to pass from here to you cannot do so, and no one can cross from there to us.' He said, 'Then, father, I beg you to send him to my father's house—for I have five brothers— that he may warn them, so that they will not also come into this place of torment.' Abraham replied, 'They have Moses and the prophets; they should listen to them.' He said, 'No, father Abraham; but if someone goes to them from the dead, they will repent.' He said to him, 'If they do not listen to Moses and the prophets, neither will they be convinced even if someone rises from the dead.'"

—Luke 16:19–31

The focal point of this chapter is the rich encyclical *Sollicitudo rei socialis (On Social Concern)* published by Pope John Paul II in 1987. The pope recalls Pope Paul VI's *Populorum progressio* and its novel discussion of integral human development. In *Sollicitudo rei socialis* we hear John Paul's impassioned concern for the poor and oppressed in his critique of the economic disparity in the world. Note his descriptive technique. The world—

212

that is, the human family—is divided. He speaks of the dramatic economic imbalance between the Northern hemisphere, referred to as the First and Second Worlds, and the Southern hemisphere, referred to as the Third and Fourth Worlds. He uses the term *Fourth World* to refer not only to very poor countries but also to "bands of great or extreme poverty" in the first-world or second-world countries.

Lying beyond the divisions and fostering the evils inherent in them, he writes, are the all-consuming desire for profit and the thirst for power. The pope's message in *Sollicitudo rei socialis*, his solution to the divisions, is to focus on the moral reality of interdependence and the virtue of solidarity.[1] By describing the different "worlds," the pope stresses the fact that they are all part of one world. The church, the sign of unity in the world, cannot remain silent in the face of the many worlds.[2]

We also hear John Paul's concern about the dominant global tension of his time, the Cold War. The Cold War refers to the serious economic, social, and political global conflict between the East (the communism of the Soviet Union and its allies) and West (the capitalism of the United States and Western Europe) from the late 1940s to the early 1990s.

The second section of the chapter examines contemporary Catholic thought on race and racism. The third section returns to the work of John Paul II with an excerpt from his 1995 encyclical *Evangelium vitae (The Gospel of Life)*, in which he addresses Catholic thought on capital punishment. The fourth section reviews an important contribution to Catholic social thought from Joseph Bernardin, who from 1982 to 1996 was the cardinal of Chicago.

Sollicitudo Rei Socialis (abridged and edited)
Pope John Paul II, December 30, 1987

INTRODUCTION

The social concern of the Church is directed toward authentic human development. In recent years this concern has been expressed through papal encyclicals. Leo XIII's *Rerum novarum* has been the point of reference. Twenty years after the publication of Paul VI's *Populorum progressio* I consider it appropriate to devote an encyclical to the theme of that distinguished encyclical.

I wish principally to achieve two objectives. On the one hand, I wish to pay homage to this historic document of Paul VI. On the other hand, I wish to reaffirm the continuity of the social doctrine and its constant renewal. Continuity and renewal are a proof of the perennial value of the teaching of the Church. The Church's teaching in the social sphere is constant as it remains identical in its fundamental inspiration, in its principles of reflection, criteria of judgment, directives for action, and above all in its vital link with the Gospel. On the other hand, the Church's teaching is ever new as it is subject to the necessary adaptations suggested by the changes in historical conditions as well as by the unceasing flow of the events in the life of people and society.

The aim of this present reflection is to emphasize, through a theological understanding of the present world, the need for a fuller and more nuanced concept of development. This encyclical will also indicate some ways of putting this concept of development into effect.

THE ORIGINALITY OF *POPULORUM PROGRESSIO*

As soon as it appeared, the document of Pope Paul VI captured the attention of public opinion because of its originality. This originality can be stated in three points.

The first is constituted by the very fact of a document, issued by the highest authority of the Catholic Church, addressed both to the Church herself and "to all people of good will," on a matter which at first sight is solely economic and social: the development of peoples. The breadth of outlook is the second point of originality of *Populorum progressio*. Paul VI declared the universality of the "social" question. Citizens of rich countries have the moral obligation to take into consideration the relationship between their conduct and the poverty and underdevelopment of so many millions of people. As a third point, *Populorum progressio* provides an original contribution to the social doctrine of the Church and indeed to the concept of development. This originality lies in the document's concluding paragraph, which can be considered a summary of the document, "Development is the new name for peace."

In fact, the social question has acquired a worldwide dimension and thus the demand for justice can only be satisfied on that level. To ignore this demand could encourage the temptation among the victims of injustice to respond with violence. Peoples excluded from the fair distribution of the goods destined by God for all ask themselves, "Why not respond with violence to those who first treat us with violence?"

Populorum progressio has permanent value. There is a close link between respect for justice and the establishment of real peace.

THE CONTEMPORARY WORLD

I now wish to conduct a brief review of some of the characteristics of today's world from the point of view of the "development of peoples."

The first fact to note is that the hopes for development today appear very far from being realized. An innumerable multitude of people—children, adults and the elderly—in other words, real and unique human persons, are suffering under the intolerable burden of poverty. There are many millions who are deprived of hope due to the fact that, in many parts of the world, their situation has notice-ably worsened. Before these tragedies of total indigence and need, in which so many of our brothers and sisters are living, it is the Lord Jesus himself who comes to question us (cf. Mt 25:31–46).

A WIDENING GAP

The first negative observation to make is the persistence and the widening of the gap between the areas of the so-called developed North and the developing South. The abundance of goods and services available in the developed North is matched in the Southern hemisphere by an unacceptable delay. It is precisely in the South where the majority of the human race lives.

Looking at all the various sectors—the production and distribution of food-stuffs, hygiene, health and housing, availability of drinking water, working condi-tions (especially for women), life expectancy and other economic and social indi-cators—the general picture is a disappointing one, both considered in itself and in relation to the corresponding data of the more developed countries. The word "gap" returns spontaneously to mind.

POVERTY INDICATORS

Other indices of underdevelopment are equally negative and indeed even more disturbing. These are illiteracy, the difficulty or impossibility of obtaining higher education, the inability to share in the building of one's own nation, the various forms of exploitation and of economic, social, political and even religious oppres-sion of the individual and his or her rights, discrimination of every type, especially the exceptionally odious form based on difference of race.

In today's world there are many other forms of poverty. The denial or the limitation of human rights impoverishes the human person as much as, if not more than, the deprivation of material goods. Such rights include the right to religious freedom, the right to share in the building of society, the freedom to organize and to form unions, as well as the right to take initiatives in economic mat-ters.

There are other tragic signs of underdevelopment, specifically the crises of a shortage of housing and the unemployment or underemployment of so many people. Also of concern here is the international debt.

ECONOMIC IMBALANCE

If a developed nation failed to meet its responsibilities in the community of nations, it would fall seriously short of its clear ethical duty.

Arms production and arms trade are serious disorders in the world. When we add the tremendous danger of atomic weapons stockpiled on an incredible scale, the following is the logical conclusion. In today's world the prevailing picture is one destined to lead us more quickly towards death rather than a concern for true development and a "more human" life.

The consequences of the economic imbalances and conflicts of the modern world are the millions of refugees whom war, natural calamities, persecution and discrimination have deprived of home, employment, family and homeland. The tragedy of these multitudes is reflected in the hopeless faces of men, women and children who can no longer find a home in a divided and inhospitable world.

TERRORISM

Today we must not close our eyes to the phenomenon of terrorism, under-stood as the intention to kill people and destroy property indiscriminately. Terrorists seek to create a climate of terror and insecurity, often taking hostages. Acts of terrorism are never justifiable.

POPULATION ISSUES

Something must be said about the demographic problem. One cannot deny the existence, especially in the southern hemisphere, of a demographic problem that creates difficulties for development. To this one must immediately add that in the northern hemisphere the nature of this problem is reversed. In the North the cause for concern is the drop in the birthrate, with repercussions on the aging of the population. In itself, this is a phenomenon capable of hindering development.

It is alarming to see governments in many countries launching systematic campaigns against birth. It often happens that these campaigns are the result of pressure and financing coming from abroad, and in some cases they are made a condition for the granting of financial and economic aid and assistance. In any event, there is an absolute lack of respect for the freedom of choice of the parties involved. Men and women are often subjected to intolerable pressures, including economic ones, in order to force them to submit to this new form of oppression. It is the poorest populations that suffer such mistreatment, and this sometimes leads to a tendency towards a form of racism, or the promotion of certain equally racist forms of eugenics.

Some Positive Signs

This mainly negative overview of the actual situation of development in the contemporary world would be incomplete without a mention of the coexistence of positive aspects.

The first positive note is the awareness among large numbers of men and women of their own dignity and of the dignity of every human being. One must acknowledge the influence exercised by the Declaration of Human Rights, promulgated some forty years ago by the United Nations Organization.

As the world is divided and beset by every type of conflict, a conviction is growing of the radical interdependence in the world. With this has developed the need for a solidarity that will take up interdependence and transfer it to the moral plane. Today people are realizing that they are linked together by a common destiny, which is to be constructed together, if catastrophe for all is to be avoided

Also to be mentioned here, as a sign of respect for life—despite all the temptations to destroy it by abortion and euthanasia—is a concomitant concern for peace, together with awareness that peace is indivisible. It is either for all or for none. It demands an ever-greater degree of rigorous respect for justice and consequently a fair distribution of the results of true development.

Among today's positive signs we must also mention a greater realization of the limits of available resources, and of the need to respect the integrity and the cycles of nature and to take them into account when planning for development. Today this is called ecological concern.

It is also right to acknowledge the generous commitment of statesmen, politicians, economists, trade unionists, people of science and international officials—many of them inspired by religious faith—who at no small personal sacrifice try to resolve the world's ills and who give of themselves in every way so as to ensure that an ever increasing number of people may enjoy the benefits of peace and a quality of life worthy of the name.

AUTHENTIC HUMAN DEVELOPMENT

Development is not a straightforward, automatic process. It is not, moreover, simply an economic concept. The mere accumulation of goods and services, even for the benefit of the majority, is not enough for the realization of human happiness. Unless economic resources are guided by a moral understanding and by an orientation towards the true good of the human race, they can easily be used to oppress persons.

CONSUMERISM

In the contemporary world side-by-side with the miseries of underdevelopment we find an equally inadmissible superdevelopment. Superdevelopment consists in an excessive availability of material goods for the benefit of certain social groups. In this condition, people are made slaves of possession and of immediate gratification. Their only thought is for the multiplication and continual replacement of the things with other better things. This is the so-called civilization of consumption or consumerism. It is characterized by "throwing-away" and "waste." An object already owned but now superseded by something better is discarded, with no thought of its possible lasting value, or of some other human being who is poorer.

All of us experience the effects of consumerism. There is crass materialism and discontent as one quickly learns that the more one possesses the more one wants. Deeper aspirations remain unsatisfied and even stifled. There is a difference between "having" and "being." To "have" objects and goods does not necessarily perfect a person. To perfect a person material goods must contribute to the maturing and enrichment of the person's "being."

One of the greatest injustices in the world is that the people who possess much are relatively few and those who possess almost nothing are many. This then is the picture. There are some people, namely, the few who possess much, who do not really succeed in "being." They have reversed the hierarchy of values and as such are hindered by the cult of "having." There are others, the many who have little or nothing, who do not succeed in realizing their basic human vocation because they are deprived of essential goods.

Note that the evil does not consist in "having," but in possessing without regard for the ordered hierarchy of goods. Development has a necessary economic dimension; goods are essential for people "to be." Human development, however, can never be limited to economic goods.

THE SPIRITUAL NATURE OF THE PERSON

In the effort to achieve true development we must never lose sight of the foundation of the nature of humans, who have been created by God in God's image and likeness (cf. Gen 1:26). Humans have both a physical and a spiritual nature.

Development cannot consist only in the use, dominion over and indiscriminate possession of created things and the products of human industry. It rather consists in subordinating the possession, dominion and use to the divine likeness in persons and to the human vocation to immortality. This is the transcendent reality of the human being, a reality that is shared from the beginning by a couple, a man and a woman (cf. Gen 1:27), and is therefore fundamentally social.

The first portrayal of humans in the Bible is as a creature and an image. This portrayal defines the deepest reality of human nature, that is to say, the origin and affinity of persons. All humans have then the obligation of a special task. The task is "to have dominion" over the other created beings, "to cultivate the garden." This is to be accomplished within the framework of obedience to the divine law and therefore with respect for the image received (cf. Gen 1:26–30; 2:15–16; Wis 9:2–3).

THE VOCATION OF THE CHURCH

Anyone wishing to renounce the task of improving the lot of humanity with the excuse that the struggle is difficult betrays the will of God the Creator. A deep study of Scripture commits us more resolutely to the duty, which is urgent for everyone today, to work together for the full development of others.

Part of the teaching and most ancient practice of the Church is her conviction that she is obliged by her vocation—she herself, her ministers and each of her members—to relieve the misery of the suffering, both far and near, not only out of her "abundance" but also out of her "necessities." One cannot ignore people in need in favor of superfluous church ornaments and costly furnishings for divine worship. It could be obligatory to sell these goods in order to provide food, drink, clothing and shelter for those who lack these things. As has been already noted, there exists a hierarchy of values between "having" and "being," especially when the "having" of a few can be to the detriment of the "being" of many others.

I wish to insist once more on the seriousness and urgency of that teaching, and I ask the Lord to give all Christians the strength to put it faithfully into practice. The obligation to commit oneself to the development of peoples is an imperative that obliges each and every man and woman, as well as societies and nations.

THE RIGHT TO DEVELOPMENT

Peoples or nations have a right to their own full development. This right includes economic and social aspects, cultural identity as well as openness to the transcendent. Development respects what is worthy of persons and thus promotes human rights—personal and social, economic and political, including the rights of nations and of peoples. Development can never be used as an excuse for one group to impose its way of life or its own religious belief on another group.

The intrinsic connection between authentic development and respect for human rights reveals the moral character of development. Human dignity is attained in conformity with the natural and historical vocation of each person. It is not simply attained by exploiting the abundance of goods and services, or by having available perfect infrastructures.

True development implies, especially for those who are responsible for the process, a lively awareness of the value of the rights of all and of each person. It likewise implies a lively awareness of the need to respect the right of every individual to the full use of the benefits offered by science and technology.

On the internal level of every nation, respect for all rights is very important. These rights include the right to life at every stage of its existence; the rights of the family, as the basic social community, or "cell of society"; justice in employment relationships; the rights inherent in the life of the political community as such; the rights based on the transcendent vocation of the human being, beginning with the right of freedom to profess and practice one's own religious belief.

On the international level there must be complete respect for the identity of each people, with its own historical and cultural characteristics. Both peoples and individuals must enjoy the fundamental equality which is the basis, for example, of the Charter of the United Nations Organization: the equality which is the basis of the right of all to share in the process of full development.

THE MORAL CHARACTER OF DEVELOPMENT

In order to be genuine, development must be achieved within the framework of solidarity and freedom. Neither can ever be sacrificed. The moral character of development includes respect for nonhuman creatures within the natural world. Respect is demanded here for three reasons.

The first is the appropriate growing awareness that we cannot use with impunity the different categories of beings, whether living or inanimate—animals, plants, the natural elements—simply as we wish. We cannot use them simply in accord with our own economic needs. On the contrary, we must take into account the nature of each being and of its mutual connection in an ordered system.

The second is based on the urgent realization that natural resources are limited; some are not renewable. Using natural resources with absolute dominion as if they were inexhaustible seriously endangers their availability not only for the present generation but also above all for generations to come.

The third refers to the consequences of development on the quality of life in the industrialized zones. We all know that the direct or indirect result of industrialization frequently is the pollution of the environment. This has serious consequences for the health of the population.

The dominion granted to humanity by the Creator is not an absolute power, nor can one speak of a freedom to "use and misuse," or to dispose of things as one pleases. A true concept of development cannot ignore the use of nature, the ability to renew resources and the consequences of haphazard industrialization. These three considerations alert our consciences to the moral dimension of development.

A THEOLOGICAL READING OF MODERN PROBLEMS

Because development has an essential moral character, it is clear that the obstacles to development have a moral character. It is necessary then to single out the moral causes that interfere with the course of development.

SINFUL SOCIAL STRUCTURES

In a world sustained by rigid ideologies, imperialism holds sway instead of interdependence and solidarity. This world is subject to structures of sin. The many negative factors working against the universal common good give the impression to many that the obstacles are difficult to overcome.

Given the present situation and the various difficulties facing the common good, it is not out of place to speak of "structures of sin." The Church recognizes sinful situations or the sinful collective behavior of social groups or nations. Social sin is the result of the accumulation and concentration of many personal sins. It is a case of the personal sins of those people who

- Cause, support, or exploit evil;
- Are in a position to avoid, eliminate or limit social evils but fail to do so out of laziness, fear, indifference, silence, or secret complicity;
- Take refuge in the supposed impossibility of changing the world;
- Produce false religious reasoning so as to avoid the sacrifice required.

Structures of sin are rooted in personal sin, and thus always linked to the concrete acts of individuals who introduce these structures, consolidate them and make them difficult to remove. And thus they grow stronger, spread, and become the source of other sins, and so influence people's behavior. Responsibility lies with individuals. A situation, institution, structure or society is not in itself the subject of moral acts. Hence a situation cannot in itself be good or bad.

Sin and structures of sin are categories that help us name the root of the evils that afflict us. These categories help us gain a profound understanding of reality. There are two typical sets of actions and attitudes opposed to the will of God and the good of neighbor: an all-consuming desire for profit, and the thirst for power so as to impose one's will upon others.

I have wished to introduce this type of analysis above all in order to point out the true nature of the evil that faces us in respect to human development. This is a question of a moral evil, the fruit of many sins that lead to structures of sin.

SOLIDARITY: THE RESPONSE TO SOCIAL SIN

The Christian response to sin is change, change of behavior, mentality, or mode of existence. In biblical language, the response to sin is conversion (cf. Mk 13:3, 5, Is 30:15). Conversion specifically entails a relationship to God, to the sin committed, to its consequences and hence to one's neighbor.

On the path toward conversion it is possible to point to the positive and moral value of the growing awareness of economic, cultural, political and religious interdependence among individuals and nations.

When interdependence becomes recognized as a moral category, the response as a moral and social attitude, as a "virtue," is solidarity. Solidarity is not a feeling of vague distress at the misfortunes of people. On the contrary, solidarity is a firm and persevering determination to commit oneself to the common good, that is to say, to the good of all. We are all responsible for all. Solidarity is based on the conviction that desire for profit and thirst for power hinder full development. The "structures of sin" are only conquered by a diametrically opposed attitude, namely, a commitment to the good of one's neighbor. Solidarity refers to the readiness to "lose oneself" for the sake of the other instead of exploiting the other, and to serve him or her instead of oppressing the other for one's own advantage (cf. Mt 10:40–42; 20:25; Mk 10:42–45; Lk 22:25–27).

Solidarity is exercised when people recognize one another as persons. Those with a greater share of goods should feel responsible for the weaker. They should be ready to share with them all they possess. Those who are weaker should not be passive. While claiming their legitimate rights, they should do what they can for the good of all. Solidarity is to be practiced within nations as well as in international relationships.

Solidarity helps us to see the "other," whether we are speaking of a person, people or nation, not just as some kind of instrument with a work capacity. Solidarity helps us to see the "other" as our "neighbor," a "helper" (cf. Gen 2:18–20), to be made a sharer. A neighbor is one who is like us and is equally invited by God to participate in the banquet of life.

In this way, the solidarity that we propose is the path to peace and at the same time to development. The motto of the pontificate of my esteemed predecessor Pius XII was *Opus iustitiae pax,* peace is the fruit of justice. Today one could say, with the same exactness and the same power of biblical inspiration (cf. Is 32:17; Jas 3:18): *Opus solidaritatis pax,* peace is the fruit of solidarity.

The goal of peace will certainly be achieved through social and international justice as well as through the practice of the virtues that favor togetherness and that teach us to live in unity.

Solidarity is a Christian virtue. Solidarity seeks to go beyond itself; it includes forgiveness and reconciliation. One's neighbor is then not only a human being with rights and a fundamental equality with everyone else, but is the living image of God the Father, redeemed by the blood of Jesus Christ and placed under the permanent action of the Holy Spirit. One's neighbor, including one's enemy, must be loved with the same love with which the Lord loves him or her. For our neighbor's sake one must be ready for sacrifice, even the ultimate one, namely, to lay down one's life for the other (cf. 1 Jn 3:16).

At that point, awareness of the common fatherhood of God, of the brotherhood of all in Christ and of the presence and life-giving action of the Holy Spirit will bring to our vision of the world a new criterion for interpreting it. This supreme model of unity, one God in three Persons, is what Christians mean by the word "communion."

MORAL PRINCIPLES FROM CATHOLIC DOCTRINE

The Church does not have technical revolutions to offer for the problem of underdevelopment. The Church does not propose economic and political systems or programs, nor does she show preference for one or the other, provided that human dignity is properly respected and promoted, and provided she herself is allowed the room she needs to exercise her ministry.

The teaching and spreading of her social doctrine are part of the Church's evangelizing mission. And since it is a doctrine aimed at guiding people's behavior, it consequently gives rise to a commitment to justice, according to each individual's role, vocation and circumstances.

The condemnation of evils and injustices is also part of that ministry of evangelization in the social field that is an aspect of the Church's prophetic role. But it should be made clear that proclamation is always more important than condemnation, and the latter cannot ignore the former, which gives it true solidity and the force of higher motivation.

It will not be superfluous therefore to reexamine and further clarify in this light the characteristic themes and guidelines dealt with by the Magisterium in recent years.

THE OPTION FOR THE POOR

Here I would like to indicate one of them: the option or love of preference for the poor. This is an option, or a special form of primacy in the exercise of Christian charity, to which the whole tradition of the Church bears witness. It affects the life of each Christian inasmuch as he or she seeks to imitate the life of Christ, but it applies equally to our social responsibilities and hence to our manner of living, and to the logical decisions to be made concerning the ownership and use of goods.

Today, furthermore, given the worldwide dimension which the social question has assumed, this love or preference for the poor, and the decisions which it inspires in us, cannot but embrace the immense multitudes of the hungry, the needy, the homeless, those without medical care and, above all, those without hope of a better future. It is impossible not to take account of the existence of these realities. To ignore them would mean becoming like the "rich man" who pretended not to know the beggar Lazarus lying at his gate (cf. Lk 16:19–31).

THE UNIVERSAL DESTINATION OF GOODS

It is necessary to state once more the characteristic principle of Christian social doctrine: the goods of this world are originally meant for all. The right to private property is valid and necessary, but it does not nullify the value of this principle. Private property, in fact, is under a "social mortgage." This means that it has an intrinsically social function, based upon and justified precisely by the principle of the universal destination of goods. Likewise, in this concern for the poor, one must not overlook that special form of poverty which consists in being deprived of fundamental human rights, in particular the right to religious freedom and also the right to freedom of economic initiative.

The motivating concern for the poor, who are the Lord's poor, must be translated at all levels into concrete actions, until it decisively attains a series of necessary reforms. Each local situation will show what reforms are most urgent and how they can be achieved. But those demanded by the situation of international imbalance, as already described, must not be forgotten.

In this respect I wish to mention specifically the reform of the international trade system and the reform of the world monetary and financial system. There is also a need to review, within an international juridical order, the current systems of technological exchanges and the structure of the existing international organizations.

SELF-DETERMINATION

Development demands above all a spirit of initiative on the part of the countries that need it. Each of them must act in accordance with its own responsibilities, not expecting everything from the more favored countries, and acting in collaboration with others in the same situation.

None of what has been said can be achieved without the collaboration of all in the framework of solidarity. This includes everyone, beginning with the most neglected. The developing nations themselves have the duty to practice solidarity among themselves and with the poorest countries of the world. An essential condition for global solidarity is autonomy and free self-determination. But at the same time, solidarity demands a readiness to accept the sacrifices necessary for the good of the whole world community.

THE UNIVERSAL MORAL CALL

FREEDOM AND SERVICE

Nations and individuals aspire to be free. Recently a new way of confronting the problems of poverty and underdevelopment has spread in some areas of the world. This approach makes liberation the fundamental category and the first principle of action. It is fitting to add that the aspiration to freedom from all forms of slavery affecting the individual and society is something noble and legitimate.

Development that is merely economic is incapable of setting persons free. Development that does not include the cultural, transcendent and religious dimensions of persons and society is even less conducive to authentic liberation. Human beings are totally free only when they are completely themselves, in the fullness of their rights and duties. The same can be said about society as a whole.

The principal obstacle to be overcome on the way to authentic liberation is sin and the structures produced by sin as it multiplies and spreads. The freedom with which Christ has set us free (cf. Gal 5:1) encourages us to become the servants of all. Thus the process of development and liberation takes concrete shape in the exercise of solidarity, that is to say in the love and service of neighbor, especially of the poorest.

INSPIRED BY SOLIDARITY

The Church has confidence in persons, though she knows the evil of which they are capable. For she well knows that in spite of the heritage of sin, and the sin which each one is capable of committing, there exist in the human person sufficient qualities and energies, a fundamental "goodness" (cf. Gen 1:31), because persons are the image of the Creator, placed under the redemptive influence of Christ.

There is no justification then for despair or pessimism or inertia. We are all called, indeed obliged, to face the tremendous challenge of the last decade of the second Millennium. The present dangers threaten everyone: a world economic crisis, a war without frontiers, without winners or losers. In the face of such a threat, the distinction between rich individuals and countries and poor individuals and countries will have little value, except that a greater responsibility rests on those who have more and can do more.

This is not however the sole motive or even the most important one. At stake is the dignity of the human person, whose defense and promotion have been entrusted to us by the Creator, and to whom the men and women at every moment of history are strictly and responsibly in debt. Every individual is called upon to play his or her part in this peaceful campaign, a campaign to be conducted by peaceful means, in order to secure development in peace, in order to safeguard nature itself and the world about us.

A CALL TO CATHOLICS

In this commitment, the sons and daughters of the Church must serve as examples and guides, for they are called upon, in conformity with the program announced by Jesus himself in the synagogue at Nazareth, to "preach good news to the poor . . . to proclaim release to the captives and recovering of sight to the blind, to set at liberty those who are oppressed, to proclaim the acceptable year of the Lord" (Lk 4:18–19). It is appropriate to emphasize the preeminent role that belongs to the laity, both men and women. It is their task to be witnesses and agents of peace and justice.

The Church knows that no temporal achievement is to be identified with the Kingdom of God, but that all such achievements simply reflect and in a sense anticipate the glory of the Kingdom, the Kingdom that we await at the end of history, when the Lord will come again. All of us who take part in the Eucharist are called to discover, through this sacrament, the profound meaning of our actions in the world in favor of development and peace; and to receive from it the strength to commit ourselves ever more generously, following the example of Christ, who in this sacrament lays down his life for his friends (cf. Jn 15:13).

CONCLUDING PRAYER

Father, you have given all people one common origin. It is your will to gather them as one family in yourself. Fill the hearts of all with the fire of your love. Fill the hearts of all with the desire to ensure justice for their brothers and sisters. By sharing the good things you give us, may we secure justice and equality for every

human being, may we bring an end to all divisions and may we build a human
society of love and peace.

RACISM AND CATHOLIC MORAL THOUGHT

In St. Louis, on January 27, 1999, Pope John Paul II gave a homily that
is often quoted. In part, he preached, "As the new millennium approaches,
there remains another great challenge facing this community of St. Louis,
east and west of the Mississippi, and not St. Louis alone, but the whole
country: to put an end to every form of racism, a plague which your Bishops have called one of the most persistent and destructive evils of the nation." Racism has been a plague on the moral face of America. It has also
been an issue in Catholic social thought.[3] This section considers Catholic
viewpoints on racism. It includes conversation on three documents. In 1988,
the Pontifical Council for Justice and Peace issued *The Church and Racism*
(in 2001, it reissued the document with an "Introductory Update"). In 2001,
Cardinal Francis George of Chicago published *Dwell in My Love*. And in
2003, Archbishop Harry Flynn of St. Paul-Minneapolis released *In God's
Image*. George and Flynn were following a long line of U.S. bishops who
have addressed racism.[4]

Racism Is Sin

It is common practice, at least since 1979, for official Catholic leaders,
including the pope, to describe racism as a sin.[5] There is good reason for
this because the formal features of sin describe well the substance of racism.
According to the *Catechism of the Catholic Church*, "Sin is an offense against
reason, truth, and right conscience; it is failure in genuine love for God and
neighbor caused by a perverse attachment to certain goods. It wounds the
nature of man and injures human solidarity. It has been defined as 'an ut-
terance, a deed, or a desire contrary to the eternal law'" (#1849). Later the
Catechism states, "Sin is a personal act" (#1868).

This sense of sin is closely related what might be the most frequent use of
the term *racism*. For many people racism refers to negative feelings and
stereotypes one has about another racial group. That is to say, racism is
prejudice. Many dictionaries define racism this way. Prejudice here is a pre-
formed or unfounded negative opinion of persons of another race. It is a sin
because it is an offense against reason and certainly a failure to love God
and neighbor. Racism is a distortion of the will and the mind.

Racism develops and depends on an emotive source and "justifications."
Racism includes a bundle of negative feelings toward members of another
race—antipathy, hatred, revulsion, and aversion. Closely related to these

feelings, and perhaps used to attempt to justify them, is a set of pseudo-rational beliefs about members of the race. There are usually four sets of such beliefs: members of the race are morally degenerate (they cannot be trusted; they steal; they have perverted or immoral sexual habits); members of the race have no work ethic (they are lazy; they are unreliable); members of the race are uninterested in personal hygiene (they are dirty; they smell; they do not bathe); members of the race are not intelligent (they are stupid; they have very little common sense).

Racism Is More Than Prejudice

While racism cannot be separated from prejudice, most anti-racist commentators, including many church officials, do not want to limit racism to a personal trait, however negative or vile this trait may be. They recognize that racism is a persistent social phenomenon, not simply a personal moral flaw. When Pope John Paul II in his homily in St. Louis called racism in America a "plague," he seemed to be suggesting that racism is more than prejudice.

The history of race and racism indicates that it is appropriate to distinguish racism and prejudice. By most accounts, *racism* and the underlying notion of *race* developed during European colonialism and the brutal systems of enslavement and the slave trade that followed. Explanations of the origins of racism seem to take one of two tracks. Some suggest that the notion of race developed from an honest attempt to understand the physical differences between Europeans and Africans.[6] In this narrative, the notion of race developed prior to and independent of racism. It accounts for the notion of race but does not, in itself, explain the development of racism. Logically speaking, according to this narrative, one can hold the view that there are many races but not be a racist. That is to say, one can at once believe that humanity is divided into racial groups and at the same time hold that all the races are inherently equal. This position, however, while able to exist in the mind, seems to have trouble existing outside the mind. Labeling differences in people for the sake of labeling differences seems to lead to hierarchical evaluative judgments. It is interesting to note the status today of the idea of race. Races are often classified in forms and surveys and population statistics. Most individuals probably identify themselves with a race. On the other hand, many people argue that race is not a true biological phenomenon; it is a political construct, created to separate and distinguish people from one another.

The other account of the development of racism and race is that they were developed to justify slavery. The Pontifical Council for Justice and Peace takes this view. The council links the beginnings of the development of racist theory with the fifteenth- and sixteenth-century European soldiers and traders. It notes that the slave trade, begun in 1562 and enduring for some three centuries, was supported by theories of the inferiorities of certain peoples. By the eighteenth century,

> a veritable racist ideology, opposed to the teaching of the Church, was forged . . . This racist ideology believed it could find the justification for its prejudices in science. Apart from the difference in physical characteristics and skin color, it sought to deduce an essential difference, of a hereditary biological nature, in order to affirm that the subjugated peoples belonged to intrinsically inferior "races" with regard to their mental, moral or social qualities. It was at the end of the eighteenth century that the word "race" was used for the first time to classify human being biologically.[7]

History offers some insight into the meaning of racism. Whether the introduction of race into human consciousness was done for scientific or vicious reasons, racism does not simply refer to an individual sin or the hatred that one person has for another. From the beginning of its public usage, race was linked to identifiable patterns of social organization. The most "conspicuous manifestations of racism" in history—among them, the white supremacism of the Jim Crow era in the United States, the apartheid system in South Africa, and the anti-Semitism that led up to and supported the Holocaust—brutally illustrate the social nature of racism.[8] Racism always includes some sort of imposition or interference in the lives of the group.[9]

It is hard to imagine the persistence of racism independent of social ideology. Given the development of the idea of racism, its actual expression in history, and its persistence, anti-racist commentators are correct when they define racism in language broader than prejudice, even though dictionaries and the general public tend not to define it in such a manner.

The social nature of racism confirms the Catholic description of racism as a sin. Indeed, the above section illustrates well what the *Catechism of the Catholic Church* describes as "social sin":

> Moreover, we have a responsibility for the sins committed by others when we cooperate in them: by participating directly and voluntarily in them; by ordering, advising, praising, or approving them; by not disclosing or not hindering them when we have an obligation to do so; by protecting evil-doers. Thus sin makes men accomplices of one another and causes concupiscence, violence, and injustice to reign among them. Sins give rise to social situations and institutions that are contrary to the divine goodness. "Structures of sin" are the expression and effect of personal sins. They lead their victims to do evil in their turn. In an analogous sense, they constitute a "social sin. (#1868–69)

In the previous section of this chapter we read Pope John Paul's description of social sin. Racism is the paradigmatic expression of social sin. It is both a personal and a social vice. A vice, in the words of the *Catechism*, "perverts emotions and feelings" (#1774). A vice, it also states, "results in perverse inclinations that cloud conscience and corrupt the concrete judgment of good and evil" (#1865). What is racism other than perverse feelings and a clouded conscience? It is a habitual distortion of the mind and heart that leads one to particular sins.

The Manifestations of Racism

Contributors to Catholic social thought often distinguish forms or categories of racism. This allows us to distinguish racism from prejudice. Archbishop Flynn distinguishes individual racism from institutional or structural racism. His definition of individual racism could serve to describe prejudice. Institutional or structural racism exists, however, "where patterns of racial superiority are embedded in the systems and institutions of society." He points out, "Some people have given racism the working definition, 'prejudice plus power.'" Racism, he suggests, involves the use of power "to keep one race in a privileged position and to exclude others."[10]

The Pontifical Council for Justice and Peace in *The Church and Racism* describes several types of racism. It defines institutional racism as racism "sanctioned by the constitution and laws of a country" (#9). Social racism refers to economic practices subjugating people to inhumane work situations based on views of social inferiority (#13). Spontaneous racism is based on an exaggerated nationalism that can arise with the introduction of immigrants into a country (#14). The council also warns of a possible new form of racism, which it refers to as "eugenic" racism (#16). The council is concerned that artificial procreation may lead to the production of humans according to racial criteria.

Cardinal George of Chicago distinguishes four types of racism: spatial, institutional, internalized, and individual. Spatial racism refers to the "patterns of metropolitan development in which some affluent whites create racially and economically segregated suburbs or gentrified areas of cities."[11] He notes that these historical demarcations of inequality created a "visible chasm between the rich and the poor" (6). Most of our institutions, writes George, have, through custom and habit, assumed and integrated an ideology of white privilege. The leadership of all our fundamental social institutions, including the church, is predominantly white. "People who assume, consciously or unconsciously, that white people are superior create and sustain institutions that privilege people like themselves and habitually ignore the contributions of others peoples and cultures" (6). George cites general indifference to high rates of violence against people of color, higher rates of abortion among people of color, higher rates of imprisonment among people of color, as well as the higher rate of the administration of the death penalty for people of color, as examples of institutional racism. All of this suggests that commentators are correct when they note that racism is "prejudice plus power." Race provides systems of advantage and disadvantage.

Internalized racism refers to the emotional or psychological phenomenon of the effects of racism on people of color: "Because of their socialization within the dominant racial and cultural system, people of color can come to see themselves and their communities primarily through the eyes of that dominant culture" (7).

The final category George describes is individual racism. He notes that this type "perpetuates itself quietly when people grow up with a sense of white racial superiority, whether conscious or unconscious" (7). George concludes his discussion with the bold statement: "When individuals automatically award superior status to their own cultural group and inferior status to all those outside it, they are acting as racists" (7).

Herein lies the problem of defining racism. Racism always comes back to the individual, but racism is never individualistic. The irony here is that the more racism is embedded in social practices—for example, in spatial or institutional racism—the less individuals need to be prejudiced in the traditional sense for racism to flourish. That is to say, when the various forms of racism function to order social relationships, racism remains alive without the strong emotional content and the pseudo-rational justification normally associated with prejudice.

Racism often has a subtle effect on people. It is as if it leaves a hidden imprint. Like a genetic predisposition to a disease, racism may lie dormant in a person until provoked by particular environmental realities.

Responding to Racism

The reality of racism is that it is a form of prejudice and yet at the same time it is more than prejudice. When allied with power, racism becomes embedded in society and its social practices. Personal feelings and stereotypes, so essential in the process of embedding racism in society, become embedded in persons. Catholic social thought offers a nuance that helps to bridge this tension between personal beliefs and public ethos. Theologian Donal Dorr, commenting on Pope Paul VI's *Evangelii nuntiandi*, writes: "Perhaps the most important structures in our world are our patterns of thinking and feeling and valuing. These are deeply personal; yet in many respects they transcend the individual. They are social realities that are often our unexamined presuppositions. They are 'within' the person without being private." He continues, "To change the collective conscience of a people is to change their value system . . . People can be oppressed by structures of their mind—by distorted value-systems and patterns of actions."[12]

Pope John Paul II's reflections on solidarity in *Sollicitudo rei socialis* clearly relate to racism. Indeed, if racism is a vice, it is an insult to the virtue of solidarity:

> It is above all a question of interdependence . . . Solidarity . . . is not a feeling of vague compassion . . . On the contrary, it is a firm and persevering determination to commit oneself to the common good; that is to say to the good of all and of each individual, because we are all really responsible for all. (#38)

> In solidarity . . . members recognize one another as persons. Solidarity helps us to see the "other" . . . as our "neighbor," a "helper" (cf. Gen 2:18–20), to be made a sharer, on a par with ourselves, in the banquet of life to which all are equally invited by God. (#39)

Because racism is complex, responding to racism is complex. Given the relationships and circumstances of interdependence people find themselves living and working within, there seem to be at least three spheres of responsibility: the interpersonal, the institutional, and the social.

The First Sphere of Interaction: Interpersonal

Only persons are moral agents, strictly understood. The responsibility of individuals in their daily lives is crucial to address racism. Archbishop Flynn writes:

> Responding to the sin of racism must begin with each of us examining our own selves on this subject. We need to be open to a change of heart. We should ask God's Spirit to remove from us all traces of racial prejudice. We should avoid racial stereotypes, slurs and jokes. We should correct any expressions or racist attitudes among family members, friends, and co-workers. We should seek opportunities to know and learn from people of other races.[13]

If racism is prejudice, it also includes strong feelings of antipathy supported by negative stereotypes of persons of another race; what is called for is personal conversion of heart and mind. The Pontifical Council for Justice and Peace argues in *The Church and Racism* that "racial prejudice . . . can only be eradicated by going to its roots, where it is formed: in the human heart. It is from the heart that just or unjust behavior is born" (#24). Three years later, in its "Introductory Update," the council wrote, "We must look first to the human heart; it is the heart that must be continually

purified so that it is no longer governed by fear or the spirit of domination" (#5).

Anti-racists use reasoned data and appeals to faith convictions to "point
out the incongruity of racist attitudes and behaviors with Christian identity. Once this is recognized and accepted, personal conversions will occur
which will eventuate in the transformation of society."[14] People will then
reflect on their attitudes and actions and blot racism or racist tendencies
from their lives.

This sphere calls for personal examination. Consider the following comments by contemporary moral theologian Charles E. Curran. His words
capture Flynn's call for personal examination:

> I was blithely unaware of how white privilege had shaped my under-
> standing of what was going on. The invisible and systematic nature of
> white privilege came through in my absolutizing my own limited privi-
> leged position and making all others the object of my good will. My
> perspective was the normative perspective from which all others were to
> be seen. My white theology was the theological standpoint from which
> all others were to be judged. I finally realized to some extent that I was
> the problem.[15]

Also note the seemingly simplistic advice of the Saint Paul Foundation
(Minnesota) research project on racism: "Encourage and support efforts to
bring diverse people together in order to improve mutual understanding,
acceptance, and respect among all racial groups." It further suggests: "Faith
communities should take a leadership role."[16] The first sphere demands
personal examination and personal contact.

The Second Sphere of Interaction:
Public Expression, Personal Commitment

The distinction between the first sphere and the second sphere is the
nature of the action and the level of commitment of the person. We move
from the personal to the public, from direct action to education and awareness. In this second sphere racism becomes "my" problem and "my" responsibility. If the first sphere concerns our private, individual actions, this
second sphere recognizes that we live and work and thus have moral responsibility within many social relationships and many social institutions.
We are members of organizations, schools, churches, neighborhoods, and
companies, not to mention families and less formal social groups. Whites
must be agents of change and advocates of practices and policies that promote solidarity and reject racism within communities and between communities.

The Minnesota research project mentioned above notes that "white
community and business leaders may be in the best position to influence

improvement in race relations." These leaders ought to develop "holistic models of inclusion and incentives for changing institutional behavior."[17]

Archbishop Flynn's concern as archbishop is, of course, the church. He too makes some suggestions:

> At the parish level, we need to make a conscious and explicit commitment to welcome those of other races and ethnic backgrounds. Too often our parishes reflect a pattern that is culturally and racially homogeneous, often reflecting the homogeneous neighborhoods in which they are located. Unfortunately, this can lead toward Catholic parishes being racially and culturally exclusive. To combat this tendency, we need to transform our parish communities so that they appreciate racial diversity, they reach out to people of other races, and they are themselves racially and culturally diverse. These goals will not happen easily or automatically. They require concerted action and a willingness to undertake strategic planning toward these ends.[18]

The Third Sphere: Social Change

The first two spheres stress individual, parish, and corporate responsibility. The third sphere builds on the first two and includes a commitment to effect social policy. Flynn writes:

> Our commitment to combat racism and promote racial diversity must also extend to the public arena. Both individually and collectively we need to resist the racism that we find embedded in the social, economic, political, and cultural institutions of our society, and we need to work for the transformation of these institutions . . . They can work to elect public officials who will work for racial justice and who will strive to undo the racial disparities and the patterns of privilege that characterize too many of our social and economic structures.[19]

Catholic social tradition inspires Catholics to address questions of racism in social structures. It also inspires the church to respond to these questions through programs and structures that empower members of all races to respond. Many dioceses and parishes, for example, have social justice committees. The church must continue to engage the plague of racism through all these measures.

These spheres capture the spirit of Pope Paul VI's words in *Octogesima adveniens*:

> It is up to the Christian communities to analyze with objectivity the situation that is proper to their own country, to shed on it the light of the Gospel's unalterable words and to draw principles of reflection, norms of judgment and directives for action from the social teaching of the

Church . . . It is up to these Christian communities, with the help of the Holy Spirit, in communion with the bishops and in dialogue with other Christian brethren and all people of good will, to discern the options and commitments which are called for in order to bring about the social, political, and economic changes which should be promoted. (#4)

To ignore prejudice and the embeddedness of racism is to be unfaithful to the Gospel and indeed to the individual call to be a Christian.

CAPITAL PUNISHMENT AND CATHOLIC MORAL THOUGHT

The following is an excerpt from Pope John Paul's 1995 encyclical *Evangelium vitae (The Gospel of Life)*. In it the pope addresses the question of capital punishment in the modern world.

Evangelium Vitae (abridged and edited)
Pope John Paul II, March 25, 1995

This should not cause surprise: to kill a human being, in whom the image of God is present, is a particularly serious sin. Only God is the master of life! Yet from the beginning, faced with the many and often tragic cases which occur in the life of individuals and society, Christian reflection has sought a fuller and deeper understanding of what God's commandment prohibits and prescribes. There are in fact situations in which values proposed by God's Law seem to involve a genuine paradox. This happens for example in the case of legitimate defense, in which the right to protect one's own life and the duty not to harm someone else's life are difficult to reconcile in practice. Certainly, the intrinsic value of life and the duty to love oneself no less than others are the basis of a true right to self-defense. The demanding commandment of love of neighbor, set forth in the Old Testament and confirmed by Jesus, itself presupposes love of oneself as the basis of comparison: "You shall love your neighbor as yourself" (Mk 12:31). Consequently, no one can renounce the right to self-defense out of lack of love for life or for self. This can only be done in virtue of a heroic love which deepens and transfigures the love of self into a radical self-offering, according to the spirit of the Gospel Beatitudes (cf. Mt 5:38–40). The sublime example of this self-offering is the Lord Jesus himself.

Moreover, "legitimate defense can be not only a right but also a grave duty for someone responsible for another's life, the common good of the family or of the State." Unfortunately it happens that the need to render the aggressor incapable of causing harm sometimes involves taking a life. In this case, the fatal outcome is attributable to the aggressor whose action brought it about, even though he or she may not be morally responsible because of a lack of the use of reason.

This is the context in which to place the problem of the death penalty. On this matter there is a growing tendency, both in the Church and in civil society, to demand that it be applied in a very limited way or even that it be abolished completely. The problem must be viewed in the context of a system of penal justice ever more in line with human dignity and thus, in the end, with God's plan for humans and society. The primary purpose of the punishment which society inflicts is "to redress the disorder caused by the offense." Public authority must redress the violation of personal and social rights by imposing on the offender an adequate punishment for the crime. Serving the punishment is a condition for the offender to regain the exercise of his or her freedom. In this way authority also fulfills the purpose of defending public order and ensuring people's safety, while at the same time offering the offender an incentive and help to change his or her behavior and be rehabilitated.

It is clear that, for these purposes to be achieved, the nature and extent of the punishment must be carefully evaluated and decided upon, and ought not go to the extreme of executing the offender except in cases of absolute necessity: in other words, when it would not be possible otherwise to defend society. Today however, as a result of steady improvements in the organization of the penal system, such cases are very rare, if not practically non-existent.

In any event, the principle set forth in the new *Catechism of the Catholic Church* remains valid: "If bloodless means are sufficient to defend human lives against an aggressor and to protect public order and the safety of persons, public authority must limit itself to such means, because they better correspond to the concrete conditions of the common good and are more in conformity to the dignity of the human person." (#55–56)

THE CONSISTENT ETHIC OF LIFE

The U.S. bishops are very active in advocating for moral social policies in the country.[20] Among other things, the bishops communicate with elected officials on matters of concern and offer public position papers on policy and social issues. They also, on occasion, write pastoral letters to Catholics and the general public on such issues. The most important of their pastoral letters are *The Challenge of Peace* (1983) and *Economic Justice for All* (1986). *The Challenge of Peace* addressed the church's teaching on war and peace in relation to the use of nuclear weapons. *Economic Justice for All* is a moral analysis of the U.S. economy in light of Catholic social thought.

Joseph Bernardin, cardinal of Chicago, was one of the leaders of the bishops during the time these two letters were written. Bernardin was the chair of the committee that produced *The Challenge of Peace*. Later he was directed by the National Conference of Catholic Bishops to lead its Pro-Life Committee. After studying the issue of war and then working on the problem of abortion, Bernardin came to see clearly what is evident in Catholic social thought, namely, that its personalistic perspective indicates a concern for a variety of life issues. Bernardin described the Catholic view as "the consistent ethic of life" or "the seamless garment." The image of the seamless garment is from the Gospel of John. After Jesus was killed, the Roman soldiers decided to divide his clothes. John says that Jesus' tunic was seamless; it was "woven in one piece from the top" (John 19:23). The soldiers cast lots to see who would get it. The image here is the unity or oneness that Jesus "wore" and preached. For Bernardin, this image captured his sense of the unity of moral issues in the Catholic tradition. The following is a compilation of a few of his speeches on the consistent ethic of life:

> Catholic teaching is based on two truths about the human person: human life is both sacred and social. Because we esteem human life as sacred, we have a duty to protect and foster it at all stages of development, from conception to natural death, and in all circumstances. Because we acknowledge that human life is also social, society must protect and foster it.
>
> Because life is sacred, the taking of even one life is a momentous event. Traditional Catholic teaching has allowed the taking of human life in particular situations by way of exception—for example, in self-defense and capital punishment. In recent decades, however, the presumptions against taking human life have been strengthened and the exceptions made ever more restrictive.
>
> The principal factor responsible for this new context is modern technology that induces a sharper awareness of the fragility of human life. War, for example, has always been a threat to life, but today the threat is qualitatively different because of nuclear and other sophisticated kinds of weapons. The weapons produced by modern technology now threaten life on a scale previously unimaginable. Living, as we do, therefore, in an age of extraordinary technological development means we face a qualitatively new range of moral problems.
>
> We face new technological challenges along the whole spectrum of life from conception to natural death. This creates the need for a consistent ethic, for the spectrum cuts across such issues as genetics, abortion, capital punishment, modern warfare, and the care of the terminally ill. Admittedly, these are all distinct problems, enormously complex, and deserve individual treatment. Each requires its own moral analysis. No single answer or solution applies to all. But they are linked!
>
> Given this broad range of challenging issues, we desperately need a societal attitude or climate that will sustain a consistent defense and promotion of life. When human life is considered "cheap" or easily expendable in one area, eventually nothing is held as sacred and all lives are in

jeopardy. Ultimately, it is society's attitude about life—whether of respect or non-respect—that determines its policies and practices.[21]

There is a relationship between "right to life" and "quality of life" issues. If one contends, as we do, that the right of every unborn child should be protected by civil law and supported by civil consensus, then our moral, political and economic responsibilities do not stop at the moment of birth! We must defend the right to life of the weakest among us; we must also be supportive of the quality of life of the powerless among us: the old and the young, the hungry and the homeless, the undocumented immigrant and the unemployed worker, the sick, the disabled and the dying.

Such a quality-of-life posture translates into specific political and economic positions—for example, on tax policy, generation of employment, welfare policy, nutrition and feeding programs and health care. Consistency means we cannot have it both ways: we cannot urge a compassionate society and vigorous public and private policy to protect the rights of the unborn and then argue that compassion and significant public and private programs on behalf of the needy undermine the moral fiber of society or that they are beyond the proper scope of governmental responsibility or that of the private sector. Neither can we do the opposite! (52)

The consistent ethic of life is primarily a theological concept, derived from biblical and ecclesial tradition about the sacredness of human life, about our responsibilities to protect, defend, nurture and enhance God's gift of life. It provides a framework for moral analysis of the diverse impact of cultural factors—such as technology and contemporary distribution of resources—upon human life, both individual and collective. The consistent ethic of life enables us to answer these questions by its comprehensiveness and the credibility that derives from its consistent application to the full spectrum of life issues. (58)

SOME QUESTIONS FOR CONSIDERATION

1. Explain Pope John Paul's concern about "having" and "being" and how this relates to his understanding of development.
2. Explain John Paul's understanding of solidarity. Describe how solidarity relates to poverty and racism.
3. Explain how John Paul's notion of structures of sin can help us understand the reality and persistence of racism and/or poverty.
4. Using the "look, judge, and act" model, discuss what Pope John Paul sees in the world, what his judgment is, and what actions he determines to be appropriate.

5. Explain the consistent ethic of life in relation to *Sollicitudo rei socialis*.
6. Review the principles of Catholic social thought from the first chapter—the dignity of the human person, the common good, subsidiarity, and solidarity—and describe how they are expressed in this chapter.
7. How do the authors of the selections in this chapter defend and support their positions? Review the discussion of moral arguments from the first chapter. Do the authors argue from authority, or do they use theological, biblical, philosophical, common sense, or pragmatic arguments?
8. Review the three spheres of Catholic social action: works of mercy and justice, public expression and personal commitment, and social analysis for social change. How do the readings in this chapter express these spheres?
9. Discuss how personalism is explained and supported in this chapter.
10. Discuss the four forms of moral discourse—narrative, prophetic, ethical, and policy—and how they are expressed in this chapter.

Prayer of Christian Action

In the midst of too much hate, too much suffering, too much injustice, and armed with confidence that the Spirit of the Lord is present to us, we must speak to this world of God's love, justice, mercy, and healing.

We must voice the healing words of Jesus Christ to a people so desperately in need of healing. We must be God's prophets, unworthy as we are, speaking the Gospel to a world that is not eager to hear us. We must illumine the problems of this age with the apostolic faith that is our treasure. We must join people of good will, whatever our differences, in restoring peace, love, and reconciliation to our society.

—Archbishop John Roach

Chapter Nine

Creating a Culture of Peace

Make Me an Instrument of Your Peace

Lord, make me an instrument of your peace; where there is hatred, let me sow love; where there is injury, let me sow pardon; where there is doubt, let me sow faith; where there is despair, let me sow hope; where there is darkness, let me sow light; and where there is sadness, let me sow joy.

O Lord, grant that I may not so much seek to be consoled as to console; to be understood, as to understand; to be loved as to love. For it is in giving that we receive, it is in pardoning that we are pardoned, and it is in dying that we are born to eternal life.

—ATTRIBUTED TO ST. FRANCIS OF ASSISI, 1181–1226

The popes of the last fifty years—John XXIII, Paul VI, John Paul II, and Benedict XVI—lived through the bloodiest century in human history. When we read their strong moral positions against war, we know that war is not an abstraction for them. The two world wars dramatically shaped their lives as well as the lives of their families and communities. These popes also experienced some of the most oppressive governments in history. They knew firsthand the evils of totalitarianism under fascism, Nazism, and communism. When we read their strong moral positions for justice we know that injustice is not an abstraction for them. The experience of the popes and of the church dictates the nature of Catholic social thought. It is at once demanding, almost idealistic, and at the same time rooted in a realistic sense of the human condition.

This vision, which we have read expressed throughout this book, is very demanding. The themes, principles, and ideas of Catholic social thought call forth the best in human nature. Yet social Catholicism is not dreamy and idealistic. There is a strong realistic strand throughout the tradition. Catholic social thought attempts to combine the experience of real humans living in society with the gospel. Catholic social thought readily acknowledges the reality of sin and conflict in the world, and at the same time it

calls persons toward personal conversion and work for social transformation. In this chapter we see this played out in the tradition's view of private
property and of peace.

The focal point of this chapter is Pope John Paul II's 1991 encyclical
Centesimus annus. *Centesimus annus* was written to commemorate the one-
hundredth anniversary of Pope Leo XIII's *Rerum novarum*. John Paul reviews Leo's great encyclical and, as one would expect, he addresses some of
the same questions that Leo addressed, for example, the meaning of work,
private property, wages, the role of government, and the moral work place.
Centesimus annus is, however, more than an update of *Rerum novarum*.
The reason for this is history. The one hundred years between these publications saw two world wars, the rise of communism, and an ideologically
divided world. Then, in 1989, European communism fell to nonmilitary
populist movements. These dramatic events changed the face of Europe and
indeed the world. The world Pope John Paul was addressing at the end of
the twentieth century, then, was very different from the world Pope Leo
faced at the end of the nineteenth century.

Centesimus annus concludes with the point that Christians and all people
must work to promote a "culture of peace." The second part of this chapter
follows up on John Paul's call by addressing Catholic social thought on war
and peace.

CENTESIMUS ANNUS

Centesimus annus is different from other social encyclicals. One of its
distinctive features is that John Paul offers a moral and theological reading
of European history in the twentieth century. Yet he is not writing as a
detached observer. The history he narrates formed his life. He grew up under the Nazi regime and studied for the priesthood in a secret seminary.
Much of his adult life was under the strict watch of the controlling Communist Party in Poland. Indeed, there is little doubt that his activities as
pope helped direct the nonmilitary populist movements that brought down
communism. Donal Dorr accurately notes that at the heart of *Centesimus
annus* are "the personal reflections of a man who had played a key role in
the transformation of Europe. In this encyclical the pope looked back on
his own struggle and that of his people, and he shared the lesson of this
experience with his world-wide audience."[1]

Section III of *Centesimus annus* is entitled "The Year 1989." Here the
pope is referring to the remarkable fall of European communism. One by
one the totalitarian regimes in Hungry, Poland, Romania, Czechoslova-
kia, and East Germany (communism in the Soviet Union, the U.S.S.R,
would end two years later) fell, mostly through nonviolent movements.
The most dramatic event occurred when the East Germans opened the

checkpoint between East Berlin (controlled by the communist government) and West Berlin. This allowed free travel between the two parts of the city for the first time in over a generation. The people responded by literally tearing down the wall, the Berlin Wall, which had been built to separate the two areas.

With the fall of European communism, John Paul offers a substantive and broad reflection on the morality of capitalism. He asks, "After the failure of communism, should capitalism be the goal of countries trying to rebuild their economies and societies?" The pope's answer, as one would expect, is nuanced. Before he answers that question, however, he offers a thorough review of all the relevant issues about capitalism: the meaning of private property, the role of work, the market (and the fact that many people in the world are cut off from participation in the market), the justification of profit, and consumerism and its effects on the environment, on the family and on the individual.

Though written a hundred years after *Rerum novarum* and responding to very different world, *Centesimus annus* and *Rerum novarum* share common ground. As theologian Daniel Finn notes, both document "the suffering of so many in the world, the Church's vision of hope, and the courage of a pope to work to bring the two together."[2]

Centesimus Annus (abridged and edited) Pope John Paul II, May 1, 1991

INTRODUCTION:
ON THE HUNDREDTH ANNIVERSARY OF *RERUM NOVARUM*

The hundredth anniversary of *Rerum novarum* is an occasion of great importance for the present history of the Church and for my own Pontificate. I wish to propose a "re-reading" of Pope Leo's encyclical by issuing an invitation to "look back" at the text itself in order to discover anew the richness of the fundamental principles that it formulated for dealing with the question of the condition of workers. But this is also an invitation to "look around" at the "new things" which surround us today. Finally, it is an invitation to "look to the future" and glimpse the third Millennium of the Christian era, filled as it is with uncertainties and with promises.

Re-reading *Rerum novarum* in the light of contemporary realities enables us to appreciate the Church's constant concern for those especially beloved by the Lord Jesus. The encyclical is testimony to the continuity in the Church of the "preferential option for the poor." Pope Leo's encyclical on the "condition of the workers" concerned the poor and the terrible conditions to which the new and often violent process of industrialization had reduced great multitudes of people.

Today, in many parts of the world, similar processes of economic, social and political transformation are creating the same evils.

Pope Leo XIII calls upon government to remedy the condition of the poor in accordance with justice. He does so because government has the duty of watching over the common good and of ensuring that every sector of social life contributes to achieving that good, while respecting the rightful autonomy of each sector. This should not however lead us to think that Pope Leo expected government to solve every social problem. On the contrary, he frequently insists on necessary limits to the State's intervention and on its instrumental character. The individual, family and society are prior to government. Government exists to protect and not stifle their rights.

TOWARDS THE "NEW THINGS" OF TODAY

ON HUMAN FREEDOM

The events that took place near the end of 1989 and at the beginning of 1990 are particularly significant. These events, and the radical transformations which followed, can be explained through Pope Leo's teachings. Pope Leo foresaw the negative political, social and economic consequences of the order proposed by socialism. He correctly judged the danger posed to the masses by the attractive presentation of this simple and radical solution to the question of the working class. This is all the more understandable when one considers the terrible situation of injustice in which the working classes of the recently industrialized nations found themselves.

Reading *Rerum novarum* we see how it points to the socio-economic consequences of an error that has even greater implications. This error consists in an understanding of human freedom that detaches it from obedience to the truth, and consequently from the duty to respect the rights of others.

This very error had extreme consequences in the tragic series of wars that ravaged Europe and the world between 1914 and 1945. Without the terrible burden of hatred and resentment that had built up as a result of so many injustices both on the international level and within individual States, such cruel wars would not have been possible. In these wars there was no hesitation to violate the most sacred human rights, even to the extent of the extermination of entire peoples and social groups. Here we recall what happened to the Jewish people under Nazi Germany.

May the memory of those terrible events guide the actions of everyone, particularly the leaders of nations in our own time, when other forms of injustice are fuelling new hatreds and when new ideologies that exalt violence are appearing on the horizon.

THE VIOLENT DIVISION OF EUROPE AFTER WORLD WAR II

True peace is never simply the result of military victory. It includes the removal of the causes of war and genuine reconciliation between peoples. For many years in Europe and the world there has been a situation of non-war rather than genuine peace. Half of the continent fell under the domination of a Communist dictatorship, while the other half organized itself in defense against this threat. Many peoples lost the ability to control their own destiny and were enclosed within the suffocating boundaries of an empire in which efforts were made to destroy their historical memory and the centuries-old roots of their culture. As a result of this violent division of Europe, enormous masses of people were compelled to leave their homeland or were forcibly deported.

An insane arms race swallowed up the resources needed for the development of national economies and for assistance to the less developed nations. Scientific and technological progress, which should have contributed to human well-being, was transformed into an instrument of war. Meanwhile, an ideology, a perversion of authentic philosophy, was called upon to provide doctrinal justification for the new war. This war was not simply expected and prepared for, but was actually fought with enormous bloodshed in various parts of the world. The precariousness of the peace that followed the Second World War was one of the principal causes of the militarization of many Third World countries and the fratricidal conflicts that afflicted them. It was also the cause of the spread of terrorism and of increasingly barbaric means of political and military conflict. Moreover, the whole world was oppressed by the threat of an atomic war capable of leading to the extinction of humanity.

At the end of the Second World War, Communist totalitarianism spread over more than half of Europe and over other parts of the world. The war, which should have re-established freedom and restored the right of nations, ended without having attained these goals. Indeed, in a way, for many peoples, especially those that had suffered most during the war, it openly contradicted these goals.

HUMAN RIGHTS AND THE UNITED NATIONS

It should be remembered that after the Second World War, and in reaction to its horrors, there arose a more lively sense of human rights, which found recognition in a number of International Documents and, one might say, in the drawing up of a new "right of nations," to which the Holy See has constantly contributed. The focal point of this evolution has been the United Nations Organization. Not only has there been a development in awareness of the rights of individuals, but also in awareness of the rights of nations, as well as a clearer realization of the need to act in order to remedy the grave imbalances that exist between the various geographical areas of the world. In a certain sense, these imbalances have shifted the center of the social question from the national to the international level.

While noting this process with satisfaction, one cannot ignore the fact that the overall balance of the various policies of aid for development has not always been positive. The United Nations has not yet succeeded in establishing, as alternatives to war, effective means for the resolution of international conflicts. This seems to be the most urgent problem that the international community has yet to resolve.

THE YEAR 1989

THE CHURCH'S COMMITMENT TO HUMAN RIGHTS

In the course of the 1980s, dictatorial and oppressive regimes fell in some countries of Latin America, Africa and Asia. These events reached their climax in 1989 in Central and Eastern Europe. An important, even decisive, contribution in this history was made by the Church's commitment to defend and promote human rights. The Church affirmed clearly and forcefully that every individual—whatever his or her personal convictions—bears the image of God and therefore deserves respect.

I pray that God will sustain the efforts being made by everyone to build a better future. This is, in fact, a responsibility that falls not only to the citizens of the countries in question, but to all Christians and people of good will. It is a question of showing that the complex problems faced by those peoples can be resolved through dialogue and solidarity, rather than by a struggle to destroy the enemy through war.

ACTIVE NON-VIOLENCE

Among the many factors involved in the fall of oppressive regimes, some deserve special mention. Certainly, the decisive factor that gave rise to the changes was the violation of the rights of workers. It cannot be forgotten that the fundamental crisis of systems claiming to express the rule and indeed the dictatorship of the working class began in Poland in the name of worker solidarity. The masses of working people rejected this ideology that presumed to speak in their name. Through their hard, lived experience of work and of oppression, these people recovered the content and principles of the Church's social doctrine.

It is important also to recognize the fact that the fall of Marxism was produced through the weapons of truth and justice, that is, through peaceful protest. The European order resulting from the Second World War has been overcome by the non-violent commitment of people who, while always refusing to yield to the force of power, succeeded time after time in finding effective ways of bearing witness to the truth. They disarmed the adversary by tenaciously insisting on negotiation, dialogue, and witness to the truth. They continually appealed to the conscience of their adversaries and sought to reawaken in them a sense of shared human dignity. Violence, on the other hand, always needs to justify itself through deceit, and to appear to be defending a right or responding to a threat posed by others.

The events of 1989 are an example of the success of willingness to negotiate and of the Gospel spirit in the face of an adversary not bound by moral principles. The struggle that led to the changes of 1989 called for clarity, moderation, suffering and sacrifice. It was a struggle born of prayer, and it would have been unthinkable without immense trust in God, the Lord of history, who carries the human heart in his hands.

LIBERATION AND DEVELOPMENT

To those who are searching today for a new and authentic theory and praxis of liberation, the Church offers not only her social doctrine and, in general, her teaching about the human person redeemed in Christ, but also her concrete commitment and material assistance in the struggle against marginalization and suffering.

Many individual, social, regional and national injustices were committed during and prior to the years in which Communism dominated. Europe cannot live in peace if the various conflicts that have arisen as a result of the past are to become more acute because of a situation of economic disorder, spiritual dissatisfaction and desperation.

What is called for now in the Third World is a special effort to mobilize resources for economic growth and common development. It will be necessary above all to abandon a mentality in which the poor—as individuals and as peoples—are considered a burden, as irksome intruders trying to consume what others have produced. The poor ask for the right to share in enjoying material goods and to make good use of their capacity for work, thus creating a world that is more just and prosperous for all. The advancement of the poor constitutes a great opportunity for the moral, cultural and even economic growth of all humanity.

Development must not be understood solely in economic terms, but in a way that is fully human. It is a question of building up a more decent life through united labor, of concretely enhancing every individual's dignity and creativity and capacity to respond to his or her personal vocation, and thus to God's call. Total recognition must be given to the rights of the human conscience, which is bound only to the truth, both natural and revealed. The recognition of these rights represents the primary foundation of every authentically free political order.

THE MORAL EVALUATION OF CAPITALISM

PRIVATE PROPERTY

In *Rerum novarum*, Leo XIII strongly affirmed the right to private property. The Church has always defended this right, which is fundamental for the autonomy and development of the person. At the same time, the Church teaches that the possession of material goods is not an absolute right, and that its limits are inscribed in its very nature as a human right. He also affirmed with equal clarity that the "use" of goods is subordinated to their original common destination as created goods. The Successors of Leo XIII have repeated this twofold affirmation: the necessity and therefore the legitimacy of private ownership, as well as the limits that are imposed on it.

God gave the earth to the whole human race for the sustenance of all its members, without excluding or favoring anyone. This is the foundation of the universal destination of the earth's goods. The earth, by reason of its fruitfulness and its capacity to satisfy human needs, is God's first gift for the sustenance of human life. It is through work that persons, using intelligence and freedom, succeed in dominating the earth and making it a fitting home. In this way they make part of the earth their own, precisely the part which they have acquired through work. This is *the origin of individual property.*

WORK

In our time, the role of human work is becoming increasingly important as the productive factor of both non-material and material wealth. Moreover, it is becoming clearer that a person's work is naturally interrelated with the work of others. Work is work with and for others. Work becomes ever more fruitful and productive to the extent that people become more knowledgeable of the productive potentialities of the earth and more profoundly cognizant of the needs of those for whom their work is done.

In our time a particular form of ownership is becoming no less important than land, namely, the possession of know-how, technology and skill. The wealth of the industrialized nations is based much more on this kind of ownership than on natural resources. Besides the earth, the principal resource for humanity is human nature itself.

THOSE MARGINALIZED FROM THE PROCESS

The modern business economy has positive aspects. Its basis is human freedom exercised in the economic field. Economic activity is a sector in a great variety of human activities, and like every other sector, it includes the right to freedom, as well as the duty of making responsible use of freedom.

Many people do not have the means that would enable them to take their place in an effective and humanly dignified way within a productive system. They have no possibility of acquiring the basic knowledge which would enable them to express their creativity and develop their potential. They have no way of entering the network of knowledge and intercommunication that would enable them to see their qualities appreciated and utilized. Thus, if not actually exploited, they are to a great extent marginalized. Economic development takes place, so to speak, over their heads.

Many other people, while not completely marginalized, live in situations where they struggle for a bare minimum. In these situations the ruthless rules of early capitalism still flourish. In other cases the land is still the central element in the economic process, but those who cultivate it are excluded from ownership and are reduced to a state of quasi-servitude. In all these cases, it is still possible today, as in the days of *Rerum novarum*, to speak of inhuman exploitation.

Unfortunately, the great majority of people in the Third World still live in such conditions. However, aspects typical of the Third World also appear in developed countries, where the constant transformation of the methods of production and consumption devalues certain acquired skills and professional expertise. Those who fail to keep up with the times can easily be marginalized, as can the elderly, the young people and, in general, those who are weakest or part of the so-called Fourth World. The situation of women too is far from easy in these conditions.

THE MARKET

It would appear that, on the level of individual nations and of international relations, the free market is the most efficient instrument for utilizing resources and effectively responding to needs. But this is true only for those needs that are "solvent," insofar as they are endowed with purchasing power, and for those resources that are "marketable," insofar as they are capable of obtaining a satisfactory price. But there are many human needs that find no place on the market. It is a strict duty of justice and truth not to allow fundamental human needs to remain unsatisfied, and not to allow those burdened by such needs to perish.

Human work and human beings are not to be reduced to the level of a mere commodity. These objectives include a sufficient wage for the support of the family, social insurance for old age and unemployment, and adequate protection for the conditions of employment.

UNIONS

We find a wide range of opportunities for commitment and effort in the name of justice on the part of trade unions and other workers' organizations. These defend workers' rights and protect their interests as persons so as to enable workers to participate more fully and honorably in the life of their nation and to assist them along the path of development.

PROFIT

The Church acknowledges the legitimate role of profit as an indication that a business is functioning well. But profitability is not the only indicator of a firm's condition. It is possible for the financial accounts to be in order, and yet for the people—who make up the firm's most valuable asset—to be humiliated and their dignity offended. The purpose of a business firm is not simply to make a profit, but is to be found in its very existence as a community of persons who in various ways are endeavoring to satisfy their basic needs, and who form a particular group at the service of the whole of society.

DEBT

At present, the positive efforts that have been made along these lines are being affected by the still largely unsolved problem of the foreign debt of the poorer countries. The principle that debts must be paid is certainly just. However, it is not right to demand or expect payment when the effect would be the imposition of political choices leading to hunger and despair for entire peoples. It cannot be expected that the debts that have been contracted should be paid at the price of unbearable sacrifices. In such cases it is necessary to find ways to lighten, defer or even cancel the debt, compatible with the fundamental right of peoples to subsistence and progress.

CONSUMERISM

It would now be helpful to direct our attention to the specific problems emerging within the more advanced economies. To call for an existence that is qualitatively more satisfying is legitimate. The manner in which new needs arise and are defined is always marked by a more or less appropriate concept of the person and the true good of the person. A given culture reveals its overall understanding of life through the choices it makes in production and consumption. It is here that the phenomenon of consumerism arises. In singling out new needs and new means to meet them, one must be guided by a comprehensive picture of human nature that respects all the dimensions of one's being and which subordinates material and instinctive dimensions to interior and spiritual ones. If, on the contrary, a direct appeal is made to instincts, while ignoring in various ways the reality of the person as intelligent and free, then *consumer attitudes* and *life-styles* can be created which are objectively improper and damaging to his or her physical and spiritual health. Of itself, an economic system does not possess criteria for correctly distinguishing new and higher forms of satisfying human needs from artificial new needs that hinder the formation of a mature personality.

It is not wrong to want to live better. What is wrong is a style of life that is presumed to be better when it is directed towards "having" rather than "being." What is wrong is a style of life that wants to have more, not in order to be more but in order to spend life in enjoyment as an end in itself. It is therefore necessary to create life-styles in which the quest for truth, beauty, goodness and communion with others for the sake of common growth are the factors that determine consumer choices, savings and investments.

THE ENVIRONMENT

Equally worrying is *the ecological question* which accompanies the problem of consumerism and which is closely connected to it. In the desire to have and to enjoy rather than to be and to grow, a person consumes the resources of the earth and his or her own life in an excessive and disordered way. A person who discovers the capacity to transform and in a sense create the world through work forgets that this is always based on God's prior and original gift of the things that are. People often think that they can make arbitrary use of the earth, subjecting it without restraint to their own will, as though it did not have its own requisites and a prior God-given purpose. Instead of carrying out the role of cooperator with God in the work of creation, people put themselves in God's place.

In all this, one notes the poverty or narrowness of people's outlook. People often are motivated by a desire to possess things rather than to relate them to the truth. People can lack the disinterested, unselfish and aesthetic attitude that is born of wonder in the presence of being and of the beauty that enables them to see in visible things the message of the invisible God who created them. People today are often not conscious of their duties and obligations towards future generations.

In addition to the irrational destruction of the natural environment, we must also mention the more serious destruction of the human environment. Although people are rightly worried—though much less than they should be—about preserving the natural habitats of the various animal species threatened with extinction, because they realize that each of these species makes its particular contribution to the balance of nature in general, too little effort is made to safeguard the moral conditions for an authentic "human ecology." God has given the earth to humans, who must use it with respect for the original good purpose for which it was given. God has also given the gift of personhood to humans, who must use it with respect for the original good purpose for which it was given.

SOCIAL ECOLOGY

The first and fundamental structure for "human ecology" is the family, in which one receives the first formative ideas about truth and goodness, and learns what it means to love and to be loved, and thus what it actually means to be a person. Here we mean the family founded on marriage, in which the mutual gift of self by husband and wife creates an environment in which children can be born and develop their potentialities, become aware of their dignity and prepare to face their unique and individual destiny.

It is necessary to go back to seeing the family as the sanctuary of life. The family is indeed sacred: it is the place in which life—the gift of God—can be properly welcomed and protected against the many attacks to which it is exposed, and can develop in accordance with what constitutes authentic human growth. In the face of the so-called culture of death, the family is the heart of the culture of life. Human ingenuity seems to be directed more towards limiting, suppressing or destroying the sources of life—including recourse to abortion, which unfortunately is so widespread in the world—than towards defending and opening up the possibilities of life. These criticisms are directed not so much against an economic system as against an ethical and cultural system. The economy in fact is only one aspect and one dimension of the whole of human activity.

Economic freedom is only one element of human freedom. When economic freedom becomes autonomous, when a person is seen more as a producer or consumer of goods than as a subject who produces and consumes in order to live, then it loses its necessary relationship to the human person and ends up by alienating and oppressing that person.

GOVERNMENT

It is the task of the State to provide for the defense and preservation of common goods such as the natural and human environments, which cannot be safeguarded simply by market forces. Just as in the time of primitive capitalism the State had the duty of defending the basic rights of workers, so now, with the new capitalism, the State and all of society have the duty of defending those collective goods which, among others, constitute the essential framework for the legitimate pursuit of personal goals on the part of each individual.

Here we find a new limit on the market. There are collective and qualitative needs that cannot be satisfied by market mechanisms. There are important human needs that escape its logic. There are goods that by their very nature cannot and must not be bought or sold.

ALIENATION IN CONTEMPORARY LIFE

The historical experience of the West shows that alienation—and the loss of the authentic meaning of life—is a reality. This happens in consumerism, when people are ensnared in a web of false and superficial gratifications rather than being helped to experience their personhood in an authentic and concrete way. Alienation can also be found in work, when it is organized so as to ensure maximum returns and profits with no concern whether the worker grows or diminishes as a person. An increased sharing in a genuinely supportive community enables the worker to grow as a person. A work place characterized by increased isolation in a maze of relationships or destructive competitiveness and estrangement in which the worker is considered only a means and not an end creates the conditions for alienation.

The Christian vision of reality recognizes that alienation is the result of a reversal of means and ends. When persons do not recognize in themselves and in others the value and grandeur of being human, they effectively deprive themselves of the possibility of benefiting from humanity and of entering into that relationship of solidarity and communion with others for which God created them. Indeed, it is through the free gift of self that one truly finds oneself. The human person's essential "capacity for transcendence" makes this gift possible. One cannot give oneself to a purely human plan for reality, to an abstract ideal or to a false utopia. As a person, one can give oneself to another person or to other persons, and ultimately to God, who is the author of one's being and who alone can fully accept this gift. A person is alienated if he or she refuses to transcend the self and to live the experience of self-giving and of the formation of an authentic human community oriented towards the final destiny, which is God. A society is alienated if its forms of social organization, production and consumption make it more difficult to offer this gift of self and to establish this solidarity between people.

Exploitation, at least in the forms analyzed and described by Karl Marx, has been overcome in Western society. Alienation, however, has not been overcome as it exists in various forms of exploitation, when people use one another, and when they seek an ever more refined satisfaction of their individual and secondary needs, while ignoring principal and authentic needs. A person who is concerned solely or primarily with possessing and enjoying, who is no longer able to control his or her instincts and passions, or to subordinate them by obedience to the truth, cannot be free. Obedience to the truth about God and the person is the first condition of freedom, making it possible for a person to order his or her needs and desires and to choose the means of satisfying them according to a correct scale of values, so that the ownership of things may become an occasion of growth. This growth can be hindered as a result of manipulation by the means of mass communication, which impose fashions and trends of opinion through carefully orchestrated repetition, without it being possible to subject to critical scrutiny the premises on which these fashions and trends are based.

IS CAPITALISM THE MODEL ECONOMIC SYSTEM?

Returning now to the initial question: can it perhaps be said that, after the failure of communism, capitalism should be the goal of the countries now making efforts to rebuild their economy and society?

The answer is complex. If by "capitalism" is meant an economic system which recognizes the fundamental and positive role of business, the market, private property and the resulting responsibility for the means of production, as well as free human creativity in the economic sector, then the answer is certainly in the affirmative, even though it would perhaps be more appropriate to speak of a "business economy," "market economy" or simply "free economy." But if by "capitalism" is meant a system in which freedom in the economic sector is not circumscribed within a strong juridical framework which places it at the service of human freedom in its totality, and which sees it as a particular aspect of that freedom, the core of which is ethical and religious, then the reply is certainly negative.

The Marxist solution has failed, but the realities of marginalization and exploitation remain in the world, especially the Third World, as does the reality of human alienation, especially in the more advanced countries. Against these phenomena the Church strongly raises her voice. Vast multitudes are still living in conditions of great material and moral poverty. The collapse of the communist system in so many countries certainly removes an obstacle to facing these problems in an appropriate and realistic way, but it is not enough to bring about their solution. Indeed, there is a risk that a radical capitalistic ideology could spread which refuses even to consider these problems, in the a priori belief that any attempt to solve them is doomed to failure, and which blindly entrusts their solution to the free development of market forces.

The integral development of the human person through work does not impede but rather promotes the greater productivity and efficiency of work itself, even though it may weaken consolidated power structures. A business cannot be considered only as a "society of capital goods." It is also a "society of persons" in which people participate in different ways and with specific responsibilities, whether they supply the necessary capital for the company's activities or take part in such activities through their labor. To achieve these goals there is still need for a broad associated workers' movement, directed towards the liberation and promotion of the whole person.

PEACE AND DEVELOPMENT IN THE WORLD COMMUNITY

POLITICAL ORDER AND THE PERSON

The Church values the democratic system inasmuch as it ensures the participation of citizens in making political choices, guarantees to the governed the possibility both of electing and holding accountable those who govern them and of replacing them through peaceful means when appropriate. Authentic democracy is possible only in a State ruled by law, and on the basis of a correct conception of the human person. If there is no ultimate truth to guide and direct political activity, then ideas and convictions can easily be manipulated for reasons of power. As history demonstrates, a democracy without values easily turns into open or thinly disguised totalitarianism.

The Christian faith recognizes that human life is realized in history in conditions that are diverse and imperfect. Furthermore, in constantly reaffirming the transcendent dignity of the person, the Church's method is always that of respect for freedom. Freedom attains its full development only by accepting the truth. In a world without truth, freedom loses its foundation and people are exposed to the violence of passion and to manipulation. Christians uphold freedom and serve it, constantly offering to others the truth that they have known (cf. Jn 8:31–32), in accordance with the missionary nature of their vocation. While paying heed to every fragment of truth that they encounter in life experience and in culture of individuals and nations, they will not fail to affirm in dialogue with others all that their faith and the correct use of reason have enabled them to understand.

Today we are witnessing a predominance of democratic ideas and a lively concern for human rights. The authentic and solid foundation of democracy is the explicit recognition of human rights. Among the most important of these rights is the right to life. An integral part of this right is the right of the child to develop in the mother's womb from the moment of conception; the right to live in a united family and in a moral environment conducive to the growth of the child's personality; the right to develop one's intelligence and freedom in seeking and knowing the truth; the right to share in the work which makes wise use of the earth's material resources, and to derive from that work the means to support oneself and one's dependents; and the right freely to establish a family, to have and to rear children through the responsible exercise of one's sexuality. In a certain sense, the source and synthesis of these rights is religious freedom, understood as the right to live in the truth of one's faith and in conformity with one's transcendent dignity as a person.

THE ECONOMY AND THE STATE

Economic activity, especially the activity of a market economy, cannot be conducted in a vacuum. It presupposes guarantees of individual freedom and private property, as well as a stable currency and efficient public services. The principal task of the State is to guarantee this security, so that those who work and produce can enjoy the fruits of their labors and thus feel encouraged to work efficiently and honestly. The absence of stability, together with the corruption of public officials and the spread of improper sources of growing rich and of easy profits deriving from illegal or purely speculative activities, constitutes one of the chief obstacles to development and to the economic order.

Another task of the State is that of overseeing and directing the exercise of human rights in the economic sector. The State has a duty to sustain business activities by creating conditions that will ensure job opportunities. The State has the further right to intervene when particular monopolies create delays or obstacles to development.

The principle of subsidiarity must be respected. A community of a higher order should not interfere in the internal life of a community of a lower order, depriving the latter of its functions, but rather should support it in case of need and help to coordinate its activity with the activities of the rest of society, always with a view to the common good.

Needs are best understood and satisfied by people who are closest to the poor and who act as neighbors to those in need. One thinks of the condition of refugees, immigrants, the elderly, the sick, and all those in circumstances that call for assistance, such as drug abusers. All these people can be helped effectively only by those who offer them genuine fraternal support, in addition to the necessary care.

"PERSONALIZED" SOCIETY

In order to overcome today's widespread individualistic mentality a concrete commitment to solidarity and charity is required. This begins in the family with the mutual support of husband and wife and the care that the different generations give to one another. The family can be called a community of work and solidarity. It can happen, however, that a family can find itself without sufficient resources. It is urgent therefore to promote policies that assist the family by providing adequate resources and efficient means of support. This includes resources for children and the elderly.

Apart from the family, other intermediate communities exercise primary functions and give life to specific networks of solidarity. These prevent society from becoming an anonymous and impersonal mass. It is in interrelationships on many levels that a person lives, and that society becomes more "personalized." The individual today is often suffocated between two poles represented by the State and the marketplace. At times it seems as though people exist only as a producers and consumers of goods, or as objects of State administration.

CREATING THE CULTURE OF PEACE

It must be remembered that persons are beings who seek the truth and strive to live in that truth. We deepen our understanding of truth through a dialogue that involves past and future generations. This open search for truth does not destroy or reject a priori. It rather puts these values to the test in one's own life and through existential verification makes them more real, relevant and personal. This then distinguishes the valid elements in the tradition from false and erroneous ones, or from obsolete forms that can be usefully replaced by others more suited to the times.

All human activity takes place within a culture. The formation of a culture includes the involvement of the whole of human nature including creativity, intelligence, and knowledge of the world and of people. The formation of a culture also includes the human capacity for self-control, personal sacrifice, solidarity and readiness to promote the common good. The Church promotes those aspects of human behavior that favor a true culture of peace. Sacred Scripture continually speaks of an active commitment to our neighbor and demands of us a shared responsibility for humanity. No one can consider himself or herself extraneous or indifferent to the lot of another member of the human family. No one can say that he or she is not responsible for the well-being of a brother or sister (cf. Gen 4:9; Lk 10:29–37; Mt 25:31–46). Attentive and pressing concern for one's neighbor in a moment of need is especially important in the search for ways to resolve international conflicts other than by war. It is not hard to see that the terrifying power of the means of destruction and the ever closer links between the peoples of the whole world make it very difficult or practically impossible to limit the consequences of a war.

Pope Benedict XV and his Successors clearly understood this danger. I myself, on the occasion of the recent tragic war in the Persian Gulf, repeated the cry: "Never again war!" No, never again war, which destroys the lives of innocent people, teaches how to kill, throws into upheaval even the lives of those who do the killing and leaves behind a trail of resentment and hatred, thus making it all the more difficult to find a just solution of the very problems which provoked the war. It must not be forgotten that at the root of war there are usually real and serious grievances: injustices suffered, legitimate aspirations frustrated, poverty, and the exploitation of multitudes of desperate people who see no real possibility of improving their lot by peaceful means.

For this reason, another name for peace is development. Just as there is a collective responsibility for avoiding war, so too there is a collective responsibility for promoting development. Just as within individual societies it is possible and right to organize a solid economy that will direct the functioning of the market to the common good, so too there is a similar need for adequate interventions on the international level. For this to happen, a great effort must be made to enhance mutual understanding and knowledge, and to increase the sensitivity of consciences. This is the culture which is hoped for, one which fosters trust in the human potential of the poor, and consequently in their ability to improve their condition through work or to make a positive contribution to economic prosperity. But to accomplish this, the poor—be they individuals or nations—need to be provided with realistic opportunities. Creating such conditions calls for a concerted worldwide effort to promote development, an effort that also involves sacrificing the positions of income and of power enjoyed by the more developed economies.

RETURNING TO *RERUM NOVARUM*

Faced with the poverty of the working class, Pope Leo XIII wrote: "We approach this subject with confidence, and in the exercise of the rights which manifestly pertain to us . . . By keeping silence we would seem to neglect the duty incumbent on us." During the last hundred years the Church has repeatedly expressed her thinking in response to social questions. Her sole purpose, entrusted to her by Christ himself, has been care and responsibility for persons. The social message of the Gospel must not be considered a theory, but above all else a basis and a motivation for action. Inspired by this message, some of the first Christians distributed their goods to the poor, bearing witness to the fact that, despite different social origins, it was possible for people to live together in peace and harmony.

The Church's love for the poor, which is essential for her and a part of her constant tradition, impels her to give attention to a world in which poverty is threatening to assume massive proportions in spite of technological and economic progress. In the countries of the West, different forms of poverty are being experienced by groups that live on the margins of society, by the elderly and the sick, by the victims of consumerism, and even more immediately by so many refugees and migrants. In the developing countries, tragic crises loom on the horizon unless internationally coordinated measures are taken before it is too late.

Love for others, and in the first place love for the poor, in whom the Church sees Christ himself, is made concrete in the promotion of justice. Justice will never be fully attained unless people see in the poor person, who is asking for help in order to survive, not an annoyance or a burden, but an opportunity for showing kindness and a chance for greater enrichment. Only such awareness can give the courage needed to face the risk and the change involved in every authentic attempt to come to the aid of another. It is not merely a matter of "giving from one's surplus," but of helping entire peoples which are presently excluded or marginalized to enter into the sphere of economic and human development. Much remains to be done.

CONCLUSION:
AN APPEAL FOR COOPERATION

The world today is ever more aware that solving serious national and international problems is not just a matter of economic production or of juridical or social organization, but also calls for specific ethical and religious values, as well as changes of mentality, behavior and structures. The Church feels a particular responsibility to offer this contribution.

I appeal to the Christian Churches and to all the great world religions, inviting them to offer the unanimous witness of our common convictions regarding the dignity of persons, created by God. In fact I am convinced that the various religions, now and in the future, will have a preeminent role in preserving peace and in building a society worthy of humans. Openness to dialogue and to cooperation is required of all people of good will, and in particular of individuals and groups with specific responsibilities in the areas of politics, economics and social life, at both the national and international levels.

The Church has constantly repeated that the person and society need not only material goods but spiritual and religious values as well. Furthermore, as she has become more aware of the fact that too many people live, not in the prosperity of the Western world, but in the poverty of the developing countries amid conditions which are still "a yoke little better than that of slavery itself," she has felt and continues to feel obliged to denounce this fact with absolute clarity and frankness, although she knows that her call will not always win favor with everyone.

In the third Millennium the Church will be faithful in making humans' way her own, knowing that she does not walk alone, but with Christ her Lord. It is Christ who made humans' way his own, and who guides them, even when they are unaware of it.

Mary, the Mother of the Redeemer, constantly remained beside Christ in his journey towards the human family and in its midst, and she goes before the Church on the pilgrimage of faith. May her maternal intercession accompany humanity towards the next Millennium, in fidelity to him who "is the same yesterday and today and for ever" (cf. Heb 13:8), Jesus Christ our Lord, in whose name I cordially impart my blessing to all.

CATHOLIC THOUGHT ON WAR AND PEACE

Catholic social thought is, as John Paul puts it in *Centesimus annus*, "at the crossroads where Christian life and conscience come into contact with the real world" (#59). This is very evident in its teachings on war and peace. The tradition forcefully argues that the solution to war can be found only in the works of justice. Peace must be built on justice. The church is critical of the idea that in the contemporary context war can be used as a means to ensure justice and peace, particularly given modern armaments and the threat posed by weapons of mass destruction. The following quotation captures Catholic thought on war. It is from the *Compendium of the Social Doctrine of the Church*, which includes references to a dozen quotations from popes and the Second Vatican Council:

The Magisterium condemns the savagery of war and asks that war be considered in a new way. In fact, it is hardly possible to imagine that in an atomic era, war could be used as an instrument of justice. War is a scourge and is never an appropriate way to resolve problems that arise between nations; it has never been and it will never be, because it creates new and still more complicated conflicts. When it erupts, war becomes an unnecessary massacre, an adventure without return that compromises humanity's present and threatens its future. Nothing is lost by peace; everything may be lost by war. The damage caused by an armed conflict is not only material but also moral. In the end, war is a failure of all true humanism, it is always a defeat for humanity: never again some peoples against other, never again . . . no more war, no more war! (#497)

Catholic thought, then, continually calls for works of peace and nonlethal responses to injustice instead of war. As Pope John Paul II stated earlier in this chapter, we must work to create a culture of peace. Yet at the same time, the tradition is not against all war. Indeed, it holds that in limited and specific times, war may be the appropriate response to injustice. This is a complicated and nuanced position. How do we create a culture of peace, or peace itself, in a world that seems at times to be marked by violence and aggression? There is no simple answer here. Yet John Paul gives a strong indication of where we begin: We must work to create peace and to avoid war. As stated in the *Catechism of the Catholic Church*, "The Church insistently urges everyone to prayer and to action so that the divine Goodness may free us from the ancient bondage of war . . . All citizens and all governments are obliged to work for the avoidance of war" (#2307–8).

Yet how does an individual or the Church or a government or an international agency create peace and work to avoid war? Commentators on these issues offer a helpful distinction here. They note a threefold task: peacekeeping, peacemaking, and peacebuilding.[3] As the U.S. bishops in *The Challenge of Peace* write, "The Christian has no choice but to defend peace . . . This is an inalienable obligation. It is the how of defending peace which offers moral options" (#73). Embedded in Catholic thought on war, as in Catholic thought on human rights and social justice, the church characteristically looks to international law and international institutions as well as to interreligious dialogue in efforts to keep peace, to make peace, and to build peace.[4]

Social Catholicism on Peacemaking and Peacebuilding: Active Nonviolence

Christians have the moral obligation to respond to injustice through nonviolent means. Nonviolent resistance to injustice is often called pacifism. Note, however, that pacifism is not the same as being passive. The word *pacifism* means "to seek peace" or "to work for peace." The word *passive*, on the other hand, means "not being active." One is passive when one does not participate or respond to injustice. Catholic thought rejects the view that one can be passive in the face of injustice. Recall John Paul's strong words quoted in the last chapter:

> The Church recognizes sinful situations or the sinful collective behavior of social groups or nations. Social sin is the result of the accumulation and concentration of many personal sins. It is a case of the personal sins of those people who
> - Cause, support, or exploit evil;
> - Are in a position to avoid, eliminate or limit social evils but fail to do so out of laziness, fear, indifference, silence, or secret complicity;
> - Take refuge in the supposed impossibility of changing the world;
> - Produce false religious reasoning so as to avoid the sacrifice required.

Christians must respond to injustice through active nonviolence. In *The Harvest of Justice Is Sown in Peace* the U.S. bishops write: "The vision of Christian nonviolence is not passive about injustice and the defense of the rights of others . . . It consists of a commitment to resist manifest injustice and public evil with means other than force" (I.B.1).

In Chapter 4 we read about Dorothy Day and the Catholic Worker movement. She was a very active pacifist. The "Significant Contributors to the Tradition" listed in Chapter 1 include other Catholics who professed nonviolence, worked for social transformation, and promoted human dignity in the face of powerful oppressors or enemies: Dom Hélder Câmara of Brazil, Cesar Chavez of the United States, and Lech Walesa and Fr. Jerzy Popieluszko from Poland.

Two distinctive nonviolent methods of promoting peace and avoiding war are peacemaking and peacebuilding. Peacemaking is the job of diplomats and politicians rather than the police or military. The objective is to settle conflict through negotiation. Thus officials debate and compromise so as to work through treaties and peace agreements. Peacemaking can occur before, during, or after overt violence.

While history is full of wars of unjust aggression, violence often begins because of injustice or perceived injustice. As Pope John Paul noted in *Centesimus annus,* it "must not be forgotten that at the root of war there are usually real and serious grievances: injustices suffered, legitimate aspirations frustrated, poverty and the exploitation of multitudes of desperate people who see no real possibility of improving their lot by peaceful means" (52). A key element in peacemaking, then, is recognizing the legitimate concerns of the parties involved and redressing injustice. Catholics and Catholic organizations around the globe are involved in such efforts. The Vatican itself is directly involved with this task. It has a diplomatic corps trained to work with nations and groups as peacemakers.

Peacebuilding is the effort to develop ordered relations between groups that are either on the verge of violent conflict or groups that have been in violent conflict. Peacebuilders aim to promote the conditions for warring factions to live in civil society. Peacebuilders, usually nongovernmental agencies, work at the grass-roots level with people in programs of social development. These programs include basic education as well as training in human rights, toleration, prejudice reduction, and conflict resolution.[5] Peacemaking and peacebuilding activities can also include the reformation of social practices and institutions, particularly those that are discriminatory or repressive, that support social tensions.

Peacebuilding is an essential feature of social Catholicism. Most Catholics are not trained as police or soldiers. Nor do they find themselves in positions of civil power to be peacemakers. Yet all Catholics and Christians find themselves in situations of conflict. They are called to live lives that testify to the power of nonviolence and reconciliation. The Vatican is also directly involved in this task. The church has many organizations that directly work with people in war-torn areas in relief aid as well as in reconciliation.

Peacekeeping in Social Catholicism: The Just-War Theory

Recall the words of U.S. bishops in *The Challenge of Peace:* "The Christian has no choice but to defend peace . . . This is an inalienable obligation. It is the how of defending peace which offers moral options" (#73). Christians have the moral obligation to respond to injustice through nonviolent means. Under certain conditions, however, the obligation to use nonviolent means may be overridden. The U.S. bishops in *The Challenge of Peace* explain this Catholic position as follows:

> We believe work to develop non-violent means of fending off aggression and resolving conflict best reflects the call of Jesus both to love and to justice . . . But, on the other hand, the fact of aggression, oppression and injustice in our world also serves to legitimate the resort to weapons and armed force in defense of justice. We must recognize the reality of the paradox we face as Christians living in the context of the world as it presently exists, we must continue to articulate our belief that love is possible and the only real hope for all human relations, and yet accept that force, even deadly force, is sometimes justified and that nations must provide for their defense. (#78)

In their letter *The Harvest of Justice Is Sown in Peace* the bishops summarize their position in two basic points:

> 1. In situations of conflict, our constant commitment ought to be, as far as possible, to strive for justice through nonviolent means.
> 2. But when sustained attempts at nonviolent action fail to protect the innocent against fundamental injustice, then legitimate political authorities are permitted as a last resort to employ limited force to rescue the innocent and establish justice. (I.B.)

There are four scenarios in which the Catholic tradition could foresee the use of lethal force: self-defense, peacekeeping, humanitarian intervention, and protection of a group of people from unjust violent aggression by another group. All governments have the responsibility to defend and promote the common good and included in that is the requirement to protect the security of the people. In *The Challenge of Peace* the bishops write: "Governments cannot be denied the right to legitimate defense once every means of peaceful settlement has been exhausted. Therefore, government authorities and others who share public responsibility have the duty to protect the welfare of the people entrusted to their care and to conduct such grave matters soberly" (#72).

The right and responsibility to self-defense is not unlimited. As the bishops wrote, such matters ought to be conducted "soberly." Two current issues of discussion on this topic are preemptive war and preventive war. Preemptive war is a war started in the name of self-defense; the purpose of the military action is to counter a serious and imminent attack from another country or group. Preventive war also is a war started in the name of self-defense; the purpose of the action is to counter a serious attack from another country or group that, it is thought, will happen in the future. Catholic thought here is cautious. The potential for war is not in itself a justifiable reason to use military force. The *Compendium of the Social Doctrine of the Church* puts it this way: "Clear proof that an attack is imminent" is necessary for justification (#501).

Humanitarian intervention refers to forceful intervention in war-torn areas by a third-party government or coalition of governments to provide humanitarian (in contrast to military) aid to civilian populations. It is often linked to peacekeeping, which refers to the activity and mission of the police or military force designed to separate social factions or countries involved in overt forms of violence. Peacekeepers aim to stop or at least limit social violence through the threat of or the use of force.

Catholic social thought for centuries has reflected on morally appropriate and morally inappropriate uses of violence. A set of conditions known as just-war theory allows the obligation to use nonviolent means to be overridden in particular circumstances. The phrase "just-war theory" has a very long tradition of use in ethics (Catholic and otherwise). When used by theologians or philosophers, the meaning and intent of the phrase is clear. When hearing the phrase for the first time, however, some people are confused by its meaning. Perhaps a better phrase would be *moral requirements concerning a particular war*. Think of this when you read about the just-war theory.

A way to begin thinking about the just-war theory is to compare it to the way we would normally think about the use of force by the police. Most people would agree to two general principles here. The first is that the *initial* moral responsibility of the police is not to use force in the line of duty. Under certain limited conditions, however, police officers are permitted to use force in the line of duty. The second is that the force used must not be excessive or inappropriate; it must be proportionate to the threat.

The just-war theory is similar. It too has two parts. The first concerns the right reasons to go to war (the conditions necessary morally to justify killing). The second concerns "right conduct" in war (the conditions limiting violence). In the following sections the two parts of the just-war theory are explained. The text is from the United States Conference of Catholic Bishops' document *The Harvest of Justice Is Sown in Peace*:

The just-war tradition consists of a body of ethical reflection on the justifiable use of force. In the interest of overcoming injustice, reducing violence and preventing its expansion, the tradition aims at

a. clarifying when force may be used,

b. limiting the resort to force and

c. restraining damage done by military forces during war.

The just-war tradition begins with a strong presumption against the use of force and then establishes the conditions when this presumption may be overridden for the sake of preserving the kind of peace that protects human dignity and human rights.

In a disordered world, where peaceful resolution of conflicts sometimes fails, the just-war tradition provides an important moral framework for restraining and regulating the limited use of force by governments and international organizations . . . We summarize its major components, which are drawn from traditional Catholic teaching.

First, whether lethal force may be used is governed by the following criteria:

- *Just Cause:* force may be used only to correct a grave, public evil, i.e., aggression or massive violation of the basic rights of whole populations;
- *Comparative Justice:* while there may be rights and wrongs on all sides of a conflict, to override the presumption against the use of force the injustice suffered by one party must significantly outweigh that suffered by the other;
- *Legitimate Authority:* only duly constituted public authorities may use deadly force or wage war;
- *Right Intention:* force may be used only in a truly just cause and solely for that purpose;
- *Probability of Success:* arms may not be used in a futile cause or in a case where disproportionate measures are required to achieve success;
- *Proportionality:* the overall destruction expected from the use of force must be outweighed by the good to be achieved;
- *Last Resort:* force may be used only after all peaceful alternatives have been seriously tried and exhausted.

These criteria *(jus ad bellum)*, taken as a whole, must be satisfied in order to override the strong presumption against the use of force. (I.B.2)

Catholic social thought presents these criteria as objective moral principles. They are held as rational, common-sense principles that can be used to distinguish wars that are morally justifiable (self-defense, peacekeeping efforts, humanitarian intervention, and protecting a nation or group from unjust aggression by another nation or group) from wars of conquest, aggression, and national self-interest, which are never morally justifiable. Note that there is no place for wars of religion or holy wars. Fighting for God is not a part of the just-war theory. Indeed, as Pope John Paul proclaimed, "Killing in the name of God is an act of blasphemy and a perversion of religion."[6]

The debate concerning the just-war theory is not with the theory itself but with the application of the criteria. Catholic thought holds, however, a certain confidence in human nature and rationality. Thoughtful persons of good will should be able to decide, for example, when all other nonviolent means have been tried. There are at least two issues currently prominent in debates over the application of the just-war theory. The first is the meaning of *legitimate authority* in the contemporary world. The question is whether or not it is sufficient for an individual country to go to war in another country on either grounds of self-defense or humanitarianism without the support of the international community or the United Nations. There is increasing support for the position that some form of international support is necessary to meet this criterion.

A second issue concerns the moral legitimacy of certain types of nonmilitary means. The just-war theory demands that force be used only after all peaceful alternatives have been tried. Nonmilitary alternatives to war include boycotts and economic sanctions. On the face of it, these are to be preferred over violent conflict, yet such measures have to be carefully considered. Boycotts and sanctions often place an intolerable burden on the poor. Leaders of countries are the last to feel the effects of boycotts and sanctions. The bishops warn that often such measures harm innocent people. In *The Harvest of Justice Is Sown in Peace* they argue:

> The troubling moral problems posed by the suffering caused by sanctions and the limits to their effectiveness counsel that this blunt instrument be used sparingly and with restraint. Economic sanctions may be acceptable, but only if less coercive means fail, as an alternative to war and as a means of upholding fundamental international norms. (II.E.3)

Indeed, the principles of the just-war theory must be considered before implementation of boycotts or sanctions.

The following section, again from *The Harvest of Justice Is Sown in Peace*, describes the second part of the just-war theory, that is, just conduct in war.

> Second, the just-war tradition seeks also to curb the violence of war through restraint on armed combat between the contending parties by imposing the following moral standards (*jus in bello*) for the conduct of armed conflict:

- *Noncombatant Immunity:* civilians may not be the object of direct attack, and military personnel must take due care to avoid and minimize indirect harm to civilians;
- *Proportionality:* in the conduct of hostilities, efforts must be made to attain military objectives with no more force than is militarily necessary and to avoid disproportionate collateral damage to civilian life and property;
- *Right Intention:* even in the midst of conflict, the aim of political and military leaders must be peace with justice, so that acts of vengeance and indiscriminate violence, whether by individuals, military units or governments, are forbidden. (I.B.2)

Even though a country (or coalition of countries) might be justified in going to war, that in itself does not mean that all their actions in the war are morally justifiable. The second set of criteria in the just-war theory, the just-conduct criteria, demands that soldiers and military officials make distinctions between combatants and noncombatants. It may at times be difficult to make this distinction, but as the bishops write in *The Challenge of Peace:* "Plainly, though, not even by the broadest definition can one rationally consider combatants entire classes of human beings such as schoolchildren, hospital patients, the elderly, the ill, the average industrial worker producing goods not directly related to military purposes, farmers, and many others. They may never be directly attacked" (#108).

Noncombatants include prisoners, whether captured soldiers, civilians, or terrorists. They are entitled to humane conditions and must be protected from abuse and torture. According to the *Catechism of the Catholic Church,* "Torture which uses physical or moral violence to extract confessions, punish the guilty, frighten opponents, or satisfy hatred is contrary to respect for the person and for human dignity" (#2297).

The just-conduct criteria also outlaw certain types of weapons, namely, those with a destructive capacity that cannot distinguish between combatants and noncombatants. Thus the use of nuclear, chemical, and biological weapons is condemned.

A current debate about the just-conduct criteria concerns postwar responsibility of the country or countries involved in the war. Just wars are not fought to punish populations. They are fought "to correct a grave, public evil." As such, all efforts ought to be made after the war to restore peace and create the conditions for justice. Such efforts would include peacemaking and peacebuilding efforts as well as commitments to rebuild and restore the necessary features of social life.

The just-war theory allows people in the military and ordinary citizens to reflect on the morality of particular wars and particular actions in war. It provides an objective public list of criteria. In this effort the church is following and contributing to a long tradition in moral reflection. One can see, for example, something similar to the first section of the just-war theory (right reasons to go to war) in international law. One can also find something similar to the second section of the just-war theory (right conduct in war) in U.S. military manuals and the Uniform Code of Military Justice.

The church has no army (other than the Swiss Guards at the Vatican), but Catholics across the globe serve in the military. Many Catholic colleges and universities have ROTC programs on campus. This indicates that the tradition does not unilaterally reject the use of force and violence to keep and ensure peace based on justice. The Catholic tradition, however, is very clear on the need to prevent war. If war is the only possible response to a clear and imminent threat and if all other means have failed, the tradition demands that the violence be targeted, limited, and controlled. The just-war theory first seeks to prevent war and only second to justify war.

World Day of Peace, Assisi

On January 24, 2002, ten months before the United States and other countries went to war in Iraq, Pope John Paul II invited leaders of all the world religions to come to Assisi, Italy, for a day of prayer for peace.[7] Some two hundred leaders from dozens of religions and denominations attended. The following two excerpts are from that remarkable event. The first is a letter from John Paul to the leaders of all the governments of the world. The second is a document endorsed by all the attendees of the World Day of Peace titled "Decalogue of Assisi for Peace." Together these documents illustrate the Catholic commitment to peace and to work with the entire human family to attain just world relations. These characteristically indicate the tradition's concern for international law and hope for international institutions and interreligious dialogue to keep peace, to make peace and to build peace.[8]

—Letter of John Paul II to All the Heads of State and Governments of the World (edited)— John Paul II, February 24, 2002

To Their Excellencies, Heads of State or Government

A month ago, the Day of Prayer for Peace in the world took place in Assisi. Today my thoughts turn spontaneously to those responsible for the social and political life of the countries that were represented there by the religious authorities of many nations.

The inspired reflections of these men and women, representatives of different religious confessions, their sincere desire to work for peace, and their common quest for the true progress of the whole human family, found a sublime and yet concrete form in the "Decalogue" proclaimed at the end of this exceptional day.

I have the honor of presenting to Your Excellency the text of this common agreement, convinced that these ten propositions can inspire the political and social action of your government.

I observed that those who took part in the Assisi Meeting were more than ever motivated by a common conviction: humanity must choose between love and hatred. All of them, feeling that they belong to one and the same human family, were able to express their aspiration through these ten points, convinced that if hatred destroys, love, on the contrary, builds up.

I hope that the spirit and commitment of Assisi will lead all people of goodwill to seek truth, justice, freedom and love, so that every human person may enjoy his or her inalienable rights and every people, peace. For her part, the Catholic Church, who trusts and hopes in "the God of love and peace" (II Cor 13, 11), will continue to work for loyal dialogue, reciprocal forgiveness and mutual harmony to clear the way for people in this third millennium.

With gratitude to Your Excellency, for the attention you will be kind enough to give my Message, I take the present opportunity offered to assure you of my prayerful best wishes.

—Decalogue of Assisi for Peace (edited)—

1. We commit ourselves to proclaiming our firm conviction that violence and terrorism are incompatible with the authentic spirit of religion, and, as we condemn every recourse to violence and war in the name of God or of religion, we commit ourselves to doing everything possible to eliminate the root causes of terrorism.

2. We commit ourselves to educating people to mutual respect and esteem, in order to help bring about a peaceful and fraternal coexistence between people of different ethnic groups, cultures and religions.

3. We commit ourselves to fostering the culture of dialogue, so that there will be an increase of understanding and mutual trust between individuals and among peoples, for these are the premise of authentic peace.

4. We commit ourselves to defending the right of everyone to live a decent life in accordance with their own cultural identity, and to form freely a family of his own.

5. We commit ourselves to frank and patient dialogue, refusing to consider our differences as an insurmountable barrier, but recognizing instead that to encounter the diversity of others can become an opportunity for greater reciprocal understanding.

6. We commit ourselves to forgiving one another for past and present errors and prejudices, and to supporting one another in a common effort both to overcome selfishness and arrogance, hatred and violence, and to learn from the past that peace without justice is no true peace.

7. We commit ourselves to taking the side of the poor and the helpless, to speaking out for those who have no voice and to working effectively to change these situations, out of the conviction that no one can be happy alone.

8. We commit ourselves to taking up the cry of those who refuse to be resigned to violence and evil, and we desire to make every effort possible to offer the men and women of our time real hope for justice and peace.

9. We commit ourselves to encouraging all efforts to promote friendship between peoples, for we are convinced that, in the absence of solidarity and understanding between peoples, technological progress exposes the world to a growing risk of destruction and death.

10. We commit ourselves to urging leaders of nations to make every effort to create and consolidate, on the national and international levels, a world of solidarity and peace based on justice.

SOME QUESTIONS FOR CONSIDERATION

1. Review and respond to Pope John Paul II's moral evaluation of capitalism.
2. Review and respond to the issues Pope John Paul II addresses that confront human dignity in the contemporary world.
3. Review and respond to Catholic teaching on peace and war. Catholic social tradition states there are two alternatives: Christian nonviolence and the just-war tradition. Which do you support?
4. Review the principles of Catholic social thought from the first chapter—the dignity of the human person, the common good, subsidiarity, and solidarity—and describe how they are expressed in this chapter.
5. Using the "look, judge, and act" model, discuss what Pope John Paul sees in the world, what his judgment is, and what actions he determines to be appropriate.
6. How do the authors of the selections in this chapter defend and support their positions? Review the discussion of moral arguments from the first chapter. Do the authors argue from authority, or do they use theological, biblical, philosophical, common sense, or pragmatic arguments?
7. Review the three spheres of Catholic social action: works of mercy and justice, public expression and personal commitment, and social analysis for social change. How do the readings in this chapter express these spheres?
8. Discuss how personalism is explained and supported in this chapter.
9. Discuss the four forms of moral discourse—narrative, prophetic, ethical, and policy—and how they are expressed in this chapter.

Prayer for Peace

Give us the depth of soul, O God, to constrain our might, to resist the temptations of power, to refuse to attack the attackable, to understand that vengeance begets violence, and to bring peace, not war, wherever we go.

For You, O God, have been merciful to us. For You, O God, have been patient with us. For You, O God, have been gracious to us.

And so may we be merciful and patient and gracious and trusting with these others whom you also love. This we ask through Jesus, the one without vengeance in his heart. This we ask forever and ever. Amen.

—JOAN CHITTISTER, O.S.B.

Conclusion

Out of the Book and into the World

The Catholic social tradition is not a simple blueprint for the good society, nor is it something one pulls out occasionally when needed. It is a life view and a life's work. It is a way of understanding one's self as a moral being and a person of faith. As a strong and vibrant voice in moral reflection for Catholics, the Catholic social tradition should be part of our broader conversations about morality. This concluding section addresses the five basic dimensions of moral reflection in relation to social Catholicism.

- What is going on?
- What moral standards ought to guide our lives?
- Who are we to be, and what are we to do?
- What does it mean to be a person?
- What reasons support our moral claims?[1]

What is going on? A foundational task of any attempt to address a moral problem is to give an accurate and objective account of what is going on. This is a significant question because how we describe a problem directs how we will respond to the problem. Much time was devoted in each official document of Catholic social thought to this. The tradition offers thoughtful, honest, and comprehensive descriptions of reality. In doing so it provides us with "diagnostic tools," that is to say, objective moral ideas (human rights, for example), to appropriately understand and describe what is happening in particular situations. Use what you have learned in this book to name and understand the realities of social situations around you and within the world.

What moral standards ought to guide our lives? Catholic social thought is often summarized by a list of principles and themes: the dignity of the person, the common good, the option for the poor, subsidiarity, participation, solidarity, rights and responsibilities, and care for God's creation. The tradition directs our attention to moral goods we ought to seek, for example, justice and peace. It also provides clear directives for action to help create just relationships within our individual, institutional, and social

269

spheres. Recall the sections of this book on racism, the environment, peace and war, the moral work place, and international relations. Be a person of principle. Be guided by the themes and goods of the Catholic social tradition.

Who are we to be, and what are we to do? While the Catholic social tradition can be summarized in themes or principles, we ought not limit our understanding of the tradition to guides for action. Fundamentally, Catholic social thought calls us to be certain *types* of people. It is about developing our "hearts and minds" as well as working to create communities of justice. This connection between the internal and the external is captured in Thomas Aquinas's definition of justice. "Justice," he wrote, "is a habit whereby a man renders to each one his due by a constant and perpetual will." There are three parts to this description. Justice is first a habit; it is part of who we are, a characteristic ingrained in our identity. Second, justice is action. The just person recognizes the uniqueness and individuality of others. The just person also recognizes the common humanity each of us shares. The just person then discerns what is due to another based on both the particularity and the humanity of the other. Finally, justice rests in the will, the part of our mind where we make decisions. All of this is to say that justice is a choice within us before it is in our actions.

The people listed in the section on "Significant Contributors to the Tradition" in Chapter 1 are there not so much because of what they did but because of who they were. They were loving, just, compassionate, caring, faithful, and active people. The things they are remembered for—their praiseworthy actions—flowed from their interiority, who they were as persons. We are to do as they did, and we are to be like they were.

What does it mean to be a person? The central task of the Catholic social tradition is to promote and defend personalism. When we come to see ourselves as persons, with all that entails, we will see that all other humans are also persons, with all that entails. Injustice starts to bother us. Violence, oppression, and war become moral problems for us. We begin to think and feel we have to do something. As a person we are responsible for and to ourselves, for and to others, for and to our community, and for and to God.

Developing personhood entails developing our conscience, the "see, judge, and act" model. Seeing includes our intellect and capacity to learn and know. Judging includes our ability to choose what kind of person we want to be and what we want to do in certain situations. Action includes our capability to do things freely and to direct our life toward the actualization of specific goals. We need to start today.

What are the reasons supporting our moral claims? An essential feature of Catholic social thought is its appeal to reason and to persons of good will. At the heart of this methodology lie theological claims about the nature of persons in relation to God, to others, and to the world. Building on this foundation, the tradition offers "public" (non-theological) supports for its themes, goods, and positions. At this level the tradition appeals to philosophical claims as well as pragmatic and experiential-based arguments. Think about your views. Be willing to articulate why you hold them. Be willing to explain why you think we ought to act in certain ways. Combine reason with your passion.

Living social Catholicism demands a dialogue between our experience and the many voices of the tradition. Within this dialogue we answer these five questions as best we can, and we move along. On the way we remember that the tradition calls each one of us to be the sort of person who acts and thinks, who responds and prays, who experiences himself or herself as an individual and as a member of multiple communities, and who lives on that vital crossroad where Christian faith meets the world.

Notes

Introduction

1. See www.vatican.va. The texts are also available in many other places, including David O'Brien and Thomas Shannon, *Catholic Social Thought: The Documentary Heritage* (Maryknoll, NY: Orbis Books, 1992).

1. The Catholic Social Tradition

1. Quoted in The Pontifical Council for Justice and Peace, *Compendium of the Social Doctrine of the Church* (Vatican City: Libreria Editrice Vaticana, 2004), #73.

2. See Michael Schuck, *That They Be One: The Social Teaching of the Papal Encyclicals 1740–1989* (Washington, DC: Georgetown University Press, 1991); for commentary on the encyclicals before Pope Leo XIII, see chap. 1.

3. See, for example, Thomas Bokenkotter, *Church and Revolution: Catholics in the Struggle for Democracy and Social Justice* (New York: Doubleday, 1998).

4. David Tracy, *The Analogical Imagination: Christian Theology and the Culture of Pluralism* (New York: Crossroad, 1981), 154, 68.

5. William Byron, "Ten Building Blocks of Catholic Social Teaching," *America* (October 31, 1998).

6. For these forms of moral discourse, see James Gustafson, *Varieties of Moral Discourse: Prophetic, Narrative, Ethical, and Policy* (Grand Rapids, MI: Calvin College and Seminary, 1988); idem, *A Sense of the Divine* (Cleveland: The Pilgrim Press, 1994); idem, "Moral Discourse about Medicine: A Variety of Forms," *The Journal of Medicine and Philosophy* 15 (1990): 25–42. See also Bernard Brady, *The Moral Bond of Community: Justice and Discourse in Christian Morality* (Washington, DC: Georgetown University Press, 1998).

7. Claudia Carlen, *A Guide to the Encyclicals of the Roman Pontiffs from Leo XIII to the Present Day 1891–1937* (New York: H. W. Wilson Company, 1939), 8.

8. Kenneth Himes, "Introduction," in *Modern Catholic Social Teaching: Commentaries and Interpretations,* ed. Kenneth Himes (Washington, DC: Georgetown University Press, 2005), 5.

9. See also the United States Conference of Catholic Bishops, *The Challenge of Peace: God's Promise and Our Response* (Washington DC: USCC, 1983). In this document the bishops made a distinction in their teaching between moral principles and moral judgment: "Indeed, we stress here at the beginning that not every statement in this letter has the same moral authority. At times we reassert universally binding moral principles. At still other times we reaffirm statements of recent popes and the teaching of Vatican II. Again, at other times

273

we apply moral principles to specific cases. When making applications of these principles, we realize—and we wish readers to recognize—that prudential judgments are involved based on specific circumstances which can change or which can be interpreted differently by people of good will. However, the moral judgments that we make in specific cases, while not binding in conscience, are to be given serious attention and consideration by Catholics as they determine whether their moral judgments are consistent with the Gospel" (#9–10).

10. Sources for this section include Robert Ellsberg, *All Saints: Daily Reflections on Saints, Prophets, and Witnesses for Our Time* (New York: Crossroad, 1997); *Catholic Encyclopedia,* www.newadvent.org/cathen/index.html; and Marvin Mich, *Catholic Social Teaching and Movements* (Mystic, CT: Twenty-Third Publications, 1998).

11. The "Peace Prayer of St. Francis" apparently dates from the early part of the twentieth century, and its author is unknown. It was found in Normandy in 1915, written on the back of a holy card of St. Francis, from which the name comes. Other histories, however, ascribe it to a time before St. Francis, and although some believe he did indeed write it, the above is the most commonly accepted history of the prayer.

12. Ellsberg, *All Saints,* 475–76.

13. Along with the principles, themes, and values of Catholic social thought, it is helpful to know definitions of the terms used in dialogue with the tradition. *Capitalism* is an economic system characterized primarily by private or corporate ownership of economic goods and the means that produce these goods. With capitalism, the prices, production, and distribution of economic goods are determined by competition in the free market. *Democracy* is a political system characterized by the rule of the majority; citizens freely elect representatives to government. *Liberalism* is the political philosophy that sets a high priority on individual personal freedom and the political, economic, and social rights based on that freedom. Liberalism is, then, the ethical foundation for capitalism and democracy. *Socialism* is an economic system characterized by collective or governmental ownership and administration of the production and distribution of economic goods. *Communism* is a political and economic system that rejects private ownership of property in favor of economic goods owned in common. It has come to be associated with totalitarian and authoritarian governments. *Totalitarianism* is a political concept that views citizens as fully subject to absolute government authority. *Egalitarianism* is the philosophy of basic human equality. This equality can be measured in political and/or economic terms. *Living wage* refers to the rate of pay that will enable a worker to support a family. *Minimum wage* refers to the state or federally mandated lowest rate an employer can pay its employees. *Rights* refer to legitimate moral claims an individual can make against the government or against other individuals. Human rights are grounded in one's human nature and thus are universal; all people have them. In Catholic social thought, human rights are the minimum conditions for the common good. These rights are often classified in one of two ways. Social/economic rights are legitimate moral claims individuals have to the material goods necessary to meet their basic needs, for example, the rights to education, health care, and a living wage. Civil/political rights are legitimate moral

claims people have to participate in society and live their fundamental freedoms, for example, the rights to vote, free speech, and conscience, including religious freedom. Legal rights are rights that are granted by law in a particular society.

14. For an excellent set of essays on this topic, see Himes, *Modern Catholic Social Teaching*. See also Mich, *Catholic Social Teaching and Movements*.

15. The Pontifical Council for Justice and Peace, *Compendium of the Social Doctrine of the Church*, #72–73.

16. John Coleman, "The Future of Catholic Social Thought," in Himes, *Modern Catholic Social Teaching*, 525.

17. *The Sacramentary* (New York: Catholic Book Publishing, 1985), 901, 902, 203, 926.

18. Several of the prayers used in this book are from The Roundtable Association of Diocesan Social Action Directors, *Living God's Justice: Reflections and Prayers* (Cincinnati: St. Anthony Messenger Press, 2006). This is an excellent resource.

19. Michael Schuck, "Early Modern Roman Catholic Social Thought, 1740–1890," in Himes, *Modern Catholic Social Teaching*, 100.

20. Caritas Internationalis, *Peacebuilding: A Caritas Training Manual* (Vatican City: Caritas Internationalis, 2002), 1.

2. Catholic Social Action

1. For a particularly helpful work, see Charles Curran, *Catholic Social Teaching: A Historical and Ethical Analysis* (Washington, DC: Georgetown University Press, 2002).

2. For a concise list of changes in papal teaching, see Michael Schuck, *That They Be One: The Social Teaching of the Papal Encyclicals 1740–1989* (Washington, DC: Georgetown University Press, 1991), 176–78. For a detailed narrative about how the church has changed its positions on slavery, usury, and marriage, see John Noonan, *A Church That Can and Cannot Change* (Notre Dame, IN: University of Notre Dame Press, 2005).

3. John Paul II, *Crossing the Threshold of Hope* (New York: Alfred Knopf, 1994), 202.

4. See Thomas Aquinas, *Summa Theologica*, II-II, Q. 47–56.

5. Richard Gula, *Reason Informed by Faith: Foundations of Catholic Morality* (New York: Paulist Press, 1989), 123.

6. For a full set of conversations on conscience, see Charles Curran, ed., *Conscience: Readings in Moral Theology No. 14* (Mahwah, NJ: Paulist Press, 2004).

7. See Gula, *Reason Informed by Faith*, 133.

8. See "Acting with Prudence," in Pontifical Council for Justice and Peace, *Compendium of the Social Doctrine of the Church* (Vatican City: Libreria Editrice Vaticana, 2004), #547–48.

9. The first time I read that Catholic social thought was "all about" the vocation for justice was in Philip Land, *Catholic Social Teaching: As I Have Lived, Loathed, and Loved It* (Chicago: Loyola University Press, 1994), 60–61.

10. Douglas Schuurman, *Vocation: Discerning Our Callings in Life* (Grand Rapids, MI: Eerdmans, 2004), 137.

11. Ibid., 123–24.

12. Mother Teresa, quoted in Georges Gorrée and Jean Barbier, eds., *The Love of Christ: Spiritual Counsels* (San Francisco: Harper and Row, 1982), 30.

13. Ibid., 24–25.

14. Ibid., 45.

15. Ibid., 51.

16. Mother Teresa quoted in Kathryn Spink, ed., *Life in the Spirit: Reflections, Meditations, Prayers, Mother Teresa of Calcutta* (San Francisco: Harper and Row, 1983), xi.

17. Ibid., 1.

18. Marvin Mich, *Catholic Social Teaching and Movements* (Mystic, CT: Twenty-Third Publications, 1998), 197–98.

19. Robert Vitillo, "Foreword," in *Credible Signs of Christ Alive: Case Studies from the Catholic Campaign for Human Development*, ed. John Hogan (Lanham, MD: Sheed and Ward, 2003), x.

20. John Hogan, "Preface," in Hogan, *Credible Signs of Christ Alive*, xi.

21. Michael Himes, *Doing the Truth in Love: Conversations about God, Relationship, and Service* (Mahwah, NJ: Paulist Press, 1995), 57.

22. See Thomas Rochon, *Culture Moves: Ideas, Activism, and Changing Values* (Princeton, NJ: Princeton University Press, 1998).

23. John Neafsey, *A Sacred Voice Is Calling: Personal Vocation and Social Conscience* (Maryknoll, NY: Orbis Books, 2006), 1.

24. Noonan, *A Church That Can and Cannot Change*, 77.

25. See Anne Patrick, "Conscience and Solidarity with Victims," 188–94, in Curran, *Conscience*.

26. The description of each group is taken from its website.

27. Dorothy Day, *Loaves and Fishes* (Maryknoll, NY: Orbis Books, 1997), 176.

3. About New Things

1. In 1879 Pope Leo XIII issued the encyclical *Aeterni patris*, which called upon the church to recognize the significance of Thomas Aquinas's work in the tradition.

2. There are thirty-nine notes in *Rerum novarum*. Thomas Aquinas is referenced nine times. The New Testament is referenced nineteen times. Pope Benedict XIV revived the tradition of papal encyclicals in 1740. Between that time and Leo's papacy, forty-six encyclicals were issued; none references Thomas Aquinas.

3. All selections from Thomas Aquinas are taken from his *Summa theologica* (New York: Benziger Brothers, 1947). The question and article from which the quotations are taken are found at the end of each paragraph. The quotations are edited and abridged.

4. Leo's successor, Pius XI, makes this point clearly in *Quadragesimo anno*: "Let us bear in mind that the parent of this cultural socialism was liberalism" (#122).

5. Karl Marx, "Contribution to the Critique of Hegel's *Philosophy of Right*: Introduction," in *The Marx-Engels Reader,* ed. Robert Tucker (New York: W. W. Norton, 1972), 12.

6. G. K. Chesterton, *Saint Thomas Aquinas* (New York: Sheed and Ward, 1933), 156.

7. John A. Ryan, *A Living Wage: Its Ethical and Economic Aspects* (New York: Macmillan, 1906). The numbers following the excerpts refer to page numbers in this text.

4. Personalism and Human Rights

1. Quoted in Robert Ellsberg, *All Saints: Daily Reflections on Saints, Prophets, and Witnesses for Our Time* (New York: Crossroad, 1997), 519.

2. See R. Bruce Douglass and David Hollenbach, eds., *Catholicism and Liberalism* (Cambridge: Cambridge University Press, 1994).

3. Jacques Maritain, *Man and the State* (Chicago: University of Chicago Press, 1951), chap. 5.

4. Jacques Maritain, *The Person and the Common Good* (Notre Dame, IN: University of Notre Dame Press, 1966), 40–41.

5. Ibid., 61.

6. Maritain, *Man and the State,* 96.

7. Thomas Bokenkotter, *The Church and Revolution* (New York: Image Books, 1998), 388.

8. Maritain, *The Person and the Common Good,* 52–53.

9. For the history of the United Nations and other information, see the United Nations website.

10. For a developed reflection on this correlation, see David Hollenbach, *Claims in Conflict: Retrieving and Renewing the Catholic Human Rights Tradition* (New York: Paulist Press, 1979). For a textual comparison of *Pacem in terris* and the United Nations' documents on human rights, see J. Milburn Thompson, *Justice and Peace: A Christian Primer* (Maryknoll, NY: Orbis Books, 1997), 91,

11. See Mary Ann Glendon, "The Sources of 'Rights Talk': Some Are Catholic," *Commonweal* 78, no. 17 (October 12, 2001): 11–13.

12. Lawrence McCaffrey, *The Irish Catholic Diaspora in America* (Washington, DC: Catholic University Press, 1984), 96.

13. Ibid., 95.

14. Jay Dolan, *In Search of an American Catholicism: A History of Religion and Culture in Tension* (Oxford: Oxford University Press, 2002), 57.

15. Dorothy Brown and Elizabeth McKeown, *The Poor Belong to Us: Catholic Charities and American Welfare* (Cambridge, MA: Harvard University Press, 1997), 2.

16. John F. Kennedy, "Address to the Greater Houston Ministerial Association," September 12, 1960. The full text—as well as the audio version—is available on the www.jfklibrary.org website.

17. John Ireland, *The Church and Modern Society: Lectures and Addresses* (Chicago: D. H. McBride, 1897), 89.

18. Leo XIII, *Longinqua oceani*, in *Documents of American Catholic History,* vol. 2, *1866–1966,* ed. John Tracy Ellis (Wilmington, DE: Michael Glazier, 1987), 502.

19. Dolan, *In Search of an American Catholicism,* 109.

20. "The Voice of Reason," *Newsweek* (August 28, 1967), 57.

21. Arthur Schlesinger, *A Thousand Days: John F. Kennedy in the White House* (New York: Black Dog and Leventhal Publishers, 2005), 44–45.

22. The primary source for this section is Robert McElroy, *The Search for an American Public Theology: The Contribution of John Courtney Murray* (New York: Paulist Press, 1989).

23. John Courtney Murray, *We Hold These Truths: Catholic Reflections on the American Proposition* (Kansas City: Sheed and Ward, 1960), 109.

24. John Courtney Murray, quoted in McElroy, *The Search for an American Public Theology,* 59.

25. Murray, *We Hold These Truths,* 272.

26. John Courtney Murray, quoted in McElroy, *The Search for an American Public Theology,* 89.

27. Murray, *We Hold These Truths,* 166–67.

28. Ibid., 37.

29. Ibid., 56–57.

30. Ibid., 78.

31. John Courtney Murray, quoted in McElroy, *The Search for an American Public Theology,* 84.

32. McElroy, *The Search for an American Public Theology,* 47.

33. John Courtney Murray, "The Construction of a Christian Culture," in *Bridging the Sacred and the Secular: Selected Writing of John Courtney Murray, S.J.,* ed. J. Leon Hooper (Washington, DC: Georgetown University Press, 1994), 102–3.

34. John Courtney Murray, quoted in McElroy, *The Search for an American Public Theology,* 115.

35. See Eric O. Hanson, *The Catholic Church in World Politics* (Princeton, NJ: Princeton University Press, 1987), esp. chap. 1.

36. Schlesinger, *A Thousand Days,* vii. Schlesinger describes the pressure on Kennedy to respond to the Soviet/Cuban threat by using military force, particularly to bomb the missile sites in Cuba. A result of this would have been the deaths of thousands of innocent Cubans. It might also have provoked the Soviets to a drastic response. Schlesinger describes Kennedy's response as "responsible management of power." He writes: "Throughout the crisis he coolly and exactly measured the level of force necessary to deal with the level of threat. Defining a clear and limited objective, he moved with mathematical precision to accomplish it" (295).

37. Roger Ruston, *Human Rights and the Image of God* (London: SCM Press, 2004), 20.

38. I thank Therese Cullen of the Catholic Worker Community in Memphis for her insight on these selections.

39. Dorothy Day, *The Long Loneliness* (San Francisco: Harper Collins, 1952), 45.

40. Ibid, 149–50.

41. Dorothy Day, *Loaves and Fishes* (Maryknoll, NY: Orbis Books, 1997), 50.

42. Ibid., 97.

43. Ibid., 198.

44. Ibid., 215.

45. Dorothy Day, *Selected Writings* (Maryknoll, NY: Orbis Books, 1992), 266–68.

46. Available on the catholicworker.org website.

47. Ibid.

5. Christ's Love Impels Us

1. Walter M. Abbott, ed., *The Documents of Vatican II*, trans. Joseph Gallagher (New York: Guild Press, 1966), xxii. This prayer was used before every session and meeting of the council.

2. See Richard McBrien, *Catholicism* (Minneapolis: Winston Press, 1981), chap. 19.

3. Allan Deck, "Commentary on *Populorum progressio*," in *Modern Catholic Social Teaching: Commentaries and Interpretations*, ed. Kenneth Himes (Washington, DC: Georgetown University Press, 2005), 293.

4. Walter Abbott, "Opening Message," in Abbott, *The Documents of Vatican II.*

5. Ibid., 2.

6. David Hollenbach, "Commentary on *Gaudium et Spes*," in Himes, *Modern Catholic Social Teaching*, 266.

7. Mother Teresa, *Love: A Fruit Always in Season*, ed. Dorothy Hunt (San Francisco: Ignatius Press, 1987), 51.

8. Donal Dorr, *Option for the Poor: A Hundred Years of Catholic Social Teaching* (Maryknoll, NY: Orbis Books, 1992), 179.

6. Liberation

1. Often mistakenly attributed to Archbishop Oscar Romero, this prayer was in fact written by Bishop Kenneth Untener for John Cardinal Dearden, who included it in a homily in November 1979. See "The Peace Pulpit: Homilies by Bishop Thomas J. Gumbleton," *National Catholic Reporter*, March 28, 2004.

2. David O'Brien and Thomas Shannon, *Catholic Social Thought: The Documentary Heritage* (Maryknoll, NY: Orbis Books, 1992), 264.

3. Eric Hanson, *The Catholic Church in World Politics* (Princeton, NJ: Princeton University Press, 1987), 59.

4. Penny Lernoux, *People of God: The Struggle for World Catholicism* (New York: Viking, 1989), 5.

5. Ibid., 6.

6. Human Rights Office, Archdiocese of Guatemala, *Guatemala: Never Again!* (Maryknoll, NY: Orbis Books, 1999), 289–90.

7. Ibid., 290.

8. Dianna Ortiz, *The Blindfold's Eyes: My Journey from Torture to Truth* (Maryknoll, NY: Orbis Books, 2002).

9. Gustavo Gutiérrez, *A Theology of Liberation,* 15th anniv. ed. (Maryknoll, NY: Orbis Books, 1988), xiii. Following page references in the text are to this work.

10. Karl Marx, *The Marx-Engels Reader,* ed. Robert Tucker (New York: W. W. Norton, 1972), 362.

11. Dom Hélder Câmara, *Spiral of Violence* (London: Sheed and Ward, 1971). Following page references in the text are to this work.

12. Tertullian, "Apology," chap. 7, in *The Ante-Nicene Fathers,* vol. 3, *Latin Christianity: Its Founder, Tertullian,* ed. Alexander Roberts and James Donaldson (Grand Rapids, MI: Eerdmans, 1980), 23.

13. Ibid., chap. 50, p. 55.

14. Catherine Cory and David Landry, eds., *The Christian Theological Tradition* (Upper Saddle River, NJ: Prentice Hall, 2003), 113.

15. Dana Gioia, "To Witness Truth Uncompromised," in *Martyrs,* ed. Susan Bergman (Maryknoll, NY: Orbis Books, 1996), 323–25.

16. William Cavanaugh, "Dying for the Eucharist or Being Killed by It? Romero's Challenge to First-World Christians," *Theology Today* 58, no. 2 (July 2001): 179–81.

17. See, for example, Jon Sobrino, *Archbishop Romero: Memories and Reflections* (Maryknoll, NY: Orbis Books, 1990), 6–13.

18. William O'Malley, *The Voice of Blood: Five Christian Martyrs of Our Time* (Maryknoll, NY: Orbis Books, 1980), 43–44.

19. Robert Ellsberg, *All Saints* (New York: Crossroad, 1997), 132.

20. Oscar Romero, *The Violence of Love,* ed. James Brockman (Farmington, PA: The Plough Publishing Co., 1998), 11. Following page references in the text are to this work.

21. Oscar Romero, *Voice of the Voiceless* (Maryknoll, NY: Orbis Books, 1985), 143–45.

22. Ellsberg, *All Saints,* 133.

23. Thomas Bokenkotter, *Church and Revolution: Catholics in the Struggle for Democracy and Social Justice* (New York: Image Books, 1998), 528.

24. Ita Ford, quoted in Ellsberg, *All Saints,* 527.

25. Jean Donovan, quoted in The Roundtable Association of Diocesan Social Action Directors, *Living God's Justice: Reflections and Prayers* (Cincinnati: St. Anthony Messenger Press, 2006), 79.

26. I never met Fr. Ellacuría, but when I was writing my dissertation in the mid 1980s I read his article "Human Rights in a Divided Society," in *Human Rights in the Americas: The Struggle for Consensus,* ed. Alfred Hennelly and John Langan (Washington, DC: Georgetown University Press, 1982). The article influenced my understanding of the time-honored principle of the common good. Usual interpretations of the common good assume a neutral or at least positive role of the state. Writing in Latin America, one could not assume that. Nor could one assume that human rights were moral principles that the powers in society would respect.

27. Ron Hansen, "Hearing the Cry of the Poor," in Bergman, *Martyrs,* 35.

28. Romero, *Voice of the Voiceless,* 189.

29. Marvin Mich, *Catholic Social Teaching and Movements* (Mystic CT: Twenty-Third Publications, 1998), 189.

30. Kenneth Himes, "Commentary on *Justitia in mundo*," in *Modern Catholic Social Teaching: Commentaries and Interpretations*, ed. Kenneth Himes (Washington, DC: Georgetown University Press, 2005), 335.

31. Ibid., 354.

32. Donal Dorr, *Option for the Poor: A Hundred Years of Catholic Social Teaching* (Maryknoll, NY: Orbis Books, 1992), 252–54, 257.

33. Dom Hélder Câmara, *The Desert Is Fertile* (Maryknoll, NY: Orbis Books, 1974), 14.

7. Human Work on God's Earth

1. Patricia Lamoureux, "Commentary on *Laborem exercens*," in *Modern Catholic Social Teaching: Commentaries and Interpretations*, ed. Kenneth Himes (Washington, DC: Georgetown University Press, 2005), 405.

2. Donal Dorr, *Option for the Poor: A Hundred Years of Catholic Social Teaching* (Maryknoll, NY: Orbis Books, 1992), 288.

3. Augustine, "Sermon 68.6," in *Sermons (51–94) on the New Testament*, vol. III/3, trans. Edmund Hill, O.P., series ed. John E. Rotelle, O.S.A. (Brooklyn, NY: New City Press, 1991).

4. This translation is from the United States Catholic Conference.

5. Pope John Paul II, Angelus in the Apennines, 1993. Available online at http://conservation.catholic.org/pope_john_paul_ii,_section_3.htm.

6. See James Gustafson, *A Sense of the Divine: The Natural Environment from a Theocentric Perspective* (Cleveland: Pilgrim Press, 1994).

7. Pope John Paul II, Lorenzago Dicardore, Italy, July 15, 1996. Available online at http://conservation.catholic.org/more_pope_john_paul_ii.htm.

8. Pope John Paul II, homily, Val Visdene, Italy, feast of St. John Gualbert, patron of foresters, 1990, quoted in *Ecology and Faith: The Writings of Pope John Paul II*, ed. Sr. Ancilla Dent, O.S.B. (Berkhamsted, Eng.: Arthur James, 1997), back cover.

9. Pontifical Council for Justice and Peace, "A Contribution of the Delegation of the Holy See on the Occasion of the Third World Water Forum," Vatican City, March 22, 2003.

8. Solidarity and Justice

1. Charles Curran, Kenneth Himes, and Thomas Shannon, "Commentary on *Sollicitudo rei socialis*," in *Modern Catholic Social Teaching: Commentaries and Interpretations*, ed. Kenneth Himes (Washington, DC: Georgetown University Press, 2005), 423.

2. Donal Dorr, *Option for the Poor: A Hundred Years of Vatican Social Teaching* (Maryknoll, NY: Orbis Books, 1992), 324.

3. For an excellent account of race and race relations in the American Catholic church, see John McGreevy, *Parish Boundaries: The Catholic Encounter with Race in the Twentieth-Century Urban North* (Chicago: University of Chicago Press, 1996).

4. See, for example, the following letters from the U.S. bishops: *Discrimination and Christian Conscience* (Washington, DC: National Catholic Welfare Conference, 1958); *National Race Crisis* (Washington, DC: National Conference of Catholic Bishops, 1968); and *Brothers and Sisters to Us* (Washington, DC: National Conference of Catholic Bishops, 1979). See also a letter written by the U.S. black Catholic bishops, *What We Have Seen and Heard* (Washington, DC: National Conference of Catholic Bishops, 1979). See also the compilation of statements of individual bishops from 1997 to 2000 in *Love Thy Neighbor as Thyself: U.S. Bishops Speak against Racism* (Washington, DC: National Conference of Catholic Bishops, 2001). For a thoughtful and critical review of this literature, see Bryan Massingale, "James Cone and Recent Catholic Episcopal Teaching on Racism," *Theological Studies* 61 (2000).

5. In the words of Pope John Paul II, "Racism is a sin that constitutes a serious offence against God" ("Angelus, August 26, 2001," available online at www.vatican.va/holy_father/john_paul_ii/angelus/2001). The idea that racism is a sin is often repeated by the National Conference of Catholic Bishops (see *Love Thy Neighbor as Thyself,* esp. 7, 18, 20, 51, 75, 102, 122, 161, 167).

6. Such inquiry may have proceeded along the following lines: Europeans asked why Africans' skin is dark. The answer given was that their skin was dark because of their constant exposure to the hot sun. Yet this reason was not sufficient. Europeans recognized that the skin of Africans stayed dark while they lived in Europe. Further, while the skin of Europeans darkened in Africa, it returned to its original color upon their return to Europe. And they wondered why the children of Africans who had never been exposed to the African sun still had dark skin. Finally, the answer given was, they are different from us; they belong to a different race. See Bernard Boxill, "Introduction," in *Race and Racism,* ed. Bernard Boxill (Oxford: Oxford University Press, 2001), 16–17.

7. The Pontifical Council for Justice and Peace, *The Church and Racism: Toward a More Fraternal Society* (Washington, DC: United States Catholic Conference, 1988), #6.

8. George Fredrickson, *Racism: A Short History* (Princeton, NJ: Princeton University Press, 2002), 156.

9. Maulana Karenga, "Introduction to Black Studies," in *Racism: Essential Readings,* ed. Ellis Cashmore and James Jennings (London: Sage Publications, 2001).

10. Harry Flynn, *In God's Image: A Pastoral Letter on Racism* (Saint Paul, MN: Archdiocese of Saint Paul and Minneapolis, 2003), 10, 2.

11. Francis George, *Dwell in My Love* (Chicago: Archdiocese of Chicago, 2001), 6. Following page references in the text are to this work.

12. Dorr, *Option for the Poor,* 253.

13. Flynn, *In God's Image,* 11.

14. Massingale, "James Cone and Recent Catholic Episcopal Teaching on Racism," 721.

15. Charles E. Curran, "White Privilege," in *Interrupting White Privilege: Catholic Theologians Break the Silence,* ed. Laurie M. Cassidy and Alex Mikulich (Maryknoll, NY: Orbis Books, 2007), 80–81.

16. The Saint Paul Foundation, "An Assessment of Racism in Dakota, Ramsey, and Washington Counties," executive summary, January 2004, 9.

17. Ibid.

18. Flynn, *In God's Image*, 14.

19. Ibid., 19–20.

20. For examples of the work they do, see www.nccbuscc.org/sdwp.

21. Joseph Cardinal Bernardin, "Address: Consistent Ethic of Life Conference," in *Consistent Ethic of Life*, ed. Thomas Fuechtmann (Kansas City: Sheed and Ward, 1988), 88–89. Following page references in the text are to this work.

9. Creating a Culture of Peace

1. Donal Dorr, *Option for the Poor: A Hundred Years of Catholic Social Teaching* (Maryknoll, NY: Orbis Books, 1992), 340.

2. Daniel Finn, "Commentary on *Centesimus annus*," in *Modern Catholic Social Teaching: Commentaries and Interpretations*, ed. Kenneth Himes (Washington, DC: Georgetown University Press, 2005), 441.

3. See Caritas Internationalis, *Peacebuilding: A Caritas Training Manual* (Vatican City: Caritas Internationalis, 2002).

4. Drew Christiansen, "Catholic Peacemaking, 1991–2005: The Legacy of Pope John Paul II," *The Review of Faith and International Affairs* 4 (Fall 2006).

5. For a more detailed discussion, see Caritas Internationalis, *Peacebuilding*.

6. Pope John Paul II, "Address of His Holiness Pope John Paul II to the Diplomatic Corps," January 10, 2002, #3.

7. From August 26, 1990, to March 6, 1991, Pope John Paul II preached numerous homilies, led many prayers, and gave speeches against what has come to be known as the Gulf War, begun by United States President George H. W. Bush in January 1991. The pope's words are collected in *John Paul II for Peace in the Middle East* (Vatican City: Libreria Editrice Vaticana, 1992). The editor of *L'Osservatore Romano*, where all the texts were originally published, notes in the introduction to the book that "the history of man has been dreadfully maimed during the early months of 1991. The documentation found herein is recollection and admonition. And, as such, it becomes hope."

8. My colleague William Cavanaugh put together a list of quotations from Catholic bishops and the pope concerning the 2003 U.S.–led invasion of Iraq and the war that followed.

"The concept of a 'preventive war' does not appear in the *Catechism of the Catholic Church*" (Cardinal Joseph Ratzinger, September 24, 2002).

"Based on the facts that are known to us, we continue to find it difficult to justify the resort to war against Iraq, lacking clear and adequate evidence of an imminent attack of a grave nature. With the Holy See and bishops from the Middle East and around the world, we fear that resort to war, under present circumstances and in light of current public information, would not meet the strict conditions in Catholic teaching for overriding the strong presumption against the use of military force" (United States Conference of Catholic Bishops, statement, November 13, 2002).

"We are against the war. That is a moral position, and there's not much that needs to be said about whether (the war) is 'preventive' or 'nonpreventive.' It's an ambiguous term. Certainly the war is not defensive" (Cardinal Angelo Sodano, Vatican Secretary of State, interview with Italian reporters, January 29, 2003).

"If a son asks you for bread, you do not give him a stone . . . To a people who for 12 years have been begging for bread, preparations are being made to drop 3,000 bombs on them! It is a crime against peace that cries out for vengeance before God. Let us pray so that the Pharaoh's heart will not be hardened and the biblical plagues of a terrible war will not fall on humanity" (Archbishop Renato Martino, president of the Pontifical Council for Justice and Peace, March 17, 2003).

"When war, as in these days in Iraq, threatens the fate of humanity, it is ever more urgent to proclaim, with a strong and decisive voice, that only peace is the road to follow to construct a more just and united society. Violence and arms can never resolve the problems of man" (Pope John Paul II, March 23, 2003, address at the Vatican to members of the Italian religious television channel Telespace).

"There were not sufficient reasons to unleash a war against Iraq. To say nothing of the fact that, given the new weapons that make possible destructions that go beyond the combatant groups, today we should be asking ourselves if it is still licit to admit the very existence of a 'just war'" (Cardinal Joseph Ratzinger, May 2, 2003, interview with Zenit news agency).

"Everyone can see that [the war] did not lead to a safer world, either inside or outside Iraq" (Archbishop Giovanni Lajolo, secretary for the Holy See's Relations with States, address to the U.N. General Assembly, October 4, 2004).

Conclusion

1. See William Schweiker, *Responsibility and Christian Ethics* (Cambridge: Cambridge University Press, 1995), 35; and James Gustafson, *Moral Discernment in the Christian Life: Essays in Theological Ethics* (Louisville, KY: Westminster John Knox Press, 2007), 198–212.

Index